Called to One Hope

Perspectives on the Life to Come

Called to One Hope

Perspectives on the Life to Come

Edited by John Colwell

A Selection of Drew Lectures on Immortality delivered at Spurgeon's College

First published in 2000 by Paternoster Press

06 05 04 03 02 01 00   7 6 5 4 3 2 1
Paternoster Press is an imprint of Paternoster Publishing,
P.O. Box 300, Carlisle, Cumbria, CA3 0QS, UK
and
P.O. Box 1047, Waynesboro, GA 30830–2047, USA

Website: www.paternoster-publishing.com

British Library Cataloguing in Publication Data
A catalogue record for this book is available from the British Library

ISBN 1-84227-063-X

Cover Design by Campsie, Glasgow
Typeset by WestKey Ltd, Falmouth, Cornwall
Printed in Great Britain by Bell & Bain Ltd, Glasgow

Contents

Acknowledgments

The editor and publisher are grateful to the following for permission to reprint essays contained in this volume:

Harper Collins, for permission to reproduce the essay by Stephen H. Travis, previously published as chapter 15 of his book *Christ and the Judgment of God* (Basingstoke: Marshall Pickering, 1986).

Paternoster Press for permission to reproduce the essay by I. Howard Marshall, previously published in *Christ in Our Place: The Humanity of God in Christ for the Reconciliation of the World – Essays Presented to James Torrance*, ed. Trevor Hart and Daniel Thimell (Exeter: & Allison Park: Paternoster & Pickwick, 1991), 313–328.

Grove Books for permission to reproduce the essay by N. T. Wright, first published as Grove Biblical booklet B 11 'New Heavens, New Earth: The Biblical Picture of Christian Hope'. Reproduced by permission of Grove Books Ltd, Ridley Hall Road, Cambridge CB3 9HU.

The editors of *Interpretation* for permission to reproduce the essay by James D. G. Dunn, 'He Will Come Again', previously published in *Interpretation* 51 (1997), 42–56.

T. & T. Clark for permission to reproduce the essay by James D. G. Dunne, previously published in *The Christ and the Spirit*, vol. 1 (1998), 424–39.

Paternoster Press, publishers of *The Evangelical Quarterly* for permission to reproduce the essay by John E. Colwell, previously published in vol. 67 (1995), 291–308.

Cambridge University Press for permission to reproduce the essay by T. F. Torrance, 'Immortality and Light', previously published in *Religious Studies* 17 (1981), 147–161.

Paternoster Press, publishers of *Evangel* for permission to reproduce the essay by D. Bruce A. Milne, reprinted from vol. 1 (1983), 8–14.

Paternoster Press, publishers of *Evangel* for permission to reproduce the essay by H. Dermot McDonald, reprinted from vols. 3.2 (1985) 10–12, and 3.3 (1985), 12–14.

Carfax Publishing, publishers of *Mortality* for permission to reproduce the essay by Paul Badham, reprinted from vol. 2 (1997), 'Religious and near-death experience in relation to belief in a future life', 7–12. Information concerning the journal *Mortality* can be found at the journal's website: www.tandf.co.uk

Introduction

'. . . called to one hope'
(Ephesians 4:4)

For the last hundred years or so there has been something of a renaissance of theological interest in the theme of eschatology, beginning perhaps with Albert Schweitzer, and finding its most popular expression (if academic theology can ever be described as 'popular') in the work of Jürgen Moltmann, a theme introduced in his *Theology of Hope*[1] and maintained through to his exploration of *The Coming of God*.[2] Nonetheless, it would seem to be the case that hope remains the Cinderella of theological virtues.

It is hardly surprising, in the context of Modernism's demand for facts and certainties, that there should be sustained focus on faith as a valid, if perhaps distinct, form of knowing. All too frequently, however, such focus has been upon faith as 'belief that' rather than upon faith as 'trust in'; a concern for historical verification; a concern for philosophical coherence; a concern (at least in some strands of the Church) for dogmatic precision. Similarly it is unsurprising, indeed it is appropriate, that love as the principal theological virtue should continue to be identified as the most profound distinctive of Christian identity. All too frequently, though, this focus on love has been the outcome of a retreat from dogma in the face of Enlightenment positivism; the reduction of Christianity to a code of ethics; an effective severing of love from any rigorous Christological reference.

In such a context hope is all too easily marginalised. Hope seems such an insubstantial – not to say unsubstantiatable – category in an intellectual climate that seeks certainties of fact or experience. In popular parlance the word refers to those best aspirations that so often issue in disappointment; the longing that the world, and our own lives within it, were other than they are in the present; the longing for prosperity and tranquillity; for health, wealth and happiness. Sadly, some distortions of the Christian message too readily embrace such self-interested aspirations, confusing them for the hope of the Kingdom, but more generally the focus of the Church seems to have remained on that which can be believed and practised in the present.

Yet Christians are 'called to . . . hope' as much as to faith and to love. Christian character is not divisible: without faith, love and hope are debilitated distortions; without love, faith and hope are debilitated distortions; without hope, faith and love are debilitated distortions. Authentic Christian faith is simultaneously loving and hopeful; authentic Christian love is simultaneously faithful and hopeful; authentic Christian hope is simultaneously faithful and loving. Christian hope simply cannot be marginalised without a fundamental corruption of the gospel.

Alongside faith and love, then, hope is a distinctive of Christian identity – not just distinctively Christian but, like faith and love when properly expounded, hope as Christian hope is distinct. It is no mere vague wishful thinking: it is 'firm and secure', 'an anchor for the soul'.[3] It is no mere optimism (which Stanley Hauerwas pointedly defines as 'hope without truth'[4]); it is 'firm and secure' because it is founded in the gospel; it is an outcome and expression for faith; it is both a goal and a motivation for love.

However, it is not just hope's relatedness to faith and love that renders it distinctively Christian. Sometimes it is necessary to state the obvious inasmuch as the obvious so frequently remains unstated: that which foundationally is distinctive about Christian hope, like Christian faith and Christian love, is simply Christ. Christians do not hope primarily for something, but for someone. Christian hope cannot be reduced to a series of mere human aspirations; it is irreducibly the expectation for the future presence of Jesus – the one who is trusted, the one who is loved. Whether we enquire into the future of the world and of human society, whether we enquire into the possibilities for the fulfilment of justice and peace, whether we enquire into our own future state beyond the grave, or whether even we enquire into the nature of final judgment (and each of these themes is explored within this collection of essays), Christian hope directs us to the person of Christ.

And for this reason, though such hope might be expressed, has been expressed, and even is expressed within this collection of essays, in a variety of ways, Christian hope is simple and singular: just as there can be only 'one body and one Spirit', just as there can be only 'one Lord, one faith, one baptism', just as there can be only 'one God and Father of all', so there can be only 'one hope'.[5] To affirm this one hope, therefore, is itself a statement of faith. Both in this passage of Scripture and in Christian tradition, hope is credal: 'He will come again in glory to judge the living and the dead, and his kingdom will have no end . . . We look for the resurrection of the dead, and the life of the world to come'. Christian hope is an affirmation and confident expectation of the coming of Christ and of the benefits of his coming.

It has frequently been remarked that credal statements, especially some of the more recent and detailed examples, are inextricably time-bound. This is not to imply, of course, that John Drew intended to make an explicit credal statement when he desired 'that instruction, assurance and inspiration should be given as to the Soul's destiny, and as to the nature and reality of the life hereafter directly or indirectly in the interests of personal immortality' – but such terminology assumes a specific credal statement, and one that is radically time-bound. It is highly unlikely that even a 'layman' (as John Drew would have described himself), less still an academic theologian, would venture to express such a desire in such terms today. Nor am I merely referring to the somewhat archaic language of the lectureship's foundation. The most crucial point to note with reference to the previous discussion is the signal lack of any explicit reference to Christ: here personal assurance concerning 'the Soul's destiny' is affirmed without its distinctive focal orientation. And it may well be this lack of explicit reference to Christ, and to his resurrection, that issues in the particular phraseology and assumptions of the statement. At some point between the framing of the Apostles' Creed and John Drew's statement of 1917 (that point being very much closer to the date of the former than the latter), Christian hope came to be expressed popularly, not in terms of the resurrection of the body, but in terms of the immortality of the soul; a hope rooted in the story of Jesus gave place to one that all too easily could be detached from that story. That the last hundred years have witnessed widespread repudiation of this development, particularly amongst scholars of the New Testament, finds expression in more than one of the lectures contained in this volume, though the more populist expectation of immortality is not left without representation.

Ironically, it is precisely the detailed and time-bound wording of the Drew Lectureship that issues in the broad and diverse interpretations represented in this collection: for the lectureship to be maintained in a context where its precise wording is questioned a degree of interpretative licence is inevitable. Whether John Drew would approve of such free interpretations is impossible to tell and actually beside the point: that which each of these lectures has in common is a commitment to explore this theme of hope and thereby to offer such 'instruction, assurance and inspiration' as is deemed by the various authors to be proper to the Christian message. And, notwithstanding the time-bound wording of the lectureship, such free interpretations could not be more pertinent. As is implicit in several of these essays, and is explicit in Richard Bauckham's paper, our supposedly post-enlightenment society finds itself markedly devoid of hopefulness. The arrogant confidence of Modernism in the inevitability of progress has given way to the uncertainties and disillusionments so characteristic of post-modernism. To live hopefully today is unusual. To live hopefully today is distinctive. To explore the nature of Christian hope in such a context then has potential, not just as an exercise in Christian theology, but as a most apposite declaration of Christian confidence. To this we are called: to live in this world as a hope-full people, and in their explorations of this hopefulness, I believe, these lectures remain faithful to the fundamental intentions expressed by their founder.

John E. Colwell
Summer 2000

Notes

1 Jürgen Moltmann, *Theology of Hope: On the Ground and the Implications of a Christian Eschatology*, trans. James W. Leitch (London: SCM Press, 1967).
2 Jürgen Moltmann, *The Coming of God: Christian Eschatology*, trans. Margaret Kohl (London: SCM Press, 1996).
3 Hebrews 6:19.
4 'Optimism – hope without truth – is not sufficient for dealing with the pretentious powers that determine a person's existence in the world.' Stanley Hauerwas, *Christian Existence Today: Essays on Church, World, and Living In Between* (Durham, North Carolina: Labyrinth, 1988), p. 211.
5 Ephesians 4:4–6.

Part 1
Biblical Perspectives

1

'Your Reward is Great in Heaven'

Rewards in the teaching of Jesus

Stephen H. Travis

'Rejoice and be glad, for your reward is great in heaven . . .' says Jesus to his disciples at the climax of the Beatitudes (Mt. 5:12). But for many modern disciples the idea of reward is more a cause of embarrassment than of rejoicing. For some the embarrassment arises because the offer of reward seems an unworthy motive for morality. The Christian who serves out of hope for reward is like the servile waiter in the restaurant who looks after your every need not because he or she is interested in your needs or because 'it's all part of the service', but because the waiter is hoping for a hefty tip. The ethic of Jesus with its teaching about rewards, wrote E. Westermarck in 1939, is sheer 'egoistic hedonism'.[1] For others, the embarrassment about reward arises because the notion of reward for work done appears to contradict the doctrine of justification by faith.

So what can you do if you feel the force of this problem? You might adopt the ethics of the Stoics or of Kant, with their slogans 'Virtue is its own reward' and 'Virtue for virtue's sake', and consequently dismiss the ethics of Jesus as a lower morality. But there are hidden dangers here. Although this approach resists all morality based on self-interest, it is difficult to avoid self-interest in the form of the sense of satisfaction you get from having done your good deed. And setting up the human race as autonomous beings without external norms is trying to be more moral than God.

Or you can rescue Jesus from criticism by adopting one of several devices. You might, for example, dismiss all the sayings about 'reward' in the gospels as inauthentic. But that is a desperate measure when the theme is so widespread and found in all strands of the Synoptic tradition. Or you might misrepresent Judaism as a religion of legalistic works-righteousness in which every deed has its pay-off from the meticulous divine Account-keeper, and thus enable yourself to conclude that Jesus by comparison is mild and spiritual in his reference to rewards. One problem with this approach – apart from the spectre of E. P. Sanders[2] confronting you at every moment – is that by careful selection of texts you could reach precisely the opposite conclusion. You could compare some of Jesus' sayings unfavourably with 'enlightened', 'spiritual' statements such as M. Aboth 1:3: 'Antigonus of Soko . . . used to say: Be not like slaves that minister to the master for the sake of receiving a bounty, but be like slaves that minister to the master not for the sake of receiving a bounty; and let the fear of heaven be upon you.'

Another variation would be to regard Jesus' references to reward as 'archaic hangovers' or 'Jewish relics' not integrated with the real thrust of Jesus' message.[3] I suppose that in principle this is a possibility, though whether it is the case will have to be determined by our exegesis of the passages in question.

One further proposed solution may be mentioned. John Reumann, among others, offers a way of reconciling the reward motif with his Lutheran scheme of justification by faith. Salvation or entry into the kingdom of God is a gift of God's grace. It cannot be earned. But beyond this there is the possibility of reward from God for one's work as a faithful servant. 'This is not salvation based on works but something on top of salvation – recompense for faithful service.'[4] This is very similar to the scheme of Palestinian Judaism as expounded by Sanders, as we shall see in a moment. Whether it is what Jesus meant, I shall want to question.

With these options in mind, then, we must look at the Synoptic Gospels. But first let me give a quick sketch of some emphases in Jewish teaching that may help us in our study of Jesus. The sketch is neither comprehensive, nor systematic; it is simply intended to give a few reference points and to correct some common misconceptions. It is based largely on Sanders' survey of the Tannaitic literature.[5]

Reward in Judaism

In general, Palestinian Jews did not believe that salvation, or membership in the covenant people, or entry into the world to come, depended on one's works. One's place in God's plan is established on the basis of the covenant and depends on God's initiative and mercy. But within this framework a belief in rewards and punishments is axiomatic: 'Just judgment is part of the concept of God.'[6]

Hence the principle of 'measure for measure' is often said to be the basis of reward for obedience or punishment for transgression of obedience. M. Sota 1:7 expresses the principle, 'With what measure a man metes it will be measured to him again.' That God recompenses people's deeds with scrupulous accuracy is shown also by the idea, already suggested in 2 Maccabees 6:12–15, and formulated clearly by Akiba, that God

> deals strictly with both (the righteous and the wicked), even to the great deep. He deals strictly with the righteous, calling them to account for the few wrongs which they commit in this world, in order to lavish bliss upon them and give them a good reward in the world to come; he grants ease to the wicked and rewards them for the few good deeds which they have performed in this world in order to punish them in the future world (Genesis R. 33:1).

This idea, of course, is a total reversal of the so-called Deuteronomic principle that earthly prosperity is a sign of God's blessing or reward for obedience.

But we would be wrong to deduce from such sayings that the rabbis had any *systematic doctrine* of reward or of justice, let alone a systematic doctrine of salvation by works. The purpose of these sayings is more practical. A rabbi says that each commandment has a reward attached to it because he wants above all things to encourage obedience. He teaches that rewards and punishments correspond exactly to deeds because he believes that God is just and reliable, not capricious. The argument of Akiba, that God rewards the wicked for their few good deeds in this life in order to punish them in the world to come, and vice versa, is a brave attempt to hang on to the justice and care of God for his people in the face of oppression by Israel's enemies.

Other things are said too which contradict the notion that God rewards according to a strict, calculating justice. Rabbis often spoke of God's mercy being greater than his justice.[7] Sometimes they emphasised that repentance cancels the punishment due for particular transgressions.[8] Certainly they were capable of warning against fulfilling the commandments *for the sake* of reward, as we saw in the quotation from M. Aboth 1:3.

Two other features of rabbinic teaching on reward should warn us against characterising it too readily as mercenary or retributive. In the first place, some rabbis expressed the notion that the 'reward' of fulfilling a commandment is to receive another commandment to fulfil. Ben Azzai (c. AD 130) said:

> Run to fulfil the lightest duty even as the weightiest, and flee from transgression; for one duty (*mitsvah*) draws another duty in its train, and one transgression draws another transgression in its train; for the reward (*sakar*) of a duty (done) is a duty (to be done), and the reward of one transgression is (another) transgression. (M. Aboth 4:2)

Thus has the retributive metaphor of reward been transformed into something not retributive at all. The 'reward' is intrinsic to the deed; it is not something 'added on' from outside.

Secondly, it must be noted how frequently rabbinic sayings introduce the word 'reward' *without* specifying what the reward consists of.[9] This suggests that they were more concerned to use the metaphor of reward as an indicator of God's reliability in blessing those who obey him, than to encourage the claiming of merit for oneself or the fulfilling of commandments from mercenary motives. One final example will illustrate this, and will at the same time draw attention to an additional point. R. Tarfon (c. AD 130) said, 'If thou hast studied much in the Law much reward will be given thee, and faithful is thy taskmaster who shall pay thee the reward of thy labour. And know that the recompense of the reward of the righteous is for the time to come' (M. Aboth 2:16). The emphasis on the *faithfulness* of the master who pays the reward is at least as important here as the apparent emphasis on the *equivalence* between 'much study' and 'much reward'. The nature of the reward is not specified. But it is said – this is the additional point – that the reward is paid in the world to come. (This does not mean that entry into the world to come is itself a reward for works done, but that the reward [whose specific content is unspecified] will be paid in the world to come. *Entry* into that world is guaranteed to members of the covenant people.) So the rewards God gives are for the world to come, as well as for this world. Rabbinic sayings use the metaphor in both contexts.

Reward in the Gospels

I propose now to look at a selection of passages in the Synoptic Gospels where the word *misthos* occurs, or where the *idea* of an equivalence between deeds and their 'pay-off' seems to be present. (Incidentally, I am never very happy about the English word 'reward' as a translation of *misthos* and its Hebrew equivalent *sakar.* The word 'reward' always sounds slightly arbitrary – a small boy who finds a lost budgerigar may or may not receive a reward. But *misthos* is an image from the world of labour. It means wages, pay for work done. You can rely on it: there is nothing arbitrary about it.) I want to look at them with four questions particularly in mind:

1 To whom is the saying addressed?
2 What does the reward consist of?
3 When is the reward paid?
4 Does the reward function as motive for action, or in some other way?

Beginning with Mark's Gospel, we find only a small amount of relevant material.

Mark 9:41

'For truly, I say to you, whoever gives you a cup of water to drink because you bear the name of Christ, will by no means lose his reward.' We are not told here what the reward consists of. It is not clear whether the reward is paid in this age or in the world to come, though the latter would seem more likely. The saying is addressed to the disciples, and it is about reward for someone else. Thus it cannot function here as the *motive* for action, since the people who might be spurred to action by the offer of reward are not themselves being addressed. So what is the significance of the saying? Jeremias suggests that to offer a cup of water in the Palestinian climate is such an obvious thing to do that there was no question even of saying thank you for it; yet God will reward even an everyday action like this.[10] The most ordinary gesture of goodwill towards a disciple is accepted by God as a mark that the one who gives the water is 'not against us [but] is for us' (v. 40).

Mark 10:28–30

These verses take us a little further. Peter has said, 'Lo, we have left everything and followed you' – with the implicit question 'What do we get out of it?' And this is Jesus' reply:

> Jesus said, 'Truly, I say to you, there is no one who has left house or brothers or sisters or mother or father or children or lands, for my sake and for the gospel, who will not receive a hundredfold now in this time, houses and brothers and sisters and mothers and children and lands, with persecutions, and in the age to come eternal life.'

Here we have a saying addressed to disciples, in a context where even the possibility – never mind the profitability – of adherence to the kingdom of God has come in for serious questioning. Jesus gives the assurance that whatever disciples may lose because of their loyalty to him, God will restore it to them in a new and glorious form. The sheer extravagance of the language – a hundred houses, a hundred mothers! – shows that the description is not meant literally. It seems that Jesus is promising the blessings of fellowship with God in the community of disciples, blessings fulfilled in experience of eternal life in the age to come. The description also stresses that the reward, the blessing of God, is out of all proportion to what a disciple can do by self-denial.

It is clear that the reward is not something granted arbitrarily from outside as compensation for the disciple's obedience. The reward springs naturally out of the relation with Jesus and his circle which the disciple has already begun to experience. The reward does not function as motive for action – the motive is 'for my sake and for the gospel'. It is there to bring assurance of God's care and reliability to disciples under threat.

In Mark's version the saying promises reward both in this age and in the age to come, though it is important to see that the two are not different rewards, but the same in different form. Schnackenburg goes so far as to say that this is the only place where Jesus promises reward in this age.[11] While Luke 18:29–30 retains the reference to both ages, Matthew 19:29–30 omits reference to this age – perhaps because he wished to prevent any idea that material reward may be part of a Christian's expectation.

Matthew 5:12

'Rejoice and be glad, for your reward is great in heaven, for so men persecuted the prophets who were before you.' (Lk. 6:23 is substantially similar.)

Once again, in this conclusion to Matthew's final beatitude, we have a promise addressed to disciples. It is not a reward offered to tempt people into following Jesus, but an offer of assurance to those who might otherwise be tempted to think that experience of persecution showed them to be out of tune with God's purpose. The nature of the reward is not made explicit. It is simply 'great' – that is, great in contrast with the sufferings, not great in contrast to some other lesser reward. But in the context of the Beatitudes the content of the reward must be a share in the kingdom of heaven. It is 'in heaven'. This does not mean that the disciple is rewarded when he 'goes to heaven', but that the reward is 'with God'.[12] So certain is it that it can be spoken of as already there, though persecuted disciples must wait for the kingdom to come before they can receive it. It is an eschatological reward, as in the similar beatitude in the Targum fragment on Numbers 23:33: 'Happy are ye, o ye righteous; what a good reward is prepared for you with your Father which is in heaven for the world to come.'[13]

As for the question about motivation, once again we see that the motive for enduring persecution is not reward but 'for my sake' (v. 11). The reward saying expresses the certainty of God's care.

Matthew 5:46

This verse, with parallel or variant material in Luke 6:32–35 says, 'For if you love those who love you, what reward have you? Do not even the tax collectors do the same?' The question of audience is a rather open one here. The paragraph in which this saying is set looks like teaching intended for a wider audience than just the circle of disciples, though it would obviously include disciples.

John Piper poses the question whether the element of reward here might 'reduce Jesus' command of enemy love to a mere expedient whereby his disciples, by using others, satisfy their own desires'.[14] It certainly looks like that, until you remember that in Jesus' teaching God's forgiveness and love *precede* the disciples' love and forgiveness of their neighbour (Mt. 18:23–35; Lk. 7:36–50). So it is not a matter of loving your enemy *in order to* gain a reward. The reward

God offers is (v. 45) to be sons of your Father in heaven (cf. Lk. 6:35), and the love of enemies flows out of this relationship.

Matthew 6:1–6, 16–18

Here Jesus defines his attitude towards the three most important demonstrations of Jewish piety – almsgiving, prayer and fasting – and warns against the religious man's temptation to seek the commendation of other men for his piety. The sayings are addressed to disciples. It speaks plainly of a reward God gives to those whom he approves, in contrast with a reward that comes to those who 'practise their piety before men'. Three times the refrain comes; 'Truly I say to you, they have their reward.' The Greek word *apechō* is often used in receipts, 'paid in full'. 'The praise of men is their full payment, and the account is closed: they have nothing owing to them from God in the age to come.'[15] By contrast, true piety will be self-forgetful.[16] It will not seek attention for itself, but will seek, and find, God. Its reward will be, not human praise, but the approval of God.

It may appear, formally, that reward from God is being offered as the carrot to persuade people to practise their piety unobtrusively. But the reward offered is not such as would appeal to the mercenary-minded. Once again, reward-language is used to offer assurance that God accepts those who seek him, and to paint the contrast between two incompatible approaches to the religious life.

Luke 14:12–14

Here we are moving in the same circle of ideas. You have to choose between having your generosity repaid by your friends, and having the blessing of God, his reward at the final resurrection. The reward God offers carries little attraction for the mercenary-minded.

Here, as in the previous two passages, we have something more radical than was normal in Judaism. Generally, Jewish teachers would encourage expectation of approval by both men and God. Jesus here says that you simply can't have both. You have to choose.

Degrees of Reward

Did Jesus teach *degrees of reward*, distinctions of status in the future kingdom of God? It is widely held that he did, and if that is the case it would fit in with rabbinic teaching about rewards. But all the passages appealed to as examples of this theme are strikingly and frustratingly unspecific about what these degrees or ranks might consist of. Jeremias, for example, appeals to Matthew 5:12, 'your reward is great in heaven'.[17] But does that necessarily imply that the reward for the persecuted is great*er* than that for others? He appeals to Matthew 10:41, 'He who receives a prophet because he is a prophet shall receive a prophet's reward, and he who receives a righteous man because he is a righteous man shall receive a righteous man's reward.' But the meaning of this verse is so problematical that it would be risky to build a doctrine on it. Another passage Jeremias cites is Mark 10:40, Jesus' reply to James and John that 'to sit at my right hand . . . is not mine to grant, but it is for those for whom it has been prepared'. But is this an affirmation that the seating plan is actually all worked out and known by God, or is it really a diversion of the question as being totally improper?

Other sayings of Jesus that suggest degrees of reward naturally include the parable of the pounds (Lk. 19:12–27), where the faithfulness of the first two servants is met with their master's promise, 'Because you have been faithful in a very little, you shall have authority over ten [or five] cities' (v. 17). This is similar to that saying of ben Azzai: 'The reward of a duty [done] is a duty [to be done]' (M. Aboth 4:2).

In the brief space I have to deal with this question, I do not wish to deny completely that Jesus echoed Jewish ideas about degrees of reward. But I doubt whether there is evidence to suggest that he had any systematic teaching about ranks in God's kingdom. He used this kind of language partly as a way of expressing his persistent theme that the kingdom of God would be characterised by surprising reversals of rank in contrast with the present age – the last would be first, and the first last (Mk. 9:35, etc.) – and partly as a way of assuring disciples that their great obedience would meet with the great blessing of God.

The following are some conclusions reached so far, before moving on to a final section:

1 All, or nearly all, of the sayings about reward are addressed to those who are already disciples. Most of them presuppose that the disciple is called to self-giving and to suffering.
2 Most of the sayings imply that the reward is given in the world to come, though Mark 10:29–30 at least implies a continuity between the reward in this age and in the age to come. This emphasis on eschatological reward is more prominent than in rabbinic Judaism, though it is certainly not absent there. Whilst stressing reward in the world to come, Jesus gives no hint of accepting the common Jewish view that prosperity in this life is God's reward for obedience.[18]
3 Although the character of the reward is never described explicitly, Jesus implies that it consists of membership of the kingdom community, experience of eternal life in the presence of God and of his people. (Mk. 10:29–30;

Mt. 5:12 in the context of the Beatitudes; Lk. 6:35; Mt. 10:41 with 10:40). The reward is not a thing, but a relationship.

4 The sayings give little support to the idea that Jesus offered reward as a crude motivation to discipleship or moral effort. They are in fact extremely paradoxical. As Bultmann put it, 'Jesus promises reward precisely to those who obey not for the sake of reward.'[19] It is only by not looking to reward that we are able to look to God, and only by looking to God can we find the blessing that God offers. So whatever the language may at first sight suggest, the real basis and motive for Jesus' demand is not reward, but God and his will. Bornkamm stressed this particularly in relation to Matthew 25:31–46, where the element of surprise rules out any possibility of regarding the offer of reward as the motivation for action.[20] As often in Judaism, Jesus' reward-language expresses God's reliability.

5 Jesus radicalised Jewish teaching by his emphasis on single-minded self-giving to God. To receive any reward at all you must deny self and be ready for any catastrophe that comes your way. All calculation of reward in relation to deed is excluded. And the reward God gives is out of all proportion to the disciple's achievement.

6 We might have felt more comfortable if Jesus had spoken in terms of 'virtue is its own reward'. Then it would be clear that reward is not some kind of retributive payment given 'from outside'. But that is one way of speaking that Jesus could not adopt, because for him human actions are never independent actions controlled by merely human norms. They are always actions carried out 'before God', they are a matter of obedience or disobedience to him. And he does not view them indifferently. In a theistic framework you have to have *some* way of saying that there is 'advantage' in loving God, that your love and obedience leads somewhere, that it is in fact approved by God, whatever anyone else may say. 'Reward' language is a popular way of expressing this, and Jesus' language was nothing if not popular.

7 Those scholars are wrong who seek to find a great gulf fixed between Jewish teaching and Jesus' teaching about reward. There is a shift of emphasis, a radicalising of demand, a greater safeguarding against misunderstanding and abuse. But the teaching of Jesus is in recognisable continuity with that of Judaism.

The Context of Jesus' Reward-Language

Jesus' language about reward can only be properly understood if it is seen in relation to three other dominant themes in his teaching.

1 First, there is Jesus' *proclamation of the grace of God*. The centre of his message is the announcement of the kingdom of God, which is already breaking into history. To establish the kingdom and to bring people into it is God's act. We cannot build it or deserve it. It is a gift: 'Fear not, little flock, for it is your Father's good pleasure to *give* you the kingdom' (Lk. 12:32, my emphasis; cf. 22:29; 4:18ff.; 6:20ff.). Nowhere is this theme brought out more clearly or more startlingly than in the parable of the labourers in the vineyard (Mt. 20:1–15). This is one of those parables in which Jesus is concerned to vindicate his gospel against its critics.[21] It presents, if you like, the tragic drama of the labourers hired at the beginning of the day, who can think only in terms of a just wage and in the end are estranged from a generous master.[22] They are all lined up, watching with astonishment as the latecomers are paid the full day's wage. Astonishment turns to fury as they themselves receive no more than the full day's wage that was agreed at the start. From their point of view it is an intolerable situation. To them the unexpected generosity of the owner is not graciousness, but injustice. So there is a conflict between two worlds of thought. There are those who insist on being able to calculate how the master's benefits should be distributed; and there is the master, to whom the spotlight now turns, who insists on dealing with employees on the basis of their need and his own reckless generosity: 'Am I not allowed to do what I choose with what belongs to me? Or do you begrudge my generosity?' (Mt. 20:15).

As always, the weight of the parable falls at the end. It is not that God rewards some people justly according to their labours, but acts *generously* towards others who respond to him late in the day. The truth is that those who think only in terms of justice completely misunderstand God. Jesus leaves his critics with the question ringing in their ears: Will you criticise God's goodness? Dare you come to terms with a God whose dealings with people cannot be calculated like wage-packets, but are characterised by incalculable grace?

This emphasis on grace as the basis of God's relations with people is underlined by the frequency with which Jesus proclaims – even while speaking in terms of 'reward' – that what God gives is out of all proportion to the service rendered by men and women. We have already noticed the passage where a 'hundredfold' reward is promised for the self-sacrifice of his disciples (Mk. 10:29–30). In the parable of the talents, the servants who are 'faithful over a little' are 'set over much' (Mt. 25:21, 23; cf. 24:47). And in Luke's parable of the watchful servants (Lk. 12:35–37), there is the totally unexpected act of the master who comes home, finds his servants alert, and rewards them by having them sit at table while he himself serves them a banquet.

But this paradoxical picture of a master giving his energies to the needs of his servants leads us to the second theme important for a proper understanding of Jesus' treatment of reward.

2 Jesus' common picture of *the disciple's relation to God as a slave–master relationship* rules out the principle of reward. The roles and expectations of master and slave were well understood by Jesus and his hearers. A master could make any demand of his servant, and expect it to be carried out. He could, for example, entrust money to the servant and expect him to use it responsibly (Mt. 25:14–30). Equally, he could demand the money back (Mt. 18:23–35). The idea of pay, normal in the contract between a master and a hired labourer (Mt. 20:1–15), was excluded in the relation between a master and his slave. If the master gave the slave any favours, it was out of kindness, not contract. The key passage here is Luke 17:7–10:

> Will any one of you, who has a servant ploughing or keeping sheep, say to him when he has come in from the field, 'Come at once and sit down at table'? Will he not rather say to him, 'Prepare supper for me, and gird yourself and serve me, till I eat and drink; and afterward you shall eat and drink'? Does he thank the servant because he did what was commanded? So you also, when you have done all that is commanded you, say, 'We are unworthy servants; we have only done what was our duty.'

In terms of Palestinian society, there is nothing unusual or harsh about the master's attitude here. The slave is in a relationship with his master in which it is his responsibility to obey. His best service is no more than the master is entitled to expect. 'So you also, when you have done all that is commanded you, say, "We are unworthy servants; we have only done what was our duty" ' (v. 10). We have done nothing to *earn* God's approval, and all our good works give us no claim on him.[23]

So the slave–master image expresses the disciple's total obligation to God. It is not a contractual relationship, in which wages can be earned. The same theme is occasionally expressed in Judaism, for example, in the saying attributed to Johanan ben Zakkai: 'If thou hast wrought much in the law claim not merit for thyself, for to this end wast thou created' (M. Aboth 2:8; cf. 1:3). But such a saying is comparatively rare. Whereas Judaism spoke readily of rewards for obedience, Jesus' use of the slave–master image rules out in principle any such contractual understanding of humanity's relationship to God.[24]

3 Jesus often speaks of the outcome of human deeds not in terms of reward or punishment imposed from outside, but in terms of the *intrinsic consequences to which they lead*. Here any idea of reward earned and quantified and paid out by God is excluded: there is an inner, organic relation between our lives and our destinies.

I am thinking, for example, of the images of sowing and reaping, of growing and bearing fruit. Matthew 7:18–20: 'A sound tree cannot bear evil fruit, nor can a bad tree bear good fruit. Every tree that does not bear good fruit is cut down and thrown into the fire. Thus you will know them by their fruits' (cf.

Lk. 6:43–44; Mt. 12:33; 15:13). The fruit you get follows inevitably from the tree you plant.

Or there is the image of the 'two ways', familiar in Judaism and found in Matthew 7:13–14. There is a way that leads to destruction and a way that leads to life. Life is not a reward for taking the right road, but is where the road unerringly leads. There is an intrinsic connection between the route and the destination.

The image of 'treasure in heaven' has the same effect. In Judaism it was a popular image. God was pictured as a banker, with whom you could keep a good deposit account by performing good deeds such as almsgiving (e.g. Tobit 4:7–11; Sirach 29:11–12; Pss. Sol. 9:9).[25] The idea was sometimes elaborated into the belief that you could store up treasure in heaven as capital, and live off the interest on the capital now (M. Aboth 3:18). In other words, your acts of charity could secure you the blessing of God in the age to come, while you could also expect to live well during this life. But Jesus' meaning is less complex and more radical (Mt. 6:19–21; Mk. 10:21; Lk. 12:33). For him it is impossible to chase both earthly and heavenly treasure. You have to choose which you are interested in. 'For where your treasure is, there will your heart be also' (Mt. 6:21). That link between 'treasure' and 'heart' is unique to Jesus. Set your heart on God and his blessings and that is precisely what you receive. There is an organic connection between what you set your heart on and what you ultimately experience in the presence of God.

The same intrinsic continuity between our actions and choices and God's reaction to them is seen in the Beatitudes (Mt. 5:3ff.; Lk. 6:20ff.). A share in the kingdom of heaven is not a reward for being poor in spirit; it is because the poor and distressed may thereby become aware of their dependence on God that they are open to the gift of life in his kingdom. Even a beatitude using the *language* of equivalent reward – 'Blessed are the merciful, for they shall obtain mercy' (Mt. 5:7) – must be interpreted in non-retributive terms. For according to Jesus the merciful are *already* blessed. Their showing mercy is a reflection of the mercy and forgiveness already shown to them by God. This is the truth underlying the parable of the unmerciful servant in Matthew 18:23–35.[26] 'One does not earn the reward; one simply receives in full at the last judgment what one has already freely experienced through Jesus Messiah, namely, the pardoning acceptance of God.'[27]

Conclusion

Given this framework, where God's grace and humanity's relationship as servant to him are fundamental, and where our choices and actions are seen to lead intrinsically to their God-given consequences, there is no danger of reward language being misunderstood. There was no point in Jesus eliminating it because it expressed in a popular way the utter reliability of God to give what he generously promises. It is fundamental for Jesus that the certainty of eternal life rests not on something in humanity but on the character and reliability of God (cf. Mk. 12:18–27).

Notes

1 *Christianity and Morals* (London: Kegan Paul, 1939), 67.

2 E. P. Sanders, *Paul and Palestinian Judaism* (London: SCM Press, 1977), has demonstrated clearly that a legalistic doctrine of salvation by works was not generally taught in Palestinian Judaism around Jesus' time.

3 This view is rightly attacked by P. S. Minear, *And Great Shall Be Your Reward* (New Haven: Yale University Press, 1941), 52.

4 *Jesus in the Church's Gospels* (London: SPCK, 1970), 247.

5 *Paul and Palestinian Judaism*, esp. 117–47.

6 Ibid., 117.

7 *Theological Dictionary of the New Testament*, 2, 197–8.

8 E.g. Sifre on Deut. 33:6, cited in Morton Smith, *Tannaitic Parallels to the Gospels* (Philadelphia: SBL, 1951), 177.

9 See examples listed by M. Smith, *Tannaitic Parallels*, 163–84.

10 *New Testament Theology* (Eng. trans. London: SCM Press, 1971), 217.

11 *The Moral Teaching of the New Testament* (Eng. trans. repr. London: Burns & Oates, 1975), 156.

12 G. Dalman, *The Words of Jesus* (Eng. trans. Edinburgh: T. & T. Clark, 1902), 206–8.

13 See M. McNamara, *Targum and Testament* (Shannon: Irish University Press, 1972), 131.

14 *Love Your Enemies* (Cambridge: Cambridge University Press, 1979), 60.

15 J. C. Fenton, *The Gospel of St. Matthew* (Harmondsworth: Penguin Books, 1963), 98.

16 See Jeremias, *New Testament Theology*, 216; G. Bornkamm, 'Der Lohngedanke im NT', in *Studien zu Antike und Urchristentum* (Munich: Kaiser, 1959), 80.

17 *New Testament Theology*, 216.

18 J. Schmid, *Das Evangelium nach Matthäus* (Regensburg: Pustet, 1959), 292; J. Riches, *Jesus and Transformation of Judaism* (London: Darton, Longman & Todd, 1980), 151–2.

19 *Jesus and the Word* (Eng. trans., rev. edn., London: Collins, 1958), 62.

20 'Der Lohngedanke', 80–81.

21 J. Jeremias, *The Parables of Jesus* (Eng. trans., rev. edn., London: SCM Press, 1963), 136.

22 D. O. Via, *The Parables: Their Literary and Existential Dimension* (Philadelphia: Fortress Press, 1967), 147–55.

[23] Cf. Jeremias, *The Parables of Jesus*, 193. Whether the parable was originally addressed to Pharisees (Jeremias) or to disciples (as in Luke) the point about obedience bringing no claim to reward remains the same. For *achreios* (v. 10) meaning 'unworthy' rather than 'useless', see LXX 2 Kgs. [2 Sam.] 6:22. On the social context see also K. E. Bailey, *Through Peasant Eyes* (Grand Rapids: Eerdmans, 1980), 114–26.

[24] Riches, *Jesus*, 151–4.

[25] Cf. *Theological Dictionary of the New Testament*, 3, 136–8.

[26] Jeremias, *The Parables of Jesus*, 210–14.

[27] R. A. Guelich, *The Sermon on the Mount* (Waco: Word, 1982), 89–90.

2

Does the New Testament Teach Universal Salvation?[1]

I. Howard Marshall

'Lord, are only a few people going to be saved?' (Lk. 13:23). Some would argue that, since Jesus himself refused to answer this question directly but rather said, 'Make every effort to enter through the narrow door', we cannot answer it and should not try to do so. We are free to assume that 'all' will be saved. Those who take this line fail to note that Jesus goes on to say that 'many will try to enter and will not be able to', which effectively rules out the position that Jesus leaves open the universalist position in this particular saying. We cannot on the basis of this text adopt an optimistic agnosticism. The question that Jesus refuses to answer directly is not whether the saved are many or all, but whether they are many or few.

I propose to take up one aspect of the question as to whether all will be saved, namely the evidence provided in the writings of Paul, since it is here, if anywhere in the New Testament that the proponents of universalism find evidence for their view.[2]

The Evidence of Paul

Discussion of the Pauline material has been placed in a new light by the work of M. E. Boring. His argument is that the evidence presented by Paul's letters gives the appearance of tension and conflict, and this arises from the fact that Paul uses two types of images in his writings. There is first of all the kind of language that talks of the saved and the lost as two groups and of an ultimate separation between them. But side by side with this we have a kind of monistic language that talks of the ultimate sovereignty of God and of the total subjugation of his enemies. So in Romans 5 we have language universal in its reference to the parallel effects of Adam and Christ that affect everybody, and in its stress that the saving deed of Christ is greater than the condemning deed of Adam. These two strands exist side by side in Paul, who can thus make 'logically inconsistent, but not incoherent, statements'.[3] Boring wants to claim that Paul makes both limited and universal statements with regard to salvation, but that he does not draw out the ultimate logical consequences of each in a way that would reveal them to be inconsistent with each other.

A variety of images

Boring is right in affirming that Paul uses a variety of images in discussing the nature of salvation. He expresses it positively in terms of inheriting the kingdom of God, being saved, being reconciled to God, being redeemed from sin, and being with the Lord. But this has its negative side. In nearly all of these images the picture is of people who are already lost and who need to be delivered. Paul is quite clear that people are on their way to destruction if they do not respond to the gospel. They are already perishing. In general, those who practise the works of the flesh will not inherit the kingdom of God (Gal. 5:21). Those who sow to the flesh will reap corruption (Gal. 6:8; 1 Cor. 6:9–10). Those who are guilty of the body and blood of the Lord will be condemned by God (1 Cor. 11:32).

Paul also has a concept of sin against the Holy Spirit (cf. Eph. 4:30). The Lord will punish people guilty of sexual immorality, for they are rejecting not man but God who gives the Holy Spirit (1 Thes. 4:6,8). This suggests that such people sin against the Spirit (cf. Rom. 12:19).

The final judgment is one of wrath and fury upon the wicked (Rom. 2:5, 8–9; 5:9; 9:22; cf. Phil. 1:28; 3:19; Col. 3:5–6; Eph. 2:3; 5:5–6), including those whose opposition to God is shown in opposition to the church (2 Thes. 1:7–10). The man of lawlessness, who symbolises opposition to God, is doomed to destruction and will be destroyed (2 Thes. 2:3, 8). Only those who do not persist in unbelief will be saved, even out of the Jews (Rom. 11:23). Salvation includes deliverance from the wrath and from destruction (1 Thes. 1:10; 5:9), and it is offered provided that people do not move away from the hope of the gospel (Col. 1:23).

These points show that often Paul operates with a framework of two types of people and two ultimate destinies.

Judgment may not be final

Within this particular type of imagery some scholars have found the possibility that judgment may not be final. A doctrine of purgatory has been detected in 1 Cor. 3:12–15 by E. Stauffer.[4] However, this is a mistaken view of the passage, which is referring rather to the way in which people may be saved 'by the skin of their teeth', as we would say. In any case, Paul is here referring to people who are believers but whose works will be tested by fire, and in the next couple of verses he speaks of people who try to destroy God's temple and will themselves be destroyed by God. The doctrine of purgatory is irrelevant to the destiny of non-believers.

Appeal can also be made to 1 Cor. 5:5 where the incestuous offender is to be handed over to Satan for the destruction of his flesh that his spirit may be saved in the day of Christ. But again the reference is to a believer, a member of the church, and Paul is dealing with the purpose, not with the guaranteed result of this mysterious process.

Universal lordship

We must next look at the kind of material noted by Boring where a different imagery from that of the saved and the lost is used and the suggestion is of a universal lordship of Christ into whose realm all people are brought.

1 Corinthians 15:22–28

In 1 Corinthians 15:22–28 we are told that, as in Adam all die, even so in Christ all will be made alive. Paul's point, however, is not to affirm that all die in Adam and all will certainly come to life in Christ, but rather that just as the death of each and all is due to Adam so the resurrection of each and all is due to Christ. He means simply that in every case where people receive life it is through their union with Christ. Against those who would dispute it Paul is arguing that it is upon the man Christ that the hope of resurrection is dependent, just as death is due to the man Adam. Wherever death and resurrection take place, they are due respectively to Adam and Christ. Death of course is universal, but this is not necessarily so of resurrection. Indeed, the next verses show that Paul thinks of the resurrection only of 'those who belong to Christ'. The resurrection is followed by the subjugation of his enemies. Boring recognises all this, but argues that Paul is moving into the image of 'God-the-king who unites all in his kingly reign'.[5] But it must be noted that subjugation is not the same thing as unification and reconciliation. Paul teaches the destruction of the cosmic forces opposed to Christ, including death.

Romans 5

All this is relevant to the understanding of Romans 5 where similar statements are made. Boring treats this passage in the same way as 1 Cor. 15:20–22, and he argues that to 'receive' grace and righteousness (Rom. 5:17) is a case of 'passive' reception rather than of 'active' taking; he claims that *lambanō* normally has this sense. This seems to misrepresent the evidence. There are places where Paul talks of receiving by faith (Gal. 3:2, 14) and where the verb appears to refer to the decision of the recipient (Phil. 2:7). Certainly Rom. 5:11 is in the context of justification by faith, and the rest of the passage must surely be understood within its context in Romans and not be treated as an isolated statement on its own.

Furthermore, we must ask what is the force of 'all' in this passage. I suggest that 'all' in Romans 5 really has primarily in view 'both Jews and Gentiles and not just Jews': that is the point that Paul is concerned to make. He is of course referring to *all* humankind and not just saying 'some Jews and some Gentiles', but the thrust of the section is that Christ's action, like Adam's, affects both Jews and Gentiles. The one/many contrast is used of both Adam and Christ to show that both affect the whole human race and not just the Jews. So Paul's aim is not necessarily to assert that all will be saved but that the work of Christ is for all, and that he alone is the Saviour in virtue of the one saving event of his death.

Eternal life is the gracious gift of God in Christ, and it is received by faith. There is no question of all people automatically receiving life apart from faith in Christ.

Romans 9–11

In Romans 9–11 we have the prophecy that all Israel will be saved and that the fullness of the Gentiles will come into the church. God has bound all men over to disobedience so that he may have mercy on them all. Here 'them all' must mean 'Jews and Gentiles alike' in the light of the earlier teaching in the letter. The problem is the identity of the full number of the Gentiles and all Israel. So far as Israel is concerned, the condition is quite plain: 'if they do not persist in unbelief' (Rom. 11:23). It is unimaginable that Paul would drop this condition. The question is then whether God can predestine 'all Israel' to believe. But here we must note: (1) Paul is writing about events in this world and not in the next. (2) There is no indication whatever that he is concerned with the destiny of those who have already died. He is thinking rather of the community of Israel in the last days. In fact there are obviously people who have died in a state of being 'hardened'.

Philippians 2:10–11

In Philippians 2:10–11 we are told that Christ will be exalted so that every knee will bow to him, and every tongue will confess that he is Lord. Boring[6] argues that this text is not to be understood in the framework of the saved and the lost; it is not concerned with salvation but with universal acknowledgment of Christ as Lord – and here Boring sides with E. Best who states that 'for a man to stand on another's neck and compel him to confess he has been vanquished is not a victory compatible with the God of the cross'.[7] Thus the text is in a way open to a universalistic understanding, but Boring would argue that it really belongs within 'the encompassing image of God-the-king and its one-group eschatology'.[8]

In assessing this argument we need to raise the question whether statements made within one encompassing image can overrule statements made in another. Boring rightly refuses to allow this move, arguing that the logical inferences of each image are never drawn; thus Paul does not push himself into explicit inconsistency. But it would be truer to say that in one set of images the question of salvation and loss is not directly in view. The question of the scope of salvation is not being raised.

Two points are important in the understanding of the passage. First, the text is making the point that all who confess God as Lord must also confess Jesus as Lord at his *parousia*. The language is drawn from Is. 45:23, which is also quoted with reference to God the Father in Rom. 14:11. Now in the passage in Romans the reference is to facing judgment and giving account of ourselves to God. But in Philippians 2 Christ occupies this divine position as judge. The passage is primarily a statement about his supreme position under the Father. Whoever confesses God as Lord must give that same honour to Christ. In other words the point is not that everybody will confess Christ as Lord but that everybody who recognises God as Lord should.

The second point is that vv. 10–11 are concerned with the purpose of God's exaltation of Christ. They do not constitute a statement that everybody will in fact acknowledge Christ as Lord, but rather a statement that the purpose of God in exalting Christ is to win for him universal acknowledgment as Lord. As G. F. Hawthorne notes, 'how these purposes will be fulfilled, or when they will be fulfilled, or whether they will be fulfilled are not questions which can be answered from the statements of the hymn itself'.[9] Nevertheless, we should note that later in this same letter Paul refers to people who are enemies of the cross and whose destiny is destruction (Phil. 3:18–19).

Two further texts

We come finally in this section to two passages in Colossians and Ephesians.

Colossians 1:20

In Colossians 1:20 God's purpose is 'to reconcile to himself all things, whether things on earth or things in heaven, by making peace through his blood, shed on the cross'. Here we have a programme of reconciliation of cosmic scope.

The passage is basically about the place of the readers in the kingdom of God's Son. Formerly they were under the power of darkness, but now they have been rescued from it and transferred to a new ruler. They have been redeemed or set free, and this took place when their sins were forgiven. In vv. 21ff. they are said to have been alienated and became enemies through their evil deeds, but now they have been reconciled by the death of Christ so that they are seen as holy, blameless and irreproachable in the sight of God. We have two descriptions of the same basic event couched in different terminology. But the latter is introduced by what is apparently a digression, a description of Jesus which describes his role in creation and in reconciliation and which thus serves to place the readers in a cosmic context with the object of showing that they are no longer subject to any power other than Christ. There is a parallel between creation and reconciliation and in each case the effect is to stress the supremacy of Christ. The everything in v. 20 must be the same as in v. 16, namely things visible and invisible, thrones, rulers, principalities and powers. They are described in neutral terms here, but elsewhere they are uniformly negative as powers opposed to God. In 2:15 Christ strips the principalities and powers and makes them a public spectacle; he leads them in his triumphal procession as enemies destined for death. Although Paul daringly applies the same metaphor to himself in 2 Corinthians 2:14, there is no reason to suppose that the evil powers are similarly redeemed by Christ.

(i) The main point that Paul is making is that it is only through Christ that this reconciliation happens. Since it is for 'everything', there is no room for any other reconciler or act of reconciliation.

(ii) In 2 Corinthians 5 reconciliation has to be accepted to become effective. This is implied here, for v. 23 goes on to speak of the necessity of remaining grounded in the faith and not moving away from it.

(iii) What is being described is what happened on the cross. It was the place where the powers were led in triumph. There is no future act of reconciliation here. A past event is described.[10]

(iv) According to Paul's earlier letters the creation is still in bondage to the powers of evil and groans to be released. Paul looks forward to the revelation of the sons of God and the redemption of their bodies: this is clearly the event described in 1 Corinthians 15 which is linked to the *parousia*. Paul has no expectations of any saving event after the *parousia*. Everything is summed up in that event. So there is an already/not yet tension in this act of reconciliation. Reconciliation has been achieved in the death of Jesus, but the offer 'be reconciled to God' continues to be presented to the world.

The situation envisaged in Colossians appears to be the same. What is being described is an act of reconciliation of cosmic scope that has taken place through the death of Christ. As a result of the proclamation of the gospel there has been a response by the readers of the letter, so that they are now reconciled and have come into submission to their Head, Jesus Christ. But the powers are still active. It is not said that they will all come under willing submission to Christ. Paul knows only the fate of judgment for rebellious humankind which refuses to accept the reconciliation. It is not clear whether there is reconciliation available for the hostile powers. The implication of 2:15 which describes the triumph of Christ over the powers at the cross is that they are under sentence of death. It may be best, therefore, to assume that when Paul speaks of the reconciliation of all things in 1:20 he is thinking primarily of the human world and the possibility of its turning away from the powers to be reconciled to God. On the other hand, it is conceivable that he envisages the possibility that the powers who have been defeated at the cross may turn in repentance towards Christ and be reconciled to God; but if this is what he means, he certainly has not said so directly and clearly.

Moreover, all this applies to the powers. There is nothing to imply that humankind are treated in any other way than on the basis of faith in Christ. There is no hint of a future act of universal reconciliation other than that which has already taken place in the cross. No future event is prophesied or described. Paul is dealing with what Christ has done, and with what has happened as a result to the readers.

Ephesians 1:10

Finally, in Ephesians 1:10 God's purpose for the fulness of time is 'to bring all things in heaven and on earth together under one head, even Christ'. The 'fulness of time' may well refer to the end-time which was inaugurated by the incarnation as in Galatians.[11] To sum up is to bring everything together or perhaps to make everything new, to unite under one head, namely Christ. So this is the purpose of the coming of Christ, which has already begun to be put into operation. But there is no suggestion that this will include people who refuse to be included. The powers of evil are still active and hostile (2:2; 6:12) and they are under God's wrath (2:3). Wrath is coming on the disobedient (5:6). As in Colossians, there is no basis here for believing that all humankind and all the hostile powers will in fact be reconciled to God. Paul's aim is to stress that all God's plans come to fruition in Christ and that his sovereignty affects the whole universe.

The effect of our discussion is to show that, while Boring is right to draw attention to the variety of imagery used by Paul, the suggestion that, if pressed, the various images would present an inconsistent picture, is to be resisted. Nothing that we have discovered in the 'lordship' passages places a question mark against Paul's use of the categories 'saved' and 'lost' nor against his belief that there will be those who ultimately face the wrath of God.

The Significance of the Evidence

We have now surveyed the relevant material in Paul. In the rest of the New Testament there is certainly no explicit teaching in favour of universalism, and there is no implicit teaching either.[12] Those who look for it in the New Testament are clutching at insubstantial straws. But is that the end of the matter? C. S. Duthie concludes his examination of the Johannine material by admitting that the evidence is slight, but claims to find 'the beginning of a movement toward universalism'. He claims indeed that the notion is 'present in sufficient strength to generate [a] tension [between the doctrines of everlasting punishment and universal salvation]'.[13]

On this there are two things to be said. The first is that this conclusion that the notion is present with what Duthie calls 'sufficient strength' is not justified by the evidence. Suppose for a moment that the case was the other way round and the clear evidence was in favour of universalism; if the evidence for everlasting punishment, as Duthie calls the alternative, were as palpably weak as the actual evidence for universalism is, no reputable scholar would treat it seriously. He would be laughed out of court for his prejudice and blindness.

If universalism were a New Testament doctrine, we should expect to find the following statements clearly made in the New Testament or, at the very least, made implicitly:

(a) That what is presented as the final judgment is not final, and that people's lot can change after death (or after the judgment).
(b) That there will be some future offer of the gospel (since it will surely be agreed that salvation can only be through Christ and through personal response to him); or, alternatively, that in some way God will change the hearts of all humankind to respond in faith to him.
(c) That everybody will in fact make this response.

None of these is to be found. All that can be found is the statement that God is not willing that any should perish but wants everyone to come to repentance (2 Pet. 3:9). But this is advanced as a reason why the Lord delays the end of the world and the judgment, not as a basis for belief that he will have mercy after the judgment.

But suppose, second, that Duthie is right and that there is a movement in the direction of universal restoration in the New Testament. What then? What is implied by a 'movement toward'?

We have surely to hold fast to the teaching of the New Testament that God loves sinners and yet that he judges them. This is in my view the major contribution of Aberdeen's greatest theological son, Peter Taylor Forsyth.[14] Against the liberalism of his day he insisted repeatedly that the character of God was not merely love, for that could be reduced to mere sentiment, but holy love, and that the holiness and justice of God must be preached as much as the love of God; it was only thus that he could make sense of the atonement, by interpreting it in moral categories. To talk of the ultimate nature of God as loving without at the same time talking of this ultimate nature as being holy and righteous is to do injustice to Scripture where God's love and holiness are not opposed but are different expressions of the same eternal fact. There is no way that the holy wrath of God against sin can somehow be subsumed under his love so that it ceases to be real. It is incorrect to say that God's justice will give way to his love or that his wrath against sin is not the ultimate reality in his nature. Since holiness is his very nature, God is implacably opposed to the action of his creatures who freely choose to sin. And this resistance must surely continue throughout eternity; it is not something that God can put away at will. Yet because he loves his creatures in their sin, he wishes to save them from the consequences of their rebelliousness, and the only way in which he can do this is the way in which he has done it, by himself satisfying the holiness of his own nature in a vicarious sacrifice for sin.

Consequently, any doctrine of universal salvation must be based not on a denial of the reality of judgment but on the claim that God will somehow deliver sinners from it. It can now be argued that God is in fact revealed in the Bible as the God who forgives sinners. On the one hand, he provides a way of atonement, foreshadowed in the sacrificial system in the Old Testament and effected fully and finally in the sacrificial death of Jesus, thereby showing himself to be both just and the one who justifies sinners. On the other hand, he extends forgiveness to those who turn to him for mercy and put their faith in him through Jesus Christ. God is thus seen to make forgiveness possible and actual.

Granted, then, that this is how God is revealed in Scripture, can we on this basis go further and say that God will act again in the same kind of way at the End, making it somehow possible for those who died in their sins to be forgiven? Would this not be of a piece with his revelation of himself as a Saviour in the death of Jesus? Would this be a legitimate extrapolation from the doctrine of the atonement?

One theologian who finds hints of such a movement is E. Stauffer who contrasts what Paul says in Galatians and Romans:

> Once Paul had written: 'the scripture hath shut up all things under sin, that the promise by faith in Jesus Christ might be given *to them that believe.*' (Gal. 3.22). But now the last reservation has disappeared: 'God hath shut up all unto disobedience, that he might have mercy upon all' (Rom. 11.32). The universalism of the divine creativity requires and guarantees the divine salvation.[15]

Here Stauffer is arguing that Paul's thought undergoes a shift towards universalism between Galatians and Romans. He seems to hold that despite the *earlier* expression of a different view in Galatians and the *parallel* or even *later* expression of a different view in John and Revelation, we go by what Romans says. Now there is no question but that Stauffer is wrong in his exegesis of Romans; he can produce no reason why the exegesis of Galatians should not control the exegesis of Romans at this point, and above all why Romans 11:32 should not be read in the context of Romans itself where the need for faith as the only way to salvation is hammered home as recently as nine verses previously; to suggest that one verse in Paul where faith is not mentioned upturns the entirety of what Paul wrote elsewhere is ludicrous.

Consequently, those who defend the movement towards universalism must admit that it is not presented explicitly in the New Testament. The question would then be whether taking this step is the same kind of thing as happens when we make ethical extrapolations from the teaching of the New Testament. For example, we can say that the New Testament shows a movement towards antislavery. And we would agree that we can walk further along this path because it brings out the latent principles of the New Testament. We can find a movement towards the emancipation of women. Both are cases where the full significance of basic ethical insights had not yet been fully recognised. Is the salvation of all as opposed to some a similar fuller insight?

We are being asked to come to a new understanding of what God will do, which goes beyond the finality of his revelation in the cross and which requires him to act differently towards sinners than he has done in the cross. The question is not really one of the extent of God's love – that he loves all and does not wish any to perish is clear biblical teaching – the question is rather whether his love leads him to act in different ways from those already revealed in Christ. It is there that the danger in universalism is to be found, for, if we adopt a doctrine of God that is not bound up with his self-revelation in Christ we have departed from the Christian doctrine of God. If, then, we adopt universalism, we are moving away from the revelation given in Christ – and in Scripture – on no other basis than our own sense of what is fitting.

Some people are, in Duthie's term, 'crypto-universalists'. They would like to believe that universalism is true and that none will be finally condemned. Of course, the Lord takes no delight in the death of the sinner, and God forgive us if we take delight in it. But the danger is that the wish can become the father of the belief that ultimately all will be saved. That is a step that we dare not take, that we cannot take, so long as we are biblical realists. What we are called to do is to proclaim the gospel of faith in Jesus Christ as the only sure hope for humankind.

Other New Testament Evidence

The teaching of Jesus

Over against the consistent picture in the Gospels of the reality of a final judgment leading to the exclusion of some from the kingdom of God it could be argued:

1 A good deal of the material may be due to the Evangelists (or the tradition) elaborating on the teaching of Jesus and giving it an emphasis or even a fresh direction that was not present in the original material. This would be especially characteristic of Matthew.

2 Ultimately Jesus says that all sins are forgivable except one, the sin against the Holy Spirit. But have we any evidence that there will be people who will in the end sin against the Holy Spirit? And does 'never' really mean 'never'?

Neither of these points is convincing.

1 This is not the place to enter into a detailed discussion of the authenticity and original wording of the various sayings of Jesus which I have cited. I would be prepared to affirm that the picture presented by the Evangelists is a uniform one, and that this picture represents the general impression of what Jesus taught.

2 Attempts to rid the saying about the unforgivable sin of its significance are quite artificial. The question is generally put in terms of the meaning of *aiōnios*, 'everlasting', and it is contended that this word expresses quality rather than temporal extent. However, this contention is baseless, since Luke's form of the saying simply has 'will not be forgiven', and Matthew has 'will not be forgiven in this age or the coming age'. Similarly Mark uses the expression in parallel to 'is never forgiven', literally 'not . . . to the age'. The only possible way round this is to suggest that 'the coming age' or 'the age' is not the final age but a penultimate period followed (although Jesus does not mention it) by the final age itself in which (although Jesus does not mention it) sin will be forgiven. We must also remember that there is no teaching in the Gospels that suggests any change in the final destiny of people once it has been settled. There is no escape for the rich man from Hades (Lk. 16:26), and the door to the banqueting hall is firmly shut (Mt. 25:10 par. Lk. 13:25).

It must also be remembered that when the saying teaches that all other sins can be forgiven, this is by no means the same thing as saying that they necessarily will be, and that the one sin which cannot be forgiven is rejection of the Spirit.

Are there, however, any implicit clues which suggest that universalism was a belief held by Jesus which he did not communicate directly to his friends? Can we find evidence that he himself held this belief which by its nature he could not share with anybody else? Obviously it would be difficult to provide such evidence, and this is why it is difficult to refute the convinced universalist who insists that Jesus could have held this belief despite the lack of open attestation. But in the total absence of positive evidence that Jesus believed that God willed the ultimate salvation of all, we have no justification for interpreting his statements about ultimate separation as being anything other than what they prima facie are and stating that they are merely warnings. When Duthie comments that despite every effort to find evidence for universalism in the Gospels 'the evidence on the other side has the stronger appearance', he is indulging in understatement. It would be more to the point to say that, if we attribute to Jesus an underlying universalism, we make nonsense of the beliefs and attitudes that we can certainly attribute to him.

Gospel of John

In the Gospel of John alongside expressions of the universal scope of the love of God we find that non-believers are condemned already (3:18). The resurrection will be to life or to condemnation (5:28–9). Jesus foreknew that there would be some who would not believe (6:64). It is possible to die in one's sins (8:24). Judas is doomed to destruction (17:12). Nothing suggests that this is anything other than the last word on sinners.

Hebrews

Hebrews stresses the reality of judgment for those who turn their backs on the salvation offered to them by virtue of the sacrifice of Christ (6:7–8; 10:31). The writer trusts that such a fate will not befall his readers, but that they will hear his warnings and respond to them, but it is to Christian believers that he says such things, and he never betrays any hint that those who do not believe in Christ now will be given a chance later (cf. 9:27).

1 Peter 3:18–20

In 1 Peter 3:18–20 Christ went after his death and 'preached to the spirits in prison who disobeyed long ago'. In 4:6 it is affirmed that 'the gospel was preached even to those who are now dead, so that they might be judged according to men in regard to the body, but live according to God in regard to the spirit'. The essential points of interpretation relevant to our problem concern the identity of those addressed by Christ, the nature of his message, and the nature of their response.

It seems reasonably certain to me that the language in 3:18–20 refers to supernatural powers and not to human beings. It also seems quite clear that the context demands that the reference is to Christ's proclamation of victory over the principalities and powers who are now in submission to him (3:20); only this message could act as encouragement to persecuted Christians who felt that they were opposed by powers stronger than themselves. And, if Christ proclaimed his victory, there is no indication that he was making an offer of salvation; on the contrary, the evil powers come into subjection to him.

It follows that 4:6 is about some different event, and much the most plausible is that Peter is commenting about the way the gospel was preached in their lifetime to Christians now dead; to the world they appear to be under judgment, but at God's bar they are vindicated and will live in his presence.

Even if this interpretation is open to question, the passage is certainly no proof of universalism. Nothing is said about *all* the dead responding positively to any such message and receiving a *post mortem* salvation. In fact, 4:5, with its comment on the way in which persecutors of the church will have to give an account of themselves to the judge of the living and the dead, points in the opposite direction. I suggest that 4:6 makes no sense in its context if it refers to such a *post mortem* preaching. And certainly it is no comfort to persecuted Christians who suffer for doing good and who try to bear witness in a malicious world to be told not to worry because Christ proclaimed forgiveness to the evil spirits and they accepted it: how does that help them to face persecution? If the point is to say that their witness to their persecutors will be as successful as Christ's to the evil spirits, then it must be replied that the most important element on this exegesis, the response of the spirits, is not mentioned at all. There is no support for universalism in 1 Peter. (For a fuller treatment see I. H. Marshall, *1 Peter* [Downers Grove, 1991].)

Notes

1 It is a pleasure to offer this discussion of an aspect of the biblical doctrine of salvation as a mark of esteem and good wishes to my friend and colleague James Torrance. The fuller lecture on which the essay is based was given under the auspices of The Drew Lecture Foundation at Spurgeon's College, London, on 19 November 1987, and my thanks are due to the Foundation for the invitation to give it.

2 The only other discussion of the biblical basis for universalism in the Drew lecture series is C. S. Duthie, 'Ultimate Triumph', *Scottish Journal of Theology* 14 (1961), 156–71. See further W. Michaelis, *Versöhnung des Alls* (Bern, 1950); H. Schumacher, *Das biblische Zeugnis von der Versöhnung des Alls* (Stuttgart, 1959); R. J. H. Shutt, 'The New Testament Doctrine of the Hereafter: Universalism or Conditional Immortality', *Expository Times* 67 (1955–56), 131–5; N. T. Wright, 'Towards a Biblical View of Universalism', *Themelios* 4.2 (Jan., 1979), 54–8; M. E. Boring, 'The Language of Universal Salvation in Paul', *Journal of Biblical Literature* 105 (1986), 269–92.

Other literature on the topic includes: J. A. T. Robinson, 'Universalism – is it heretical?', *Scottish Journal of Theology* 2:2 (1949) 139–155; T. F. Torrance, *Scottish Journal of Theology* 2:3 (1949), 310–318; J. D. Bettis, 'A critique of the doctrine of universal salvation', *Religious Studies* 6 (1979), 329–344; R. J. Bauckham, 'Universalism: a historical survey', *Themelios* 4:2 (1979), 48–54.

3 Boring, 'Universal Salvation', 288.

4 E. Stauffer, *New Testament Theology* (London, 1955), 212.

5 Boring, 'Universal Salvation', 280.

6 Boring, 'Universal Salvation', 282–3.

7 E. Best, *The First and Second Epistles to the Thessalonians* (London, 1972), 368.

8 Boring, 'Universal Salvation', 283.

9 G. F. Hawthorne, *Philippians* (Waco, 1983), 94.

10 P. O'Brien, *Colossians, Philemon* (Waco, 1982), 53.

11 Many commentators, however, apply the phrase to the end of time: F. F. Bruce, *The Epistles to the Colossians, to Philemon and to the Ephesians* (Grand Rapids, 1984), 261–2.

12 For a survey of the New Testament evidence see 'Other New Testament Evidence' below.

13 C. S. Duthie, 'Ultimate Triumph', *Scottish Journal of Theology* 14 (1961), 161.

14 P. T. Forsyth, *The Work of Christ* (London, 1910). Duthie, 'Ultimate Triumph', 169, claims that Forsyth was nevertheless a crypto-universalist. According to L. McCurdy (private communication), Forsyth's position is not altogether clear and the evidence may be read in contradictory ways: he held 'the tension between universal atonement and personal freedom, except in one passage'. In *The Justification of God* (London, 1916, 1948), 161, Forsyth speaks of 'a goal of universal salvation, worked out by a method of particular election' which can continue after death. His view may perhaps be best summed up in his statement 'we are obliged to leave such questions as universal restoration unresolved' (*The Work of Christ*, 161).

15 Stauffer, *New Testament Theology*, 224.

3

New Heavens, New Earth

N. T. Wright

Introduction

I come to address the question of immortality with a warning ringing in my ears. A recent book by Professor James Barr *The Garden of Eden and the Hope of Immortality* (Oxford: OUP, 1993) says that those who speak about immortality should be paid danger money for doing so. The subject, declares Barr, arouses strong passions. He cites the violent letters and comments that were addressed to Oscar Cullmann and Krister Stendahl after they had written on this topic. Whether Barr's own book will provoke equally strong reactions remains to be seen.

I have three starting-points as I approach this huge subject. The first is a personal one. It is not just that my Drew Lecture, on which this chapter is based, was delivered on Armistice Day, and that I had two great-uncles who died in the First World War; nor just that, as I was putting the finishing touches to this lecture the night before delivering it, Radio 3 played the wonderful *German Requiem* by Johannes Brahms, with its glorious setting of 'Blessed are they that mourn, for they shall be comforted.' It is more because, pastorally, I am very much aware that everybody's life sooner or later is touched by the awesome question of what, precisely, happens next. The question is still asked, even in our postmodern world, as was graphically shown me not long ago when a woman, engaged in doctoral study in theology, told me of her husband's recent death. She said 'What I want to know is, *where is he?*' These human issues are real questions, not just ideas to play with.

My second starting-point is more academic (which, despite current popular usage, does not of course mean 'irrelevant'!). I had a student some years ago who decided to study Buddhism as one of her options. I sent her to study with the senior Professor in that department in Oxford. She came back puzzled. During the course of a tutorial, he had asked her to compare and contrast the Buddhist view of the soul with the Christian view; and she had had to confess that she could not. She did not know what the Christian view of the soul was, and, despite only just having begun Buddhism, already knew more about the soul within that scheme of thought. The Professor was incensed (I said it was a dangerous subject to get into), and actually wrote me a letter asking how someone could study Christianity for two years, as she had done, without knowing what the soul was. I wrote back and said that it was quite easy to study, as one does, Old Testament, New Testament, a fair amount of Church History, Ethics, and so forth, without ever being confronted head-on by the question 'What is the Christian view of the soul?' It is not a topic upon which many undergraduates have to write essays in traditional theological courses.

But what then *do* we mean when we use the word 'soul', as some of us still do, and as we find in the Bible, the liturgy, the hymn-books (particularly the hymn-books, about which I shall say more presently), and so on? This question has been pointed up by Barr's recent book, just mentioned, and in another recent book, *The Meanings of Death*, by John Bowker (London: DLT, 1993). Bowker argues on the one hand that Marx and Freud are wrong: hope for something beyond death is not mere projection; and, on the other hand, that death possesses a dignity acknowledged across the different cultures and religions, even though as Christians we want to nuance this in specific ways. I do not want to discuss these books here, but rather merely to commend them for further study. Barr will make you think furiously (perhaps in both senses); Bowker will provide a lot of wisdom as well as reflection.

My third starting-point arises out of my own research as a student of the New Testament. I have come to the conviction that the rise of the early church in the 40s and 50s is completely inexplicable, historically speaking, unless you have a strongly historical, bodily view of the resurrection of Jesus of Nazareth. This may seem obvious to some, but it is remarkable how many New Testament scholars manage not to raise the question in that way, and continue to work with a minimalist view of the resurrection, developing theories about how it was that the church began which somehow avoid the question.[1] But it is clear that the resurrection of Jesus does not fit the prevailing worldviews of the time. The Greeks were not expecting 'resurrection' at all, and indeed would have been frustrated to think of re-embodiment. The Jews did not expect that *one* person would rise again from the dead, in the midst of ordinary history, but that God would raise all the true Israel to life at the end of the age. Belief in Jesus' resurrection is thus not simply the product of wish-fulfilment on the part of certain people who held certain expectations and who projected them onto 'reality'. How then do we plot and map the range of first-century beliefs about death and what happens afterwards? That has been one of my concerns as a historian and theologian of the early church, and forms my third starting-point.

Thesis: the integrated Christian hope

With these starting-points, I want now to propose a basic thesis, which to some will seem so blindingly obvious that they will wonder why it needs saying at all, while to others it may seem more than a little controversial. After that, I shall fill the thesis in in certain ways and suggest certain results. The basic thesis is this: that the Christian hope is not simply for 'going to heaven when we die', but for 'new heavens and new earth, integrated together'. Let me spell that out a bit.

Christians regularly speak of their hope in terms of 'going to heaven when they die'. One hears it in hymns; one finds it in prayers – not least (in my tradition) in liturgical prayers, but also when people pray extempore. One hears it in sermons, both explicitly and implicitly. The point seems to be that there is something called 'eternity', which is regularly spoken of as though it has only the loosest of connections with space and time, and one day we are going to step into this eternal existence, whether in the form of heaven or of hell, which has almost nothing to do with this earth and this present history. I suggest that this view, widely held though it is, is far less warranted by the New Testament than would normally be supposed; can be at the very least very seriously misleading, and at worst quite positively damaging to a healthy Christian faith; and should be challenged by a more biblical picture altogether. I suggest instead that what we find in the New Testament, and what I commend, is the Christian hope for a new, or renewed, heaven and a new, or renewed earth, with these two integrated together.

I want to advance this view in five stages. The first is the longest, and looks at some biblical texts.

Biblical Foundations: Clearing the ground

Jesus and the writers of the New Testament have very little to say about 'going to heaven when you die'. When I point this out to my students, as I do from time to time, they look shocked. Why? Very often, people have come to the New Testament with the presumption that 'going to heaven when you die' is the implicit point of it all, of Christianity and indeed of all religion. They acquire that viewpoint from somewhere, but not from the New Testament. But when they then read the New Testament, they think they find it there. We shall look at various texts.

'Kingdom of heaven'

The first book in the New Testament is St Matthew's Gospel; and Matthew has Jesus speaking again and again about 'inheriting the kingdom of heaven'. Now, as all those who have ever taken serious courses in New Testament study will know, the phrase 'kingdom of heaven' in Matthew does not mean 'a place, called "heaven", to which you go after death'. It is, rather, a reverent, typically Jewish, way of saying 'kingdom of God', as in Mark, Luke, John, Paul and elsewhere. And the phrase 'kingdom of God' does not mean 'a place over which God rules', particularly not conceived of as a place other than the present world. It means, rather, 'the *fact that* God rules'. We would do better to translate it as '*kingship*, or *kingly rule*, of God'.[2] This then ties in to the first-century Jewish expectation that God alone would be king. Kingdom-expectation is revolutionary: God will be king, and all the jumped-up pseudo-kings will be put in their place. That is what it means when Jesus uses the phrase.

Matthew's Gospel is actually radically subverted when it unwittingly becomes the tool of people who want to buttress the 'going-to-heaven-when-you-die' view of Christianity. Matthew's Gospel, read like that, offers the Sermon on the Mount, and much else besides, as the guide-book, the rule-book, to enable people to get there in the end. So, just as when people say 'I'm a "Sermon-on-the-Mount" Christian', meaning 'I have a vague memory of some rather fine ethics I once heard somewhere, and I can probably claim some kinship with Jesus on this basis', usually flagrantly ignoring the context, and two-thirds of the content, of the Sermon itself, I suspect that likewise that same Sermon is regularly abused as meaning that if you keep these ethics you will 'go to heaven when you die'. And I suspect that a good deal of ordinary old-fashioned English Christianity exists more or less on that foundation. I suggest that this is a thorough misunderstanding.

'Eternal life'

The second set of texts to which the 'going-to-heaven' view will appeal is the phrase 'eternal life', which occurs quite frequently in Paul and John. But 'eternal life' does not mean 'continuing existence'. It refers neither to a state of timelessness, nor simply to 'linear time going on and on'. In its original Jewish context the phrase fairly certainly refers to 'the life of the age to come'. The 'present age', according to some Jewish thought, would give way to 'the age to come'. One of the great beliefs of the early Christians was that God had already kick-started the 'age to come', even though the 'present age' was still in some sense continuing. The new world order that God was to bring to birth had, they believed, already begun, and those who were Christ's had already entered upon it. The life proper to the new age, the new *aiōn* in Greek, had already begun. The phrase 'eternal life' should not, therefore, be read as though it meant a spaceless, timeless existence. It should refer to a new dispensation which God will create in the renewal of all things. Perhaps we should translate *zōē aiōnios* differently, to make the point.

'Salvation kept in heaven for you'

The third piece of evidence is 1 Peter 1:4, which speaks of 'an inheritance which is imperishable, undefiled, unfading, kept in heaven for you, who are being protected by the power of God through faith for a salvation ready to be revealed in the last time'. My sense is that many people read that passage as referring to a place, called 'heaven', where salvation is to be found, and to which we have to go in order to get it. I want to suggest, conversely, that that idea of something being 'kept in heaven for you' does not mean that you have to go and live in heaven in order to enjoy it. 'Heaven' in the Bible is not usually a reference to a future state, but to God's dimension of present reality, that dimension which is normally hidden from our gaze but where God's purposes are stored up. The point is that salvation is being kept safe in heaven for you, in order then to be brought *from* heaven to where you are, so that you can enjoy it there. It is rather like a parent, in the run-up to Christmas, assuring a child that 'there is indeed a present kept safe in the cupboard for you'. That does not mean that on Christmas Day and thereafter the child is going to have to go and live in the cupboard in order to enjoy the present there. Rather, it means that at the appropriate time the present will be brought forth out of its safe hiding-place, so that it can enrich the life of the child in the world of real life, not just in the cupboardly world.

'Our citizenship is in heaven'

This way of reading 1 Peter 1 is reinforced by another passage in the New Testament: Philippians 3:19–21, 'Our citizenship is in heaven', or, as Moffatt translates it, 'we are a colony of heaven'. What does that mean?

Many have thought that if our citizenship is in heaven that means that heaven is our real home, the place to which we will eventually go. But that is not how the language of citizenship functions. The point of being a citizen of a mother city is not that when life gets really tough, or when you retire, you can go back home to the mother city. The people to whom Paul was writing in Philippi were Roman citizens, but they had no intention of going back to Rome. They were the means through which Roman civilisation was being brought to the world of Northern Greece. If and when the going got tough there, the emperor would come *from* Rome to deliver them from their enemies in Philippi, and establish them as a true Roman presence right there. So, Paul says, 'from heaven we await a saviour, the Lord Jesus Christ, who will change our lowly body to be like his glorious body'. This is, I suggest, much more integrated with a theology of new heavens and new earth than with a theology of going from the present space-time world to a non-spatio-temporal one. It ties in with other passages such as Galatians 4:21–31, which speaks of the Jerusalem 'which is above'. The purpose is not to escape to that Jerusalem, any more than the muddled Galatians thought they had to go and live in terrestrial Jerusalem in order to be proper Christians. No: they were under the dangerous influence of the terrestrial Jerusalem, and Paul is saying, in effect, 'you must be under the influence of, and act as the agents of, the heavenly Jerusalem'. Philippians 3 and Galatians 4 both speak of the dimension of the present reality which is to be informed by the mother city, not of a sense of escaping from present reality to that mother city.

Mark 13: sun, moon, stars – and Jerusalem

The next biblical passage is Mark 13 and its parallels, the wrongly so-called 'little apocalypse'. This passage is not about the end of the space-time world; it is about the fall of Jerusalem.[3] The language of sun, moon and stars being destroyed is a part of a metaphor-system, designed to invest present reality with its theological significance. This usage is rooted in the Old Testament, where prophets regularly used 'cosmic' language of this sort to describe what we would call 'earth-shattering' events in the social and political spheres. Talk of sun, moon and stars goes back, in particular, to passages like Isaiah 13, which is *describing* the fall of Babylon and *investing* that event with its full cosmic or God-level significance.[4]

All depends on the recognition, and appropriate decoding, of the metaphor – a problem which might afflict us all. If we were to describe the fall of the Berlin Wall as an 'earth-shattering event', someone in a couple of thousand years' time might misread that as a reference to a literal physical earthquake which created a new situation in which East and West learned to live with each other. That misreading, I suggest, is exactly what first-century readers would see in the modern reading of Mark 13 as a reference to the end of the space-time universe. The most natural first-century Jewish reading of it would be as a reference to what we would call 'earth-shattering events'. What sort of things would count as the 'sun and the moon falling from heaven, and the powers of the heavens being shaken'? Well, for example, having four different emperors on the throne within a year (remember, of course, that the Roman emperor was the ruler of most of the known world), each one having got there by means of a military coup. That is what happened in AD 69. Then, when Jerusalem was captured and burnt the next year, the only language that would be appropriate would be that of cosmic collapse. It was the end of the world for all sorts of people – with the awful corollary that they still had to wake up to another morning and somehow get on with life in the form it had now taken.

There is a lot more to be said about all this, but this must suffice for the present.[5] The key thing to realise is where the normal reading of apocalyptic will lead. If you read apocalyptic as referring to the destruction of the *world*, as is so often done, you buy into a worldview which is neither the early Jewish nor the early Christian one, but is a rather different sort of thing, having more affinities either with Gnosticism (the physical world is evil and to be destroyed) or Stoicism (the cosmos will all burn up, and will then be reborn like a phoenix in exactly the same form) than with mainstream Christianity.

Revelation 21: the heavenly city

The final biblical passage I shall look at here is Revelation 21. Revelation is not all about 'the future', as though it were an Old Moore's Almanack for events yet to occur. This mistake is deeply rooted in many traditional readings of the book, and has woven itself into much popular piety. Consider, for instance, Charles Wesley's wonderful hymn 'Love Divine, All Loves Excelling'. In the final verse, reaching a great climax, he writes:

> Finish then thy new creation,
>   Pure and spotless let us be;
> Let us see thy great salvation,
>   Perfectly restored in thee,
> Changed from glory into glory,
>   Till in heaven we take our place,
> Till we cast our crowns before thee,
>   Lost in wonder, love and praise!

I hasten to say that I would rather have many a Wesley hymn, albeit allowing for some (as I see it) misreadings of Scripture, than most hymns of the nineteenth century, and many of the twentieth. But in this verse the great Methodist songster has done three things over which I think we must raise a question mark. First, he has apparently restricted 'new creation' to the work of God in human beings (assuming that the second line explains what he means by the first); the aim of salvation is that we shall be 'perfectly restored'. What then of Paul's great vision of the whole creation being set free from its bondage to decay (Rom. 8, on which see below)? Second, he has quoted 2 Corinthians 3:18 ('Changed from glory into glory') as though that text referred to a future transformation. But that text clearly refers to the *present* process whereby Christians, looking at the work of the Spirit in one another, are transformed from one degree of glory into another – a process to be completed hereafter, no doubt, but the thrust of what Paul says in the whole passage relates to the present, not the future.[6] Third, and the germane point for our present discussion: Wesley seems to assume that Revelation 4 and 5, the glorious scene in heaven with the elders casting their crowns before the throne of God (4:10), is a vision of the *future*, the eventual state of the blessed. But this is clearly not the case. It is a description of *present* reality: creation worshipping God, and the people of God taking up the song and personalising it. When the seer is told (4:1), 'Come up here, and I will show you what must take place after this', the initial vision is not of the things that are to take place later; it is of the throne-room *within which* the future will be revealed in subsequent chapters of Revelation. A great many popular pictures of 'heaven', conceived as a purely future state (perhaps even up in the sky somewhere), are similar misreadings of the wonderful picture-language by which Revelation describes the heavenly dimension of present reality.

Nor is Revelation, in Austin Farrer's phrase, a kind of 'Cook's Tour' of heaven, telling you 'what things will be like when you get there'. Rather, it is a disclosure of what is true all along in God's dimension of reality, for which the biblical name is 'heaven'.

What then *does* Revelation say about the future? One thing that is true of the heavenly reality is that, like the gift in the cupboard, there is there a secure future for God's people. That future, however, according to Revelation 21, is *not* that people will escape up to heaven, but that the new Jerusalem will come down *from* heaven, so that the dwelling of God will be with his human creatures, and that, eventually, heaven and earth will not be separated, but, in being renewed, will be integrated with each other. The great claim of Revelation 21 and 22 is that heaven and earth will finally be united. This is the polar opposite of all kinds of Gnosticism, with their ultimate separation of heaven and earth – a worldview which is all too suspiciously close to some forms of devout Western Christianity.

This, then, is the first and easily the longest of the stages by which I am advancing my claim. The passages in the New Testament which would most naturally be called up to support the idea of 'going to heaven when you die' do not in fact do so. Rather, they point to God's heaven, God's life, God's dimension, impregnating, permeating, charging (in Hopkins' sense) the present world, eventually producing new or renewed heavens and new or renewed earth, integrated with each other.

Biblical Foundations: Romans 8

The second stage by which I advance my thesis is to suggest, more positively, that the weight of biblical theology as a whole actually falls on the renewal of heaven and earth. There is no space here to expound this in detail, so I choose one particular central passage to make the point. The prediction of new heavens and new earth at the end of Isaiah (66:22) can of course be called as witness; but the most obvious passage is Romans 8:18–28. Here, in one of the most central statements in the New Testament about what God intends to do with the whole cosmos, the matter is set out quite clearly. This passage is regularly marginalised in mainstream Protestant interpretations of Romans (chs. 9–11 suffer a similar fate). If you insist on reading Romans simply as a book about how human beings 'get saved', in the sense of 'going to heaven when they die', you will find that these verses function as a kind of odd, apocalyptic appendix. That, in consequence, is how the tradition has often regarded them, both in the 'radical' scholarship of Lutherans like Bultmann and Käsemann and in the 'conservative' readings of much evangelical scholarship. In fact, the passage is the deliberate and carefully planned climax to the whole train of thought in Romans 5–8, and indeed Romans 1–8, as a whole.

Paul's whole argument is that the renewal of God's covenant results in the renewal of God's creation. (That, incidentally, is the sequence of thought also in 2 Cor. 3–5.) Romans has expounded the fall of Adam (1:18–32, made explicit in 5:12–21). How is the fall of Adam reversed? Clearly, through Christ: but when Paul talks of the work of Christ (and of the Spirit, which implements the work of Christ) he uses explicit 'new covenant' language to do it. Israel is God's means of rescuing the world, but Israel herself needs renewal if this is to happen. Romans 5:20 is the key: the law came in to increase the trespass, but where sin abounded grace super-abounded. In 7:1–8:11, which unpacks 5:20, Paul speaks of the renewal of the covenant: what the law could not do, because it had to work with sinful human flesh, God has done in Christ and by the Spirit.

But the result of the renewal of covenant, according to regular prophetic Jewish literature, is the renewal of creation. That is why, in Romans 4:13, Paul says that the promise to Abraham and his seed was that they should inherit – not the land, as one might expect, but the world, the cosmos. When God does for his people what he intends to do for them, the whole cosmos, the whole creation, will be renewed as well. The wilderness and the barren land will celebrate. In Romans 8:18–27 we have the exodus-motif, which Paul has applied to the *people* of God in 8:12–17, applied now to the cosmos as a whole: the whole creation 'will be set free from its bondage to decay, and share the liberty of the glory of the children of God'. This in turn is the completion of an exodus-motif which has run through several chapters of Romans, not least chapter 6, where God's people come through the waters (baptism, in parallel with the Red Sea[7]), and so are freed from slavery (sin, in parallel with Egypt), whereupon they are given, not the Torah this time, but the Spirit. And it is the Spirit that will lead them into their promised land, the renewed and liberated cosmos.

This is not, then, a theology in which human beings are set free from space-time existence and escape into a 'salvation' which is detached from the created world. It is a theology which answers explicitly to the problem of the cosmos as set out in Genesis 1–3, where the integration of humans with the whole creation gives way to the subsequent dislocation and fracturing of that integration: thorns, thistles, and pain, shame, toil and sorrow for humans and the cosmos. Notice the way in which, throughout Isaiah 40–55 and reaching a climax in the final verses of the last chapter, the liberation of God's people from exile is inextricably linked with the rejoicing of all creation, the wilderness and the barren land celebrating along with Israel:

> For you shall go out in joy, and be led back in peace;
> the mountains and the hills before you shall burst into song,
> and all the trees of the field shall clap their hands.
> Instead of the thorn shall come up the cypress;
> instead of the briar shall come up the myrtle;
> and it shall be to YHWH for a memorial,
> for an everlasting sign that shall not be cut off.
> (Is. 55:12–13)

This is the kind of picture, we may suppose, that Paul has in mind when he holds out the salvation which arises out of the new covenant in Christ and the Spirit: the creation itself will enjoy its exodus, its liberation.

This is the theology upon which Paul then builds the more specific argument of Romans, in 9–11 and 12–16. It is not Paul, therefore, who speaks of leaving the cosmos to its own devices and of finding a salvation elsewhere. It is Gnosticism, that twists apocalyptic into escapism.[8] This, then, is the second step in my argument: that biblical theology as a whole, witnessed here by one recognisably climactic passage within it, points firmly in the direction of the liberation of heaven and earth, rather than towards an escapist salvation. The new world will be more real, more physically solid, than the present one, as was brilliantly envisaged in C. S. Lewis's *The Great Divorce*. We speak of people being 'shadows of their former selves'; if 2 Corinthians 5:1–10 is correct, we should think of ourselves as being shadows of our future selves in God's purpose.

'Heaven' as God's Dimension of Present Reality

The third step in my argument is to suggest that a proper Christian understanding of heaven is not as 'a place remote from the present world' but rather as a *dimension*, normally kept secret, of present reality. I have already anticipated this in one or two places and must now fill it out somewhat further.[9] The idea that heaven is a distant place, perhaps up in the sky somewhere, is of course easily recognised as misleading today; most people know that that is not actually what we mean by such language. However, I suspect that a great many influential writers, not least hymn writers, in the last few centuries, have been influenced by some form of Deism, with a God who is somewhat removed from present reality, and so all too easily have written about God's dwelling place as 'way beyond the blue' and so on. This produced the farcical situation where Nikita Kruschev could claim that the early Russian astronauts had gone to look for God in space, and had not found him, thus disproving his existence. As C. S. Lewis said at the time, some of us would have been rather worried if they *had* found God, or paradise, in outer space. Rather, 'heaven' is *God's dimension of present reality*.

One of the best examples in Scripture of how this works out is in 2 Kings 6:15–19. Elisha and his servant are surrounded by the Syrian army. The servant, not unnaturally, says 'Alas, master, we are undone'. Elisha replies, telling him to be calm: 'Those who are with us are more than those who are with them'. Is this simply something he has to take on trust? Yes and no. Elisha prays: 'Lord, open the young man's eyes'. The Lord opens his eyes, and he sees the mountain full of horses and chariots of fire round about Elisha. A sudden unveiling of what was there all along, but normally unseen: that is what the opening of heaven (or, in this case, the opening of eyes so that they see the heavenly reality) is all about. When we read in apocalyptic writings 'I saw heaven opened' (as in Rev. 4:1 and elsewhere) this does not mean, even within the apocalyptic literary convention, that the seer had some kind of spiritual telescope through which he could see, miles and miles up in the sky, a door being opened, through which he could peep into 'heaven' itself. Rather, the opening of heaven is like what happened to Elisha and his servant. A veil which is normally present is suddenly pulled away, so that what is usually invisible becomes visible. That, I think, is a more biblical way of envisaging heaven.

It is interesting that the Eastern Orthodox Church seems to have got more of a handle on this than we have in the various Western churches. The construction of an Orthodox church is such as to divide the building by a screen, covered with icons; east of the screen, where much of the liturgy takes place, all is designed to symbolise heaven; and west of the screen, where the people are, symbolises earth. The liturgy takes place in 'heaven', since in Orthodox eucharistic theology that is exactly what is going on: heaven and earth are not distant spheres, separated by a great geographical or ontological distance, but actually overlap and interlock, supremely in Jesus but thereafter in the Eucharist. That is why, among many other things, the gospel is brought out to the people, moving from heaven to earth. The Orthodox have thus retained something of the old sense, present in the Temple in Jerusalem, that the sacred space in question is not merely a signpost of a different reality, but actually partakes in the reality itself. For a devout and well-taught Jew, the Holy of Holies was not just a place on earth where one might sense more particularly the presence of God; it was the place on earth where heaven and earth intersected, in a quite literal sense. Western churches in the Gothic tradition have made a similar point by the use of soaring arches and vaulting, and particularly by the use of light through high windows. A Gothic cathedral symbolises by its structure that we are worshipping with the angels, archangels and all the company of heaven, not least when we make music that rolls around the rafters and joins in (symbolically? why not actually?) with the music of the angels.

All this has an interesting spin-off in terms of one element of usual Christian language, namely that the old split between 'natural' and 'supernatural' is ill-conceived. When we find ourselves talking about 'nature' and 'supernature', as we still do, I think we are running some conceptual risks. It would be more biblical, in my view, if when we wanted to make this sort of distinction we spoke instead about 'earthly' and 'heavenly'. There is a distinction between earthly and heavenly, and we do well to recognise it, not simply to pretend they are just the same thing, or to collapse one category into the other. There is a duality, a two-sidedness to God-given, God-created reality. But if we talk about 'natural' and 'supernatural', we can easily slide back into that Deist framework of thought in which God lives in the 'supernatural' world and occasionally 'intervenes' in the 'natural' world; or, worse, into a neo-Gnosticism in which the 'natural' world is either trash or actually evil.

It is against the 'interventionist' view that theologians like John Hick and David Jenkins have protested. Faced with this protest, some traditionally-minded Christians have assumed that, in order to shore up their belief in the gospel, they must go bail for a total 'supernaturalism' as conceived in the eighteenth century, with all its language of 'miracle' and so on, as though there were an 'interventionist' God who occasionally reached in and stirred the pot, but who was normally absent.[10] That is not the biblical view of God. The biblical view of God is as the one who is constantly present, who breathes with the breath of the world, and gives his own breath to his human creatures, who feeds the young ravens when they call upon him, and so on. It is our perspective, clouded of course by sin, that compartmentalises God's world up into nature, supernature and such like. If we go on in that way, we will play into the hands of the New Agers and others like them. We live today in a period that is increasingly religious but decreasingly Christian. In that setting, simply to think that we have got to talk about 'the supernatural' all the time will render us unable to distinguish between the true God and the many false gods who are being hawked around. 'The supernatural' is not the same thing as the Christian view of God. That, then, is my third step: a proper understanding of heaven, leading to a proper distinction between heaven and earth, as opposed to the false antithesis of nature and supernature.

The Meaning of Resurrection

So to the fourth step. The traditional Christian doctrine of resurrection actually requires a robust sense of the new heavens and the new earth. I have discovered that some Christians, when using the word 'resurrection', for instance in saying the Creed, mentally translate that word out so that it simply means 'survival', a disembodied 'life after death'. The result of this is that when David Jenkins, then Bishop of Durham, expressed doubts over the physicality of Jesus' resurrection, many ordinary Christians heard him to be saying that he doubts survival. That is what they thought he was talking about. Of course, he was not; he was talking simply about what did and did not happen on Easter morning in relation to Jesus' body, the tomb, and so on.

Equally, many who today believe in the physical resurrection of Jesus do so simply because that is one plank in their second-order defence of a 'supernaturalist' worldview. Belief in the resurrection of Jesus is, for them, the supreme example of God's miraculous power; alternatively, the resurrection somehow 'proves' Jesus' 'divinity'. But resurrection as an idea began in a very different setting.[11] It began in parts of the Old Testament as a function of the national hope. Ezekiel 37 is a wonderful picture of the return from exile, using resurrection as a great and evocative metaphor for what that return would mean. The idea developed through the period of the Maccabees in the second century BC, as people came to realise that, if there was any justice anywhere in the world, those who had died rather than compromise their loyalty to God and his Torah must be raised to life to share the new age of world history which God would eventually bring forth.

But this picture of resurrection is not simply about 'survival', nor yet about the 'supernatural'. The Jews believed anyway that God would in some sense or other look after them after death; that is not what their belief in 'resurrection' was getting at.[12] Many Jews of Jesus' and Paul's day believed not only in some sort of 'survival' but also that God would have a new world for them to live in one day, and that loyal Jews would inherit this recreated world. 'Resurrection', as an idea, is designed to function within the overall belief in a renewed world, not as a thin 'survival' with the present cosmos simply abandoned. When it comes to early Christianity, the resurrection of Jesus seems to have triggered the announcement of the claim of the one true God upon the whole world. The message of the early Christians was not that the world was going to be destroyed and that one had better escape, nor that there was after all an after-life and that they had a way of accessing a happy version of it, but that the whole world belonged to the one true God, and that he was claiming the allegiance of his long-rebellious subjects within it.

Results of Different Views

My fifth step ties the threads together. If we speak simply of 'going to heaven when we die', we run into serious problems in terms of its knock-on effects. It has the effect, if one is not careful, of inducing a Gnostic spirituality, in which the cultivation of the 'spiritual' life becomes more important than our responsibility in God's world. It encourages an individualistic view of salvation rather than the New Testament one. (Bishop Michael Marshall makes a good distinction, stressing that we should speak of 'personal' rather than 'individual', and 'corporate' rather than 'collective'. 'Personal' and 'corporate' entail each other; 'individual' and 'collective' rule each other out.) The idea of escaping from the world to a non-spatio-temporal heaven encourages an unbiblical attitude towards creation, so that anyone who engages in ecological activity, or perhaps even feeding the hungry, is seen as somehow selling the pass. One should be doing something more 'spiritual'.

One can understand the longing for escape from this world in a context where people are suffering untold persecutions. 'This world is not my home; I'm just a-passing through' is comprehensible when sung by a black slave in the old American South, for whom the present world simply did not hold out any prospect of hope. (I am told, however, by sociologists of that period that even then the so-called 'Negro Spirituals' were 'heard' as coded messages, both of escape from the US to Canada and as calls to some sort of resistance or revolution – though I suspect for many who sang them they functioned simply as expressions of despair in this present world.) But it seems to me inexcusable and inescapably sub-Christian if one persists in saying 'I'm just passing through' if one is in fact living a comparatively comfortable life in this world. 'Passing through', taken literally, is a far more Gnostic idea. I have, says the Gnostic, an immortal spark within me, which started off somewhere else, is in a state of transience here, and is then off on its travels somewhere else, perhaps to some kind of 'heaven'. It is remarkable how many people in our world would still say, if asked, that this is what Christians are supposed to believe.

Resurrection and Immortality

My basic thesis is now complete. It remains to fill in some important details.

If my point is to be sustained, it should be clear that it actually requires something not always granted within theologies of resurrection. Within this scheme there is a necessary place for a concept of immortality – for *a* concept of immortality, but not the Platonic concept. It is, rather, a revision, in the light of Christ and the Spirit, of the *Jewish* concept (perhaps I should say, of *a* Jewish concept) of immortality. Resurrection and immortality are not simply to be played off against one another, as used to be done. Things are not that easy. We have to make some distinctions. Here pressure of space demands that I over-simplify a rather complex argument.

In his recent book, James Barr confuses, I think, different types of immortality. He confuses the idea of persons simply going on living, and never dying at all, with the idea of a soul continuing after death – and then with variations within that. He is so concerned, in attacking Cullmann and Stendahl, to make space for *any* sort of immortality at all being found in the Bible that anything, it seems, will do as evidence. There is, however, a well-known view of immortality which is not found in the early Jewish world and the New Testament (with the possible exception of Philo), namely, the Platonic view of the body as a shell which the immortal soul happens to inhabit for a while. I want in particular to emphasise the proper understanding of Wisdom of Solomon 3; I suspect that a great many discussions of immortality have referred to this passage at some point or other:

> The souls of the righteous are in the hand of God, and there shall no torment touch them; in the sight of the foolish they seemed to have died, but they are at peace. (3:1–3)

It is a well-known passage, sung regularly at funerals and memorial services, not least in its Latin text, *Iustorum animae in manu Dei sunt.* It is regularly heard, I suspect, as a statement of a generalised, perhaps Hellenised, 'immortality', meaning that the final state of human beings, at least righteous ones, is to live with God as disembodied souls. What you almost never hear is what the passage goes on to say: that, after these people have rested awhile, out of the sight of their tormentors and persecutors,

> at the time of their visitation they will shine forth, and run like sparks through the stubble; they will govern nations and rule over peoples, and the Lord will reign over them for ever. (3:7–8)

What is this whole passage about? It is about the Jewish hope of the coming kingdom of the true God, ruling over the world in justice and peace. Those who at present are resting will rise again to be God's agents in that renewed world. This falls within the Jewish martyr-literature; it is cognate with the books of the Maccabees. Part of the whole point of the passage is that the wicked, who were persecuting the righteous, celebrated a triumph over them, supposing them to be dead and gone. But the righteous are in fact at peace, *and will rise again to rule the world* and overturn the apparent victory of their oppressors.

The book Wisdom is not in the Protestant canon, as it was not in the ancient Jewish one. We are not committed to this way of putting things – though we may note that there are several analogies between this passage and parts of the New Testament, as we shall see presently. What matters is this: Wisdom 3, the main passage regularly cited as evidence for first-century Jews believing in the Greek view of 'immortality', proves nothing of the sort. It is evidence for a particular way of construing the Jewish hope. Those who are suffering and dying at the moment will disappear; the wicked will celebrate a triumph over them; but they will be at rest, with God; and they will rise again to rule over God's renewed creation.

Something of that same shape, though redefined by Christ and the Spirit, is what we find in the New Testament. When Jesus says to the brigand, 'Today you will be with me in Paradise' (Lk. 23:43), he is referring to this same concept. 'Paradise' is a regular Jewish way of referring, not to the final destination of God's people, but to the temporary place of rest before the rising again from the dead.[13] When Jesus says to the Sadducees that God is the God of Abraham, Isaac and Jacob, and that therefore they are alive 'to him' (Mk. 12:18–27 and parallels), this might seem to be simply talking about 'survival' ('Oh yes, they're still alive somewhere'). But within the wider Jewish context that idea of being still alive somewhere, rather like the gift in the cupboard, is the sign that they are going to rise again to a new life, a full life. As often within rabbinic discussions, the final step in the argument, like the final moves in a high-level chess game, is left unstated; both parties know when the game is really over. What Jesus needed to prove was simply that the patriarchs were still alive in the presence of God; the strong implication is that God will one day renew all things, and then those who are now 'alive to him' in this way will be given new, re-embodied, life.

Paul's language about departing 'and being with Christ' (Phil. 1:23) belongs here as well. He has taken a regular Jewish view about the dead being 'alive to God', and has re-thought this, as so many things, in the light of Jesus Christ. Paul does not suppose, however, that this state of simply being 'with Christ' is the end of the matter; the time will come when Jesus will himself 'change the body of our humiliation to be like the body of his glory' (Phil. 3:21). When Paul also uses the language of 'sleep', as he does in 1 Corinthians 15:51 and 1 Thessalonians 4:13–15, this is a metaphor, but not a misleading metaphor.

When one sleeps, one is still alive, albeit, as we sometimes say, 'dead to the world'. There is a sense of peculiarity, of retreating for a while from the present hurly-burly of things, in order then to awake to a fuller life again. There is continuity; and I suggest that for Paul, and for the other early Christian writers, the resurrection of Jesus has, literally and metaphorically, put flesh and bones on to the rather vague Jewish hope of an immortality succeeded by a resurrection.

'Departing and being with Christ', or 'living to God', then, are for the New Testament writers ways of expressing a *temporary stage*, ahead of the time when God will restore all things, and will renew his people to bodily life, in the midst of his new creation. Paul believes, after all, that God has given his own Spirit to his people; and if God has deigned to dwell within his people, by his own Spirit, then God is well able to keep by that same Spirit those who are his until, again by that same Spirit (Rom. 8:10–11), he gives to them their renewed bodies.[14] And, in the renewal of our bodies, we may assume that there will be continuity without the suggestion of absolute physical identity. God does not need to search for the same atoms and molecules that once constituted us; if he did, there would not be nearly enough to go round, since we all wear second-hand clothes in that respect. We are all of us, as C. S. Lewis says, like the curve in a waterfall; our bodies are in a state of physical flux. Any resurrection to physical life will involve a massive act of new creation. No doubt that was so for Jesus himself, though because the new creation of his body preceded the decomposition of his original body there was a close continuity which we do not need to imagine in the case of those of whom Christ, in Paul's language, is the first-fruits.

Results

What are the results of construing the Christian hope in this way?

It gives us a view of creation which emphasises the goodness of God's world, and God's intention to renew it. It gives us, therefore, every possible incentive, or at least every Christian incentive, to work for the renewal of God's creation and for justice within God's creation. Not that we are building the kingdom by our own efforts. Let us not lapse into that. Rather, what we are doing here and now is building *for* God's kingdom. It is what Paul speaks of in 1 Corinthians 3:10–15: there is continuity between our present work and God's future kingdom, even though the former will have to pass through fire to attain the latter. It is also clearly implied in 1 Corinthians 15:58: the conclusion of Paul's enormous exposition of the resurrection is not an outburst of joy at the glorious life to come, but a sober exhortation to work for the kingdom in the present, because we know that our work here and now is not in vain in the Lord. In other words, belief in the resurrection, the other side, if need be, of a period of disembodied life in the Lord (cf. 1 Cor. 15:29), validates and so encourages present Christian life, work and witness.

A suspicious reader might, perhaps, think that this is sliding down the hill towards some kind of naturalism or even pantheism. That would be quite wrong. This same theology, precisely because it speaks of a *renewed* heaven and earth, rules out any sort of pantheism such as (for instance) you find in New Age theology at the moment. It emphasises that creation is good, but in need of renewal and restoration by a mighty act of God, parallel to the resurrection of Jesus. We cannot divinise nature as she stands; were we to do so, we would be locking ourselves in the cabin of a ship that is going down, since nature as she stands is subject to the long, slow (to our eyes) process of decay. 'Change and decay in all around I see'; but that does not mean that the cosmos is evil, merely that it is not divine.

The Christian hope cannot, therefore, collapse into individualism ('me and my salvation'). If we allowed it to, we might be making a similar mistake in our theological context to that of first-century Israel in her theological context. We would imagine that God's whole purpose focused on us and us alone, instead of seeing grace as summoning us to be God's agents in mission to and for the whole world. (This, I suggest, is the way to a proper construal of being in the image of God – not simply that we as humans are somehow like God, a rather impressive thing to be, but that we as God's image are to reflect his saving, healing love into the rest of God's creation.)

As for the use of language, therefore, I suggest that it is all right to use the word 'heaven', so long as we remember that it refers to God's dimension of present-to-hand reality. If we talk about 'going to heaven', we strictly speaking should remember that that means 'going to be with God, with Christ, until the time when God makes new heavens and new earth and gives humans new bodies appropriate for citizens of this realm'. The language of 'going to heaven' is so ingrained in us that I sometimes despair of correcting the false impressions that are thereby given; but I think the attempt must be made. Another example from a popular hymn 'Sun of my soul, thou saviour dear', after a devout and humble sequence of prayer, the last verse suddenly turns from Christianity to Buddhism:

> Come near and bless us when we wake,
> Ere through the world our way we take;
> Till in the ocean of thy love
> We lose ourselves in heaven above.

One suspects that many devout Western Christians are blithely unaware of the way in which that thought, of the soul leaving the physical world and becoming lost, a drop in the ocean of disembodied reality manages at a stroke to deconstruct the New Testament picture of the future life.

Should we continue, then, to speak of 'souls' at all? I see no problem with the word in principle (as Lewis Carroll suggested, you can use words however you like as long as you pay them extra on Thursdays); you can say 'soul', as long as you are committed to meaning by that 'a whole human being living in the presence of God'. Soul-language, within a Christian context, is a shorthand for telling a story of that sort, a story about the way in which human beings *as wholes* are irreducibly open to God. It is not, within Christian theology, a shorthand for a story in which a partitioned human being has a soul in one compartment, a body in another, and quite possibly all sorts of other bits and pieces equally divided up. We can then continue to use the word 'soul' with fully Christian meaning; but we should be careful, because the language has had a chequered history, and may betray us.

The language of 'soul' is telling a story; the trouble with shorthands is that they can become absolutised. The story is of a person as a person living with God and towards God, 'departing and being with Christ'. I prefer not to push beyond where Scripture takes us on such things; Paul does not speculate as to what more precisely happens when one has thus 'departed'. In 2 Corinthians 5:1–5 he is stressing that the eventual goal is a totally renewed body, not a disembodied spirit. It is natural for us to use the language of separation of body and soul, in order that we then have a word available to talk about the person who is still alive in the presence of God while the body is obviously decomposing. But we should not think of the 'soul' as a 'part' of the person that was always, so to speak, waiting to be separated off, like the curds from the whey.

The language of immortality itself, then, has to be held within the whole sweep of thought from creation to new creation. Some churches, I have noticed, have stopped saying merely, of the departed, 'may they rest in peace', and have added 'and rise in glory'. That, it seems to me, is a thoroughly proper thing to say of those who have gone on ahead of us. Another example from popular piety would be the hymn 'For All the Saints', in which we find the two things clearly separated: first, 'Paradise', where the blessed are resting in anticipation of the final day, and then the resurrection:

The golden evening brightens in the west;
Soon, soon to faithful warriors cometh rest:
Sweet is the calm of Paradise the blest. Alleluia!

But lo! There breaks a yet more glorious day;
The Saints triumphant rise in bright array:
The King of glory passes on his way. Alleluia!

That, it seems to me, is an example of a Victorian hymn getting it exactly right. Rest in Paradise (or, if you prefer, in 'heaven'); then the resurrection, the great renewal of all things, the marriage of heaven and earth.

Christian hope, therefore, is for a full, recreated life in the presence and love of God, a totally renewed creation, an integrated new heavens and new earth, and a complete humanness – complete not in and for itself as an isolated entity, but complete in worship and love for God, complete in love for one another as humans, complete in stewardship over God's world, and so, and only in that complete context, a full humanness in itself.

Of course, the most glorious feature of the whole renewed creation, the new heavens and the new earth, will be the personal presence of Jesus himself. 'When he appears we shall be like him, for we shall see him as he is' (1 Jn. 3:2). Or, as another hymn puts it, 'And our eyes at last shall see him/Through his own redeeming love' (though the hymn then spoils it somewhat by implying that this seeing will be in 'heaven above', rather than in God's complete new-heaven-and-new-earth new creation.) Since the Greek word for 'presence', particularly for 'royal presence', is *parousia*, it seems to me that that word is misunderstood if we think of it as simply 'coming'. Jesus will indeed 'come again', from the perspective of those still labouring here in the present earth; but I believe it is more appropriate, and more biblical, to see Jesus' personal presence, within the glorious renewed cosmos, as the ultimate feature of Christian hope.[15] But that is another subject, for another occasion.

Notes

1 Cf., for example, J. D. Crossan, *The Birth of Christianity* (San Francisco: HarperSanFrancisco, 1998). For Jewish views of the resurrection, see my *The New Testament and the People of God* (hereafter *NTPG*) (London and Minneapolis: SPCK and Fortress, 1992), ch. 10.

2 On the whole subject see my *Jesus and the Victory of God* (hereafter *JVG*) (London and Minneapolis: SPCK and Fortress, 1996), esp. chs. 5–10.

3 On this chapter see *NTPG*, ch. 10, and, above all, *JVG*, ch. 8.

4 On this theme see particularly George B. Caird. *The Language and Imagery of the Bible* (2nd edition; Grand Rapids: Eerdmans, 1997).

5 See my *The Myth of the Millennium* (London and Louisville: SPCK and Westminster John Knox, 1999), ch. 2.

6 See N. T. Wright, *The Climax of the Covenant: Christ and the Law in Pauline Theology* (Edinburgh and Minneapolis: T. & T. Clark and Fortress, 1991), ch. 9.

7 See 1 Cor. 10:2.

8 See Christopher C. Rowland, *Christian Origins: From Messianic Movement to Christian Religion* (London and Minneapolis: SPCK and Augsburg, 1985).

9 Cf. the chapter entitled 'Heaven' in my *Following Jesus* (London: SPCK, 1994).

10 On 'miracle' etc. cf. *JVG*, 186–8.

[11] For further details on what follows, cf. *NTPG*, 320–334.

[12] There is some debate at present on the subject of *Sheol*, the OT abode of the dead: what people thought it was, who went there, and such like. I cannot go into this here.

[13] An important study of this whole area is Andrew T. Lincoln *Paradise Now and Not Yet: Studies in the Role of the Heavenly Dimension in Paul's Thought with Special Reference to His Eschatology*, SNTS Monograph Series, 43 (Cambridge: CUP, 1981).

[14] This has all kinds of overtones for how we read Genesis 1–3, but this again would take us too far afield in the present essay.

[15] I have said more on this subject in ch. 14 of Marcus J. Borg and N. T. Wright, *The Meaning of Jesus: Two Visions* (San Francisco and London: HarperSanFrancisco and SPCK, 1999).

4

He Will Come Again

James D.G. Dunn

One thing we can be sure about: over the next four years the subject of eschatology will gain increasing prominence.[1] As we draw steadily nearer to the close of another millennium, enthusiastic speculation regarding the eschaton is bound to rise. I am no prophet, nor even the son of a prophet; still I make that prediction with confidence. Those who believe that they have been given a preview of the divine timetable for history's grand finale could hardly fail to see significance in such an auspicious date. And high on the eschatological agenda for anyone influenced by Christian tradition is bound to be the topic of the second coming. Anyone looking for the imminent coming of Christ could hardly fail to find the year 2000 a likely candidate.

Does such speculation increase our hope? Or does it increase our embarrassment? There seems no way of avoiding either the one or the other. For the coming again of Christ is quite central in the earliest Christian documents, as also in the creeds, doctrinal statements, and liturgies of the churches. From the earliest formulation that we have in Aramaic, 'Maranatha, Our Lord, come' (1 Cor. 16:22), to the eucharistic acclamation, 'Christ has died, Christ is risen, Christ will come again', the hope is constant and is repeatedly reaffirmed.

So what are we to say about this hope today? In a day when the currency of eschatological hope is subject to the inflation of rising expectation (which also means that the currency is losing its value) what are we to say? In the face of repeated disappointments of that hope and many earlier devaluations of that currency over the centuries, what are we to say? 'He will come again', we boldly confess. But what are we actually saying? What do Christians believe?

The Nature of Christian Hope

It only takes a little study of the theme to remind us of two important features of biblical hope. On the one hand, biblical hope is a *confident* hope. This is one of the points at which biblical vocabulary differs from Hellenistic vocabulary. In classical Greek thought there is an inescapable sense of uncertainty about the future – rather like our own use of the term: 'I hope I may see you next summer (but I am not confident that I will)'. But in biblical thought hope is closely allied to trust, trustful hope, hope as confidence in God. Of this trustful hope, Abraham is the great example, as one who in trustful hope accepted God's promise of a son when he and his wife were long past childbearing (Rom. 4).

At the same time, however, biblical hope is a constantly *redefined* hope. It is a hope in which the balance between the 'already' and the 'not yet' has never been finally resolved. Let me try to document this briefly.

Two of the great paradigms of the eschaton in the Bible are the entry into the promised land and the return from exile. The letter to the Hebrews, for example, makes effective use of the idea of the promised rest of the promised land. The Christian pilgrimage is like the people's wandering in the wilderness; and so, according to Hebrews 4, 'there remains a rest for the people of God' into which they have still to enter. In other words, the great goal of the promised land is incomplete, only a shadow of what is still to come.

Similarly the exile became for many Jews an image of being under the curse of God because of disobedience, and the longed-for return from exile became an enduring metaphor for their restoration as God's favoured nation. So the great prophets of the school of Isaiah depict the restoration of Israel and the longed-for return to Judaea in classic images of eschatological renewal and of paradise restored – the child playing over the hole of the asp, and the wolf and lamb feeding together (Is. 11:6–9; 65:25). And the seer of Revelation is not the only one to use Babylon as the metaphor of the final opposition to God (Rev. 14:8; 17–18).

In both cases (entry into the promised land and return from exile), the hope fulfilled fell short of the hope expressed, and the realisation of hope was understood as only a partial fulfilment of that hope. Yet, the partial fulfilment did not undermine or falsify the hope but became the springboard for a fresh articulation of hope. The 'already' did not completely express the fullness of hope, so that the unrealised 'not yet' became the basis of hope re-expressed.

So also with the first coming of Christ. It was itself the fulfilment of eschatological hope. Yet the figure expected by John the Baptist was to be one who would bring final judgment – the unfruitful trees to be cut down and cast into the fire, the chaff likewise to be burnt with unquenchable fire (Mt. 3:10, 12). The hope of the royal Messiah was for one who would restore the glory of his father David's reign (e.g. Ps. 2:7–9; Ezek. 34:20–31). What a surprise Jesus was!

What a disappointment to so many. The predictions of kingly glory and of judgment on the nations were not fulfilled. Jesus did not fulfil all hopes for the age to come. In the light of Jesus' coming, Christians had to redefine the biblical hopes they inherited – above all as the hope of a Messiah who must suffer and die.

At the same time, the images used by Jesus – the blind receiving sight, the deaf hearing, the lame walking, the poor having good news proclaimed to them (Mt. 11:5) – were the Isaianic images for the age to come, for paradise restored (Is. 29:18–19; 35:5–6; 61:1–2). There *was* fulfilment. In some sense the new age had come. And yet at the same time, it had not yet come. For still today we pray, as Jesus himself taught, 'May your kingdom come' – the kingdom which he also said 'had come upon them' in his ministry of exorcism (Mt. 12:28). The 'not yet' remains; the 'already' has not exhausted the fullness of the 'not yet'. The hope is reaffirmed even as it is redefined. Thus again is illustrated the nature of biblical hope. It is both realised and renewed, without the one causing the other to be denied.

Consequently we should not be alarmed to realise that Jesus' own expectation is unclear to us, and probably was unclear to him. What did he hope for? Scholars are confused on this, because the data is confusing. He proclaimed the coming of the kingdom; that is clear: 'The kingdom of God is at hand; repent!' (Mk. 1:15). But did he mean by that the restoration of Israel or the coming of the end of the world? The former might seem a disappointingly narrow hope to attribute to Jesus. But why then does Luke have the disciples ask the risen Jesus, 'Will you at this time restore the kingdom to Israel' (Acts 1:6)? And the latter, the end of the world, poses still more difficult questions for us. Was Jesus' hope for his own generation not after all fulfilled? Jerusalem was destroyed indeed, but have the stars fallen from heaven and the angels come to gather the elect (Mk. 13:25, 27)? So Jesus' own hope belongs to the same tradition of biblical hope realised but not completely, an 'already' which still leaves a 'not yet' outstanding as the substance of hope freshly reminted.

And what of Jesus' talk of the coming of the Son of Man? The language is ambiguous. Did he mean a coming of the Son of Man to God – a hope of vindication and exaltation? So the clear echo of Daniel's vision in all the relevant New Testament passages might suggest (Dan. 7:13–14). Or did he envisage the Son of Man, or himself as the Son of Man, coming again from heaven to earth? So some expressions of the hope seem to indicate (Mk. 14:62). And yet, can we be sure? Here again is a meshing and mixing of hope realised and hope redefined, of the 'already' and the 'not yet'.

Consider the similar way in which the event of Pentecost is presented as the fulfilment of eschatological hope. The outpouring of the Spirit 'on all flesh' is a typical way of envisaging the new age (Joel 2:28–32). But the prophecy of Joel, fulfilled at Pentecost, according to Acts, includes talk of the sun turned to darkness and the moon to blood in anticipation of the coming of the day of the Lord (Acts 2:20). This, according to Luke's version of Joel's prophecy, would happen 'in the last days' (2:17). Despite the absence of such cataclysmic end-time happenings, Luke regards this hope as fulfilled at Pentecost. The hope is fulfilled, but not in the way that the prophet seems to have envisaged. The hope is reaffirmed even as it is redefined.

It is not surprising, then, when we turn to focus on the hope of Jesus' coming again, that there should be a similar ambiguity. Jesus spoke of the coming kingdom. But if it was not tied to the restoration of Israel, to what extent was it fulfilled in Pentecost? Was it there that some saw the kingdom of God come with power before they tasted death (cf. Mk. 9:1)? And if he spoke of the coming of the Son of Man other than as referring to his own vindication after death, why is this language not picked up elsewhere in the New Testament, in the other earliest Christian expressions of *parousia* hope?

Can we rule out the possibility, popular earlier in this century, that the Maranatha prayer, 'Come Lord Jesus', was used as a eucharistic prayer: 'Come to us Lord as we gather two and three in your name to partake of your body and blood'; 'Make yourself known to us in the breaking of the bread, as you did to the two at Emmaus' (Lk. 24)? Can we not speak of a 'coming again' in the Lord's Supper? And John's Gospel seems to suggest that Jesus' promise to his disciples that he would not leave them desolate but would come to them was to be fulfilled in the coming of the Spirit of Truth, the place of the first Paraclete filled by the coming of the other Paraclete (Jn. 14). Here again we find a tension built into the *parousia* hope, a tension between the 'already' and the 'not yet', between reaffirmation and redefinition.

We should note the confusion we bring upon ourselves when we take the scattered references to and pictures of the hoped-for coming again and try to build from them a single coherent whole. The simple fact is that biblical hope has never been a matter of straightforward prediction. Confident, yes! Confident in God, above all! But confident as to knowledge of all that would be involved in the fulfilment of that hope? No! Jesus himself warns us of the dangers of speculating on this point and of building anything on these speculations. The one thing we can be sure of is that the life of the world to come will not be determined by the rules governing present-day society (Mk. 12:18–27). Again, no one knows the day or the hour, not even the angels, not even the Son, but only the Father (Mk. 13:32). There is an unknown quality, an unknowableness about God's future, which means that confidence in God can remain strong without being specific; the hope is in God, not in the particulars of what God will do. Again, God can repent and have a change of mind: the unfruitful tree can be given another year to show whether it is after all fruitful (Lk. 13:6–9), and Nineveh can repent and be spared, even if the prophet Jonah is outraged at the seeming falsification of his prophecy of doom. We may indeed be confident in God. But in the matter of final judgment, as far as human schemas are concerned, God is unpredictable, since divine mercy runs far beyond what we would think proper or could ever predict.

The nature of biblical hope, therefore, should be allowed to guide us in the formulation of Christian hope, and not least on the subject of eschatology in its traditional sense, 'the final things'. Central to that eschatological hope is the coming again of Christ, and our articulation of that hope must be in tune with the nature of biblical hope as a whole. This means that the hope can be reaffirmed with confidence, but the elements that go into any description of what is hoped for are subject to the 'principle of indeterminacy'. The repeated redefinition involved in the restatement of biblical hope leaves us no choice. The tension between the 'already' and the 'not yet' means that the shape of the 'not yet' is in part clarified, since it will accord with the 'already', and in part obscured, since it remains unclear what all belongs to the 'not yet'. This brings us to our second main line of reflection.

The Language of Christian Hope

It is a striking feature that much if not most of the biblical language related to the coming again of Christ is the language of vision. The imagery that comes to mind is that of the Christ coming in clouds. 'Behold, he is coming with the clouds', cries the seer of Revelation at the beginning of his series of heavenly visions (Rev. 1:7 RSV) – imagery captured so well in Wesley's great hymn, 'Lo, he comes with clouds descending'.

Now we know that in apocalyptic visions clouds functioned as a means of heavenly transport (e.g. Mk. 13:26; 14:62; Acts 1:9; 1 Thes. 4:17; Rev. 11:12), and as a symbol of divine majesty and authority. Thus in Ezekiel's archetypal vision of the chariot throne of God, the vision is of 'a great cloud' that came out of the north, in the midst of which appeared the fire and the living creatures and the chariot itself (Ezek. 1). So also in the other archetypal vision of Daniel, the one like a son of man came with the clouds of heaven (Dan. 7:13). It is important for us to grasp that the symbolic force of this language would have been fully appreciated by the prophets and seers. They would not have expected their readers simply to take it at face value, any more than Daniel would have expected his readers to think the extraordinary beasts, which came up out of the sea earlier in his vision (7:3–8), were intended to denote actual beasts. The apocalyptic visionary worked with symbolic language all the time.

This is clearest in the Revelation of John. It is filled with symbolism – bowls and trumpets, strange portents and bizarre beasts. It is the one book in the New Testament where the normal rules of biblical exegesis do not apply: in

Revelation a *literal* interpretation is usually a *false* interpretation. It is in the nature of apocalyptic vision that what is seen and described is more symbol than anything else. So with reference to Jesus' coming again, the language of hope is the language of vision, the language of symbol. If we forget this in interpreting the Christian hope, we simply store up for ourselves trouble and confusion – as the history of interpretation of Revelation illustrates all too well.

Another way to put this is to recognise that in talking of Christ's coming again we are talking about events that transcend history, that bring history to an end as we have experienced it hitherto. In this we may see a parallel between *Endzeit* (the end-time) and *Urzeit* (the beginning-time). Despite a certain amount of discomfort in some quarters, we can begin to recognise that the biblical accounts of creation depict events beyond time. We use the word 'myth', not in the sense of *un*historical, but to denote that which is *beyond* history, that for which scenes drawn on the template of human history can function only metaphorically or allusively. How else can we speak of what precedes history as we know it? Again, as Christians have struggled to come to terms with the meaning of myth, it is not a question of falsehood, but of a truth that can only be expressed by picture language and imagery. The myth of the beginnings of the world and of humankind is true in the way that a great poem or a great painting may be true.

Somewhat to our surprise, cosmologists and astrophysicists have been coming to equivalent conclusions for some time, with such concepts as curved space, antimatter, and time so accelerated that what proponents of the big bang claim to have happened within the first second simply outruns the scope of rational imagination. Augustine was more perceptive than most of his readers recognised for centuries when he said that God created *with* time – not that he created in time, nor that he created time, but that he created with time. The fact is that when we speak of events outside the realms of our normal space-time complex, we simply cannot avoid using language in a metaphorical, analogical way, when the words used can no longer have a straightforward one-to-one correlation with that to which they refer.

The same is true for the other end of time, marked by the second coming. Once we leave aside the more bizarre imagery of the apocalyptic visions, we are left with a fairly small number of metaphors. The principal ones are the coming in clouds, the throne and judgment seat, and the resurrection, which simply denotes getting up or arising. They are all metaphors. Their truth is not to be thought of as exhausted by or dependent upon reading them as literal descriptions, any more than the truth of the cosmos is exhausted by or dependent upon viewing it in terms of Newtonian physics. We recognise that there is no contradiction between Christ's coming in clouds and the physical fact that clouds are too insubstantial to provide a platform for any solid body. The language we use at such times is an attempt to express what we cannot fully express by language, and can only begin to express when language functions as metaphor, metaphor functioning as another way of depicting reality.

Another aspect of the same feature comes to focus in one of the principal texts relating to the second coming, the words of the angel to the disciples at Jesus' ascension: 'Men of Galilee, why do you stand looking up toward heaven? This Jesus, who has been taken up from you into heaven, will come in the same way as you saw him go into heaven' (Acts 1:11). Clearly the language used expresses the cosmology of the time, in which heaven is a place above the earth. So for Jesus to go to heaven could only be expressed, could only be seen in terms of the conceptuality of the time, as a 'being taken up into heaven'. This is the issue Bultmann saw so clearly, and tried to resolve, however inadequately, in his essay on demythologising.[2] The language used by the ancients could only express what they saw and understood within the horizon of their own conceptuality. Again, it is not a question of truth or untruth. It is simply that language is the coming to birth of conceptions, ideas, and insights that have not yet been conceived and cannot yet come to expression in language.

The fact then that we self-styled 'moderns' are heirs of a different conceptuality, enriched by centuries of discovery and reflection, the fact that we see the cosmos differently and can no longer think of heaven as 'up there', should neither disturb us nor cause us to see Bultmann's problem of myth as a threat. Of course, we can still smile tolerantly when Yuri Gagarin, the first Russian cosmonaut, says, 'There is no God; I've been up there, and I didn't see him'. Of course we use the word 'heaven' both for the vault above and for the 'place' where God is, and do so without confusion or embarrassment. Of course, we can still speak of the 'ascension' of Jesus, even though the metaphor is of a physical 'going up'. The issue simply reminds us that all our metaphors are drawn from our experience and understanding of reality but go beyond that experience and understanding. It is not the case of ancient metaphor confronting modern fact, so much as of ancient metaphor compared with modern metaphor. For in all things that transcend human experience we have no choice but to use metaphor.

And if this is true of the ascension, and if indeed the ascension is the pattern for the coming again, as Acts 1:11 affirms, then presumably the same is true of the coming again. As with vision and myth, so with metaphor, all are a recognition that Christians speak of that of which our everyday experience and conceptuality and language give us only inklings, 'rumours of angels', the 'already' but not yet the 'not yet'. Even those who attempt to describe 'near-death' experiences find the same problem and inadequacy of language. To speak of the second coming as metaphor or myth, then, is not to deny it or to play it down, but to recognise the character of the language of hope. And to deny the language of hope its metaphorical character is to particularise and specify the terms of that hope in a way that Jesus and the biblical writers repeatedly warn us against.

Christians acknowledge this all the time in their worship and liturgies. They are not tempted to abandon their faith by the inadequacies of the metaphors they use in talk of heaven and the hereafter. They enthusiastically sing of being gathered by the crystal sea, of sitting on thrones and casting crowns before him, of endlessly acclaiming 'Worthy is the Lamb', of lying prostrate before the throne and gazing upon the Father, and so on. Do they mean this language literally? Surely not. To take it literally is *not* to take it seriously; on the contrary, it is to diminish it. If ever we think we have fully grasped the reality of heaven in the words we use to describe it, we are to be pitied, not commended.

Francis Thompson's poem 'Little Jesus' includes these lines:

> Didst Thou sometimes think of *there*
> And ask where all the angels were?
> I should think that I would cry
> For my house all made of sky;
> I would look about the air,
> And wonder where my angels were;
> And at waking 'twould distress me –
> Not an angel there to dress me! . . .
>
> And didst Thou play in Heaven with all
> The angels that were not too tall,
> With stars for marbles? Did the things
> Play *Can you see me?* through their wings?[3]

Do we squirm uncomfortably in our seats at such extravagance? We should not. Thompson catches well the tone of childish wonder. And who of us would want to say that a child's vision of heaven is wrong or inappropriate? – especially with the words of Jesus himself ringing in our ears: 'Unless you change and become like little children you will never enter the kingdom of heaven' (Mt. 18:3). Many of us, after all, have no doubt sung many times, 'There's a friend for little children above the bright blue sky'. Would we wish to deny its sentiments in the presence of our children? The vision of heaven we express in our words has to be appropriate to our level of understanding, however inadequate. And that is as true of our adult language of heaven as it is of a child's. For in the mysteries of the faith we are all children, however mature we may be in the Spirit, and our language, however sophisticated, shares something of Thompson's naive innocence.

How could it be otherwise? When the author of Revelation in his description of heaven says, 'and the sea was no more' (Rev. 21:1), was he expressing a hope framed in terms of his own presumably unhappy experience of the sea, or was he affirming that heaven would be a place of disappointment for all who love the sea? Or when 2 Thessalonians envisages the climax of hostility to God as 'the son of perdition', 'the lawless one [masculine]' taking his seat in the temple of God (2 Thess. 2:3–10), are we to understand that such a preview of the end events can only be realised by a male figure sitting down in a rebuilt Jerusalem Temple? No! This is the language of image, and we abuse the language, diminish its imagery, and disdain its writers if we insist that it can have no other than a literal reference.

To take but one other example – from the other place – we are all accustomed to picturing the biblical vision of hell in terms of a fire that burns without being quenched. The imagery was in part drawn from the fires of Gehenna, the constantly smouldering rubbish dump outside the walls of Jerusalem. And this imagery has been constantly repeated in art and literature through the centuries. Are we to take that imagery literally? What then of Dante's portrayal of the deepest circle of hell as a deep frozen lake in which the souls of the tormented are forever trapped?[4] Or C.S. Lewis's portrayal of hell as a depressingly gloomy, smoggy city?[5] Are these alternative images rendered false by the predominant canonical one? Surely not. Were Dante and Lewis wrong to depart from the biblical metaphor? Surely not. A metaphor by its very nature is not and cannot be a literal description. The more appropriate answer is to say that all three are attempts to portray an unimaginable human future in terms drawn from the most horrific experiences of human life. Here once again language falls far short of what we are trying to say.

To sum up our second line of reflection, then, the language of Christian hope, and particularly the hope of heaven and of Christ's coming again, shares a basic deficiency with all our language about the divine and the beyond. It simply cannot express a reality that goes beyond anything those who speak with human speech have experienced. Even their visions are still only visions, and when put into words are constrained by the concepts and words available to them from the store of human discourse. Or else they hear things 'that are not to be told, that no mortal is permitted to repeat' (2 Cor. 12:4). For in both cases the reality envisaged far surpasses the power of human speech to express. As with our talk of the beginning of all things, so with our talk of the end. It is all metaphor, whether the metaphor of a garden paradise or the metaphor of a 'big bang', whether the metaphor of a descent from heaven on clouds, or the metaphor of a wedding feast. There is no single or multiple description of heaven or of Christ's return which is adequate to express a reality beyond words, a reality beyond our experience and understanding.

In short, in this, as in all our talk of God, our language is an icon, and functions properly only when it functions as an icon, that is, as a window through which we look to the spiritual reality beyond. As with all icons, the danger is always present that we will turn the icon into an idol, that we will cease to look through the metaphor and instead focus our attention on the metaphor itself, and so give the language the devotion that belongs to God and to Christ alone. In terms of our present topic, the danger is that we will forget the symbolic character of our talk of Christ's coming again (the reality confessed is far greater than our human language can express), and that we will focus our attention upon the language in a pedantic way that turns our attention away from God and Christ and leaves us expressing our devotion to idols made of human words and verbal images.

The Christ-focus of Christian Hope

This brings us to our third and final line of reflection, to the key issue: What, then, is Christian hope? What are Christians confessing when they confess that Christ will come again? The short answer is: They are confessing Christ. They are confessing God in Christ. They are confessing God's purpose summed up in Christ.

First we need to recall that an eschatological hope is something distinctive within the monotheistic traditions that stem from the religion of Israel. The religions of the East typically have a cyclical view of time; the religions of the West a linear view. I still remember the impact this point made upon me when I first encountered it in John Baillie's *The Belief in Progress.*[6] We see some affirmation of this basic worldview in the irreversible forward steps that have characterised our own entry into the modern period – the development of printing, of aviation, of radio and television, and the revolution in information technology, none of which are reversible.

We should not downplay the extent to which such progress has been inspired, made possible, and to a degree validated by Christian theology and eschatology – just so long as we do not make the mistake of the Victorians and the nineteenth-century liberal Protestants, assuming that scientific progress must lead to moral progress. The events of the twentieth century surely exposed that fallacy once and for all! The more realistic appropriation of Christian eschatology should have reminded us long before World War I that Christian visions of the future have included plenty of scope for evil as well as for the final triumph of good.

In the attempt to speak of eschatology, in the attempt to envisage the future and the end, Christ is the distinctive Christian contribution. For Christians the coming again of Christ is a way of affirming that Christ is the goal and climax of human history. The forward-moving line of human progress reaches its end in Christ. In this Christians share the traditional hope of Jews past and present: the world to come will be inaugurated by the coming of the Messiah. In the words of Isaiah, reworked by Paul, 'Out of Zion will come the deliverer; he will banish ungodliness from Jacob' (Rom. 11:26, citing Is. 59:20–21). The only difference is that Christians believe they know who that deliverer, who that Messiah is – Jesus the Christ. But the hope is essentially the same, reaffirmed even as it is redefined. The hope is expressed in the language of metaphor, but it is a confident hope nonetheless.

Moreover, we should recall again the slogan that in Jewish-Christian eschatology the end-time will be as the beginning-time. It reminds us that the role of Christ at the end may be analogous to the role attributed to him at the beginning. The idea of Christ as agent in creation is as old as Paul: 'For us there is one Lord, Jesus Christ, through whom are all things and through whom we exist' (1 Cor. 8:6); 'who is the image of the invisible God, firstborn of all creation, for in him all things were created . . . all things have been created through him and for him' (Col. 1:15–16).

What did Paul mean by such language? The growing consensus of scholars is that Paul did *not* intend to affirm that Jesus of Nazareth as such was there in the beginning; that would be a step on the road to bitheism. Rather Paul was using the language developed by Jewish wisdom writers to speak of divine Wisdom: Wisdom who, in the poem of Proverbs 8, was with God at the time of creation like a master workman or little child, daily God's delight and rejoicing always (Prov. 8:30); or who, according to Jesus ben Sira, came forth from the mouth of the Most High, and covered the earth like a mist, who was given to Israel as her inheritance and is now embodied in the Torah (Sir. 24:3, 8, 23). This is the wisdom by which God has made all things, the wisdom by which the earth was founded (Ps. 104:24; Prov. 3:19).

And what is this wisdom? It is simply God's wisdom. The poems of Proverbs and ben Sira are simply vivid elaborations of the basic metaphor, imagination-stirring ways of saying that creation was not irrational or purposeless but an act of God's wisdom. The cosmos is not nonsense. It is creation; it makes sense – God's sense! In other words, the figure of Wisdom is simply a way of speaking of God's action and relation to creation. That is why the Wisdom of Solomon can speak of the acts of God towards humanity and on behalf of the patriarchs and Israel as the acts of Wisdom. For Wisdom is the face of God turned to God's world and God's people.

So when Paul and other New Testament writers use such language of Christ, they are speaking not of some divine being other than the one God of Israel. Like their predecessors the Jewish wisdom writers, they are speaking of the way in which God relates to God's world and God's people. And what they are saying is that Christ demonstrates the character of God's outgoing creative and redemptive power. As ben Sira and other Jewish writers saw this divine Wisdom embodied in the Torah, so Paul and the other Christian writers saw this divine Wisdom embodied in Christ. Christ reveals God to us, the God who creates in wisdom. Christ is the climax, the epitome, the incarnation of that divine Wisdom. He shows us what God is like; he reveals to us what creation is all about. Apart from anything else, Christ as Wisdom underlines the insight, rooted deep in our Scriptures, that spirituality is not something divorced from creation, that in no way should salvation be seen as rescue from creation. In wisdom christology, creation and redemption are two sides of the same coin.

What does this say to our present concerns? If indeed the end is to be as the beginning, then could it be that the language describing Christ's involvement in the end plays an analogous function to the language describing Christ's involvement in the beginning? Is the same basic insight involved here? That the end will be as Christ-focused as the beginning, that Christ embodies the character of the end in as definitive and final a way as he embodies the character of the beginning? Christ coming again in new creation is, as Christ, agent of the old creation? But if so, the point is the same in both cases: to speak of Christ as a way of confessing faith in God, as a God whose initial purpose was not only wise but will in the end and *as* the end achieve the goal intended for it in the beginning.

Something of this is surely expressed in two biblical passages central to our concerns. First, Psalm 8:4–6, as taken up and interpreted in the New Testament, Hebrews 2:6–8 in particular: the purpose of God in making humankind – made a little lower than God, crowned with glory and honour, given dominion over the works of God's hands, with all things subservient – has not been fulfilled in humankind as we know it. But it has been fulfilled in Christ – made a little lower than the angels, but now crowned with glory and honour (Heb. 2:6–9), to whom all things will be made subservient (1 Cor. 15:25–27). Christ in his dominion over all fulfils the purpose of God in making humankind in the first place. Second, 1 Corinthians 15:20–28: when this dominion over all is completed, including the last enemy, death, then Christ himself will be subservient to God, 'so that God may be all in all'. Final-time is indeed as primeval-time, when the process begun with God alone in creation *ex nihilo* climaxes in God alone as all in all.

Here again we can conclude that any christology, any eschatology that sets creation and salvation in antithesis is at odds with the Christ-focus of both. Moreover, any spirituality or theology that separates Christ from God, or focuses on Christ in forgetfulness of God, is at odds with the consistent and fundamental God-centred monotheism of the scriptures. Consequently, the confession of Christ's coming again is, like the confession of Christ's role in creation, a confession primarily of God's wisdom and purpose finally and most fully illuminated by and embodied in Christ. The doctrine of the second coming is at its heart the Christian attempt to say that God's final purpose, like God's original purpose, is Christ-focused, is Christ-shaped.

Finally, Christians already know the character of the end, because they know the character of Christ. Christ as the midpoint of time shows us what the unveiling of God's purpose for the end will be like, just as it shows us what the unveiling of God's purpose in the beginning was like. Christians already know the end, because they already know Christ.

This is surely the great lesson to be learned from the strong emphasis on realised eschatology in Christianity's early scriptures. In Christ the end has somehow already arrived. The kingdom of God has come in Jesus' exorcisms (Mt. 12:28). The resurrection of the dead has begun in his resurrection (Rom. 1:4); it is the 'first-fruits', the beginning of the eschatological harvest of the dead (1 Cor. 15:20). So too the Spirit is the downpayment and guarantee of that complete redemption (Rom. 8:23) which will include the transformation of the body enlivened by the psyche into a body enlivened by the Spirit (1 Cor. 15:45–50). Or in alternative terms, the Spirit-Paraclete is the coming again of the first Paraclete (Jn. 14; 1 Jn. 2:1).

All this imagery was born from the strong conviction of the first Christians that they were already experiencing the powers of the age to come (Heb. 6:4–5); they already knew the end because they were already recipients of its blessings. They were already part of the 'new creation' (2 Cor. 5:17; Gal. 6:15). That was why delay of the *parousia* was never as serious a problem for early Christians as so many theologians of this century have thought, simply because the imminence of the end was not constitutive of their view of the end. What was constitutive was their recognition of its character as defined by Christ – the kingdom to come already manifest in the ministry of Jesus of Nazareth; the Spirit of the end-time understood as the Spirit of Christ, the Spirit that inspired the ministry of that Jesus. As Oscar Cullmann pointed out, the delay of Christ's coming again was no great problem for the first Christians because the spring of their hope was in Christ's first coming.[7] In similar terms, the unclarity of their unrealised eschatology was no problem because its defining moment lay in the realised eschatology of Easter and Pentecost.

The struggle with which the first Christians had to hold together the potentially divergent strands of their faith and hope points in the same direction. If Paul is any guide, the overlapping and sometimes conflicting images and metaphors that they used to express their worship would have come to nothing if they did not find their resolution in Christ. What did it mean for them to speak of their being 'in Christ', of being baptised 'into Christ', of coming to the Father 'through Christ', of their community as 'the body of Christ', of the Spirit as 'the Spirit of Christ'? Certainly not that they thought of Christ as dead and gone. Certainly not that they were merely celebrating Christ the great teacher: to collapse such language into an affirmation of the influence of Jesus' teaching is to cut out the living heart of the earliest Christian worship.

But how did they conceive of him, the living, present Christ? How did they picture this Christ in their minds? Christ as Jesus of Nazareth sitting on a throne in heaven beside God? Christ as a kind of universal atmosphere or fluid in which they lived? Christ as a huge, cosmic body? Pursuit of such questions is likely to be as fruitless as the quest for the 'primal man' myth of pre-Christian Gnosticism, a wild-goose chase that dominated much New Testament scholarship in the middle decades of this century.

The point is that the first Christians were ransacking their language and imagery to express the conviction that Christ, the risen Christ, Christ from the other side of death, Christ the embodiment of God's wisdom, Christ as the face of God turned to creation, was still with them, still determining their being as they focused their worship of God through him. They could not give further content to their faith except in and through this language and imagery. 'In Christ' said it all. To say more was to say less.

Is it not the same with Christian talk of Christ's coming again? To tie that confession to a literal coming of Jesus in the clouds of heaven is to limit it. To reduce it to the level of a live television report of Jesus' descent on the Mount of Olives, which could be seen simultaneously all over the world, on all channels, is to lose sight of the deeper significance of the language, to linger on the letter and lose the Spirit. Not that the language should be abandoned. Not at all! The words of the confession are the means by which Christians express this great conviction, this great truth of universal significance. Christ will come again! But the imagery itself is not the reality. The reality is far greater than the imagery. We must not fall into the trap of making the icon into an idol.

Conclusion

Perhaps it would be helpful to see a parallel between the confession of Christ's coming again and the confession of Jesus as the Son of God. By the imagery of 'son' we do not mean that Jesus was literally God's Son through sexual intercourse between God and a woman. That would be to reduce Christian confession of Jesus' divine sonship to the level of the lewd legends of Zeus in his amorous dallyings with earthly women. But that does not mean we must abandon the language of divine sonship for Jesus. Not at all! Christian worship and thought down through the centuries, from the beginning, has recognised that there is no better way of expressing the intimate relation between God and Jesus. That is to say, we recognise that the language is metaphorical, that it is, strictly speaking, inadequate to the task. But we recognise equally that there is no better, no more fitting imagery than that of Jesus as God's Son.

So too with the hope of Christ's coming again. There is an uncertainty about it that pervades all human prediction about God's future purpose. It is the language of vision and metaphor. It is therefore, strictly speaking, inadequate to the task, as is all human speech about God. But it is the best we have and we should neither be embarrassed about it nor abandon it. For it tells us and enables us to tell the world that the future is not random and pointless; God's purpose still prevails and drives forward to the climax of history. It tells us and enables us to tell the world that the future has a Christ-shape and a Christ-character. The future will not come to us as a total surprise. For the God we encounter at the end of time will be the God who encounters us at the midpoint of time, God in Christ. And the Christ we encounter at the end of time will be the Christ we encounter in the Gospels, the Christ we encounter in Christian worship, in the Spirit, in Christ and through Christ to God the Father. We believe that this Christ will come again. 'Maranatha. Come, Lord Jesus'.

Notes

1 This paper was first delivered as a lecture for the Presbyterian Church (USA) Theology Convocation, 'We Believe in One Lord Jesus Christ', in Pittsburgh, 19–22 April 1995. Since then it has also been delivered as the Drew Lecture at Spurgeon's College, London, in October 1995, as the Christ and Cosmos Lecture in Durham, also in October 1995, and as the A.B. Bruce Lecture at the University of Glasgow in January 1996.

2 Rudolf Bultmann, 'New Testament and Mythology', in *Kerygma and Myth*, ed. Hans-Werner Bartsch (London: SPCK, 1953; German orig. 1941), 1–44.

3 Francis Thompson, 'Little Jesus', in *The Oxford Book of Children's Verse*, eds. Iona and Peter Opie (New York: Oxford University Press, 1973), 307–8.

4 'The Inferno' of Dante's *The Divine Comedy*.

5 C.S. Lewis, *The Great Divorce* (New York: Macmillan, 1946).

6 John Baillie, *The Belief in Progress* (London: Oxford University Press, 1950).

7 Oscar Cullmann, *Christ and Time* (Philadelphia: Westminster, rev. edn., 1964).

5

Life Before and After Death in the Old Testament

Rex Mason

To join such a dazzling array of scholars and saints as those who have delivered the Drew Lecture before is a daunting one[1]. I can only think that I was approached since, at my age, I must be thought to be nearer the experience of the theme of the lecture than anyone else who has given it before me. And, seriously, this does affect what I shall say. None of us knows at any stage of our life whether we are on the last chapter of its story or not. But to know that one *is* facing what must be its last chapter (even if one secretly hopes it may be a chapter of a length which, while tedious to others, will be of comfort to oneself) does affect one's outlook on life, death and what lies beyond. And I hope to show one or two ways in which this is so for me and how it affects my thinking on 'immortality'.

Since I am neither philosopher nor theologian I determined to deal with the various ways in which the theme is treated in the Old Testament. I drew comfort from the thought that, of the two previous occasions when the lecture had dealt with this subject, one was given in 1924 when Wheeler Robinson spoke on 'The Old Testament Approach to Life after Death', and the other in 1954 when H.H. Rowley spoke on 'The Future Life in the Thought of the Old Testament'. Outstanding as both these must have been, and we have Rowley's excellent lecture always before us in his book *The Faith of Israel*,[2] I drew comfort from the reflection that their excellence would have faded from the frontal lobes of the memory of at least the great majority of today's audience. But, since determining on the subject I have been outflanked much more recently by Dr John Day, my friend and colleague at Oxford, who has recently published an article called 'The Development of Belief in Life after Death in

Ancient Israel', which appeared in none other than a book entitled *After the Exile*, a book of essays presented to me by Old Testament colleagues in honour of my seventieth birthday. As with all John Day's work, it is so carefully researched, so judicious in its arguments and balanced in its judgments, in a word so scholarly, that it must really be regarded as the last word on the subject[3]. Nevertheless, I wish to look at the subject from a slightly different perspective from any of the three scholars I have just mentioned, and that alone can be the fig leaf of justification with which I attempt to cover my apparent nakedness when compared to their erudition and thoroughness.

I start from the singular fact that, for the greater period of time when they were producing the literature that comprises what we know as the Old Testament, the people of Israel apparently had no lively expectation of life after death. I put it that way because they clearly did not think that men and women became totally extinct at death. Dead people went to Sheol, a place beneath the waters that surrounded the cosmos, and where they were believed to experience only the most shadowy kind of existence: they had no great expectation of a lively and full experience there. Job, for example, is hardly writing the ideal estate agent's blurb for the place when he says:

> If I look for Sheol as my house,
> If I spread my couch in darkness,
> If I say to the Pit,
> 'You are my father',
> And to the worm, 'My mother' or 'My sister',
> Where then is my hope?
> Who will see my hope?
> Will it go down to the bars of Sheol?
> Shall we descend together into the dust?
> (17:13–16)

Generally it is a place of darkness, of hopelessness, and there is no real praise or experience of God there. 'Among the dead no one remembers you; in Sheol who praises you?' (Ps. 6:5), a verse I once heard Frank Fitzsimmonds paraphrase as 'If you let me die you'll lose a customer.' Of course, some apparently conflicting things are said about Sheol in the Old Testament. No one was attempting to write a textbook on the subject. As well as such passages as Psalm 6:5 and many others we can also find the magnificent Psalm 139:8, 'if I make my bed in Sheol, you are there', but that is really poetic language speaking of the universality of God's power and sovereignty. We have to remember that many of the references to Sheol do occur in poetry and we must reckon with the use of metaphor, simile and all the rich panoply of literary devices. A similar contradiction might be found in the view, on the one hand, that those in Sheol are ignorant of all that goes on in the world above them. Koheleth says, '. . . the dead know nothing . . . in Sheol, for which you are bound, there is neither doing nor thinking, neither understanding nor wisdom' (Eccl. 9:5, 10). On the other hand, the shades are pictured as rising up to greet the king of Babylon when he dies, knowing full well what he's been up to on earth, and taunting him with the words 'So you too are as impotent as we are, and have become like one of us! Your pride has been brought down to Sheol' (Is. 14:10–11). The main thrust of the passage is of course the prophet's conviction that the tyrant of Babylon will be destroyed by God.

That some at least believed in such a continuing existence after death is shown by the practice of necromancy. This is roundly denounced in the law and in what we might call the 'official' versions of Yahwism, but it obviously went on in popular practice. That there can be such a discrepancy between the 'official records' and the reality on the ground should not surprise Baptists. After all, we have the official statistics of the Baptist Union Handbook, and we know how they often compare with the number we find in a particular church on any given Sunday morning! We know necromancy was practised because of the very denunciations themselves. Listen to what a minister denounces in his sermons and you can get a fairly accurate picture of the life of any congregation and the society that is its context. And, of course, we have recorded such incidents as the raising of the spirit of Samuel by the medium of Endor at Saul's behest (1 Sam. 28:3–25). Samuel knows full well what has happened and what will happen on earth. In its present form and context that story owes something to the anti-Saul and pro-David stance of early court records, but its relevance here is that it would have been pointless if no one ever had experience of any such practice. But, even granted the whole range of poetic statements about Sheol, together with such evidence as the practice of necromancy and what is known of funerary rites from ancient Israel, no one can claim that passing from life on earth to existence in Sheol is ever spoken of as good news.

There was perhaps another way in which continuing life after death was hoped for and did bring real comfort to many Israelites. To begin to appreciate it we need to see something of their understanding of just what human life consisted of. The Hebrews thought of human beings as what we might call a 'psychic' whole, or even a 'psychosomatic' whole. They did not have the Greek dualistic concept of a human life consisting of a distinct entity, the 'soul', imprisoned in a physical body. We could speak either of an animated body or even an embodied spirit and be fairly close to the way they understood human life. It is an idea expressed in the creation story (Gen. 2:7) 'Then the LORD God formed man from the dust of the ground' – of course a pun on the Hebrew words ארם (*man* or *human being*) and אדמה (*earth* or *ground*) – and breathed into his nostrils the breath of life; and man became a living being (ה'ה לגבשׁ). As Aubrey Johnson has shown, the Hebrew word נפשׁ has a semantic range from a basic meaning 'throat', through to the thought of the 'breath' drawn through the throat, to 'life', because breath is the animating principle of all life.[4] But that it does not answer to the Greek thought of 'soul' is shown by the fact that animals can be spoken of in just the same way. In Genesis 9:10 God promises Noah that he is going to establish a covenant with him 'and with every living creature (כל־נפש החיה) that is with you, the birds, the domestic animals . . .' The uniqueness of human beings according to the creation story is not that they possess נפש, but that of them alone it is said that God created them 'in his image' (Gen. 1:27) and later it is shown how the 'spirit' (רוח) of human beings is capable of being 'invaded' by the 'spirit of God'.

Human beings appear to have been thought of as having shared mortality with animals from the first. Traditional Christian theology has often argued that Adam and Eve were originally created immortal and that death only became a reality after their fall, a view sometimes based on Romans 5:12, just as sin came into the world through one man, and death came through sin . . .' and on an understanding of Genesis 3:19, which sees it as the climax of God's curse on Adam: 'you are dust, and to dust you shall return'. On the other hand, Genesis 3:22 seems to suggest otherwise, for here God is reported as fearing that, by eating the fruit of the tree of life, human beings might transcend their mortal lot: 'Then the LORD God said, "See, the man has become like one of us, knowing good and evil; and now, he might reach out his hand and take also from the tree of life, and eat, and live for ever". . .' However, whatever its origin, mortality is now the common lot of all created life, human and animal.

At death, the נפש is 'breathed' or 'poured' out. Job says that the only ultimate hope of the wicked is 'the breathing out of their נפש' (Job 11:20) while the Servant is said to have 'poured out his נפש until death' (Is. 53:12). Yet as we have seen, this did not necessarily mean immediate and total extinction. At least for a time vital powers seemed to remain. So the son of the woman of Zarephath was so ill 'that there was no breath left in him' (1 Kgs. 17:17). Yet, when Elijah prayed for him, 'The LORD listened to the voice of Elijah; and the נפש of the boy came into him again . . .' (v. 22). Something of a person's 'vital powers' could live on in parts of his body, for, after Elisha's death, a man killed by raiding Moabites was thrown hurriedly into the prophet's grave where 'as soon as the man touched the bones of Elisha, he came to life and stood on his feet' (2 Kgs. 13:21). This is no doubt why a proper burial was regarded as so important. It was a sign of terrible judgment from God if a king's body was left unburied and thus prey to wild animals and birds of carrion (e.g. 1 Kgs. 14:11), and this is why Amos saw it as such an outrage that the Moabites had burned the bones of the king of Edom (Amos 2:1). It may be more metaphorical, but we must recall that God could say to Cain, '. . . your brother's blood is crying out to me from the ground' (Gen. 4:10). But, in such ways, some human beings, at least, were thought of as living on after death.

There was also a real sense that someone lived on in his children, and that was why the promise of descendants was so important. A negative testimony to this is provided by the example of Absalom who set up a memorial pillar to himself because, he said, 'I have no son to keep my name in remembrance' (2 Sam. 18:18). Some have argued that the Nehemiah memoirs, with their repeated refrain 'Remember for my good, O my God, all that I have done for this people' (e.g. Neh. 5:19) were written for a similar purpose. If Nehemiah would have had to be a eunuch to have served in the queen's presence (2:6) then, in the absence of children, his memoirs would have served to perpetuate his name. Such an argument, though, is tenuous and inconclusive.

However, none of this adds up to what we should call a lively hope for anything positive and rich beyond death. Yet, the striking thing is, the collection of literature that makes up the Old Testament is by no means negative or pessimistic. The Israelites were life affirming, not life denying. Their very word for 'life', חיים, is a plural form, often called a 'plural of intensity'. Of course every shade of human emotion and experience is expressed there. There are the cries of those who are suffering physically, mentally and spiritually. There is the near despair of those who have lost everything that made life dear. There are cries of agony, of doubt, of complaint. There is the bitterness of bereavement. A Jeremiah and a Job can speak very plainly to God indeed, pouring out their sense of bitterness and betrayal. Psalmists mince no words when complaining to God on their own behalf or on behalf of others. And this is part of the rich human tapestry of the Old Testament and is an expression of its spiritual treasury, for in such open and honest talk to God we hear the heartbeat of authentic prayer. Yet, for all this, the note of praise and sheer joy is dominant. The Psalms of praise throb with what Mowinckel described as 'enthusiasm for God'. The story of their nation reveals, and the prophets proclaim, the sheer grace, love and goodness of their covenant God. In the Psalms they respond to him with grateful and awestruck praise. Their Wisdom writers celebrate and explore God's realm of creation. In fellowship with God, in good relationship with all his covenant people, in the joy of their family ties, surrounded by the good things of a land flowing with milk and honey, they experience and affirm this intensely positive fact of חיים. They know it is surrounded by shadows. They know that, at the end, they sink down into Sheol. But they rejoice in all the good life God gives now. Indeed, we can think of the range of their experience rather like a voltmeter. Over at the plus end of the scale is חיים in all its fullness. At the minus end of the scale, death in Sheol represents the weakest form of life. So the approach of any kind of suffering represents a diminution of full life. The needle is swinging away from the plus to the minus sign. Any suffering is an approach of death. And, as we have seen, to die is to go down through the waters to Sheol. So this provides a rich set of metaphors for speaking about the experience of life. The psalmist cries:

Save me, O God,
For the waters have come up to my neck (נפש).
I sink in deep mire,
Where there is no foothold;
I have come into deep waters,
And the flood sweeps over me.
(Ps. 69:1–2)

And deliverance from any deep trouble can be described using the same metaphor:

He reached down from on high, he took me;
He drew me out of mighty waters.
(Ps. 18:16)

Such cosmic metaphor is almost certainly the seedbed of later Christian baptismal theology. But we have to remember that it *is* metaphor. And this means it is not always clear whether an Old Testament writer is speaking about actual death and resurrection, or whether he is using such picture language to describe any form of suffering and the experience of deliverance from it. The point of note in all this is, however, that, despite being much of the time without any lively hope of life after death, their experience of life and of God is as joyful, as positive and as affirming as it is.

Can we trace the development of more specific hope of life beyond death and the stages by which they came to such hope? Such is the uncertainty of the date of all the constituent parts of any of the Old Testament literature, that I am doubtful as to whether we can chart a chronological progression with all its intermediate and developmental stages fully mapped. But what I want to suggest is that there are certain paths along which they did advance to the concept, whatever the calendar date of any particular point along one of those paths. And the first *is a conviction concerning the faithfulness and righteousness of God.* God cannot ultimately be defeated by any evil power, terrestrial or supernatural, nor even by the sin and faithlessness of his own people. In the end he must be a God who keeps his promises and who vindicates his purposes for his own people and for all the world.

We begin with an eighth-century prophet, Hosea. He has no doubt that God will judge Israel for their religious apostasy in worshipping Ba'al, apostasy he likens to prostitution and the rejection of their 'marriage' relationship with Yahweh. Yet, the God they have wronged loves them still, as Hosea was called to love Gomer, and so the prophet exhorts them to return:

Come, let us return to the LORD;
For it is he who has torn, and he will heal us;

He has struck down, and he will bind us up.
After two days he will revive[5] us;
On the third day he will raise us up.
(Hos. 6:1–2)

The prophet is clearly speaking of the judgment of Israel in exile and promising that God will ultimately restore them again. He is thus using the language of death and resurrection metaphorically, in a way we have seen was familiar in Hebrew usage. Probably, just as Hosea daringly uses the fertility language and metaphors of the Canaanite religion of Ba'al to describe Israel's relationship with their true lover, Yahweh, so here he is drawing on the language of the dying and rising God, also familiar from the Ba'al epics, to describe Yahweh's redemption of his people. Such language is used even more strikingly later in the book: Hosea 13:14 reads:

Shall I ransom them from the power of Sheol?
Shall I redeem them from Death?
O Death, where are your plagues?
O Sheol, where is your destruction?
Compassion is hidden from my eyes.

Here the thrust is different. God is saying that he will *not* rescue his people. But clearly the idea is that he has the power to do so. Again, we are in the realm, not of physical death and resurrection from the grave, but of metaphor, of national death and survival spoken of in terms of exile and (possible) restoration. But metaphorical language can have potency. It can soon suggest a literal, rather than a metaphorical reality alone. The Hosea metaphor certainly had influence because it seems to have inspired Isaiah 26:19, a verse occurring in Isaiah 24–7, often described as 'the Isaiah Apocalypse':

Your dead shall live, their corpses shall rise.
O dwellers in the dust, awake and sing for joy!
For your dew is a radiant dew,
And the earth will give birth to those long dead.

John Day has pointed to the many parallels between Isaiah 26:19 and Hosea 13 and 14. We may mention just two here: both passages are preceded by the imagery of Israel travailing vainly in birthpains, and both use the imagery of reviving and refreshing 'dew', another feature of Ba'al fertility language. In the Isaiah passage the power of metaphor to metamorphise into more literal reality is clear, but commentators are divided over whether this is a clear allusion to the resurrection of individuals who have died, or to the renewal of a community that has suffered grievously. The Hosea passages clearly refer to the renewal of the national fortunes. The Isaiah passage *probably* does, but the legitimate doubt over its interpretation shows how metaphor can so easily become the seedbed in which the picture it paints becomes reality.

But the powerful use of the same metaphor continued. For in a familiar passage, Ezekiel uses it of the renewal of the nation of Israel after the exile. In a vision (ch. 37) he sees the nation of Israel as a valleyfull of dead bones and is asked by God whether they can live. With perhaps understandably wise caution he replies, 'O Lord GOD, you know' (v. 3). He is commanded to prophesy to the dead bones, which might seem a somewhat useless exercise, but is one that has often been repeated in the history of preaching since. The prophetic word of God, however, carries the same power of the Spirit as the creative word of God. In a passage meant to recall the Genesis account of creation, in which we read that 'the LORD God formed man from the dust of the ground, and breathed into his nostrils the breath of life; and the man became a living being' (לנפשׁ חיה, Gen. 2:7), Ezekiel sees that the divine 'spirit' brings the nation to life and gives them such power as to transform them into an army. Throughout the passage there is the play on the Hebrew word רוּח, which means 'wind', 'breath' and 'spirit' (with just the same semantic range as the Greek word πνευμα). Again, it is metaphor, and speaks of the release and renewal of God's people following exile. But in testifying to the power of God to vindicate his name, his purposes of righteousness, and his age-long promises, it must be nourishing the seed of something that is to flower into something bigger and finer.

Such faith in the ultimate vindication by God of those who have been unjustly persecuted is also seen in the promise of restoration, perhaps of resurrection, of the Servant in the famous Servant passage in Isaiah 53. The Servant was 'cut off from the land of the living . . . They made his grave with the wicked . . .' (vv. 8–9). His נפשׁ was made a 'sin-offering' (v. 10). Yet, this Servant will see his offspring and shall prolong his days' and 'through him the 'will of the LORD shall prosper' (v. 10).

The identity and ministry of the Servant in these chapters has been endlessly debated, and shows every sign of continuing to be so. There is no space here to enter that debate in detail of any kind. I will satisfy myself, with a thoroughly enjoyable arrogance, simply by saying that the interpretation of the Servant as 'Israel', always the way Jews have taken it, has much to commend it. Throughout Isaiah 40 to 55 the 'servant' is uniformly used of Israel. In the second 'Servant song' that identification is specifically made in a verse that has no textual evidence of any strength against it (49:3). It is no problem that the same passage goes on to speak of a mission of the Servant *to* Israel, since the 'true' Israel will always be distinct from and smaller than Israel κατα σαρκα. The observation that the Servant has suffered unjustly would be strange if it came from God's mouth, since the prophet makes clear that Israel was sent into exile on account of her sins. But surely the speakers in the central section of the final song are the Gentile kings? For, having just been told by God that

> . . . he shall startle many nations;
> Kings shall shut their mouths because of him;
> For that which had not been told them they shall see,
> And that which they had not heard they shall contemplate.

They most naturally follow that immediately by saying:

> Who has believed what we have heard?
> And to whom has the arm of the LORD been revealed?
> (52:15–53:1)

So it is the Gentile kings, who have themselves invaded and spoiled Israel and carried her away into exile for no action of Israel towards them, who now come to see that it was through this suffering servant, Israel, that the true God has now revealed himself to them. They have been saved by the servant's vicarious suffering. And such an interpretation fits into the whole message of these chapters which is that, in redeeming Israel, God is going to show his universal might and power so clearly and strongly that all nations will come to acknowledge him as the one true God. They are doing just that in Isaiah 53. Nor need we fear for the way this chapter has been so famously interpreted in the New Testament. For every page of the Gospels reveals that Jesus, in his ministry, comes as the 'true Israel', to fulfil that mission to which Israel had been called and for which they had been redeemed, but which they so signally had failed to accomplish. Seen in this way, the 'resurrection' of the Servant in Isaiah 53 is another example of a metaphor for the exile and restoration of Israel, and is a powerful statement of the assurance that God will vindicate his righteousness and fulfil his promises.

No example of this repeated metaphor could have had stronger influence, for it demonstrably inspires the first quite explicit statement of a belief in the resurrection of the dead in the Old Testament. I say 'the first' in the sense that there is no possibility of doubt over Daniel 12:2–3. We do not have to ask whether this is metaphor or 'the real thing'. It is 'the real thing'. Not that it promises a general and universal resurrection of all dead. It will affect 'many' of both the 'wise' and the 'evil', and the reference must be to those faithful who had perished in the fires of persecution and so apparently missed the victory of God's kingdom, and to the wicked who by their death conveniently avoided the judgment which awaits them.

Daniel 12:2–3 is all about the vindication of God's righteousness, a vindication that can only be fully achieved as he exercises his power to raise the dead. And it interprets this resurrection in the light of Isaiah 53. The book of Daniel traces the history of events from the time of the Babylonian exile, through what it sees as a succeeding Median, then Persian and, finally, Greek empire. It sees this whole period as a time of suffering on the part of the people of God. Indeed, there is some evidence to suggest that it sees it all as a continuing exile, a kind of continuing 'Babylonish captivity of the people of God'. In chapter 9 Daniel is reading in the book of the prophet Jeremiah and finds that the period of desolation is to last seventy years (v. 2). But, in answer to his prayer, Gabriel tells him that the prophecy really means 'seventy weeks of years' (v. 24). That this is not just an isolated, detached, convenient way of adjusting the prophecy to the event is suggested by its probable allusion to the Chronicler's picture of the Babylonian exile. The Chronicler says that the Babylonians captured and sacked the city and exiled the people 'to fulfil the word of the LORD by the mouth of Jeremiah, until the land had made up for its sabbaths. All the days that it lay desolate it kept sabbath, to fulfil seventy years' (2 Chr. 36:21). The land had become so polluted by the sin of its inhabitants that the theological purpose of the exile was to cleanse it by letting it lie fallow for seventy 'sabbaths'. From the 'seventy sabbaths' of the Chronicler to Daniel's 'seventy weeks of years' is not a quantum leap, especially as Gabriel goes on to say this is just what the intervening period has been intended to achieve: 'Seventy weeks are decreed for your people and your holy city: to finish the transgression, to put an end to sin, and to atone for iniquity . . .' (9:24). The book contains unmistakable references to Antiochus who 'lifts himself up' and 'makes war against the saints' in a time of ever increasing ferocity and terror. In fact, while Jews had often suffered during their history, it was in the time of Antiochus Epiphanes that they were first persecuted for keeping their faith. Antiochus needed to consolidate his disparate empire in the face of Rome's threat by uniting it in a common form of emperor worship and he needed funds for his military campaigns so badly that he rifled the temples of his subject peoples. When loyal Jews opposed him on both counts he showed he was in no conciliatory mood. However, the book of Daniel also sees that his time is strictly limited and that God has his 'time' when he will intervene, overthrow the tyrant, and set up his own kingdom among the saints.

However, here a question had to pose itself, especially as we are in the time of the later Wisdom literature when the problem of evil and the suffering of the righteous is becoming ever more acute. A time, also, when the people have been encouraged to believe there is only one God. It is not that the God of Israel is stronger than all other gods, it is that there *are* no other gods. He alone is creator and saviour. But once you have arrived at a clear monotheistic faith, then the problem of evil becomes even more acute. There are signs in the book of Daniel that we are already beginning to move to the idea of evil forces in heavenly places and that the struggle taking place on earth is only a projection of a cosmic struggle between God and the spiritual powers of evil. But, although the writer is in no doubt of God's ultimate victory, what of the faithful who have died under persecution? Is it just that they should miss this great scene of victory in heaven and on earth because they have died too early? And what of those evil persecutors who have escaped the judgment that awaits them by conveniently dying before it takes place? It is in this context that the concept of a resurrection occurs: 'Many of those who sleep in the dust of the earth shall awake, some to everlasting life, and some to shame and everlasting contempt' (Dan. 12:2). But the faithful, those who are called the *maskîlîm*, the 'wise', that is, those who had the discernment to read the signs of the times and act accordingly, are shown not only to be heirs to resurrection. Their suffering and death is interpreted in the light of that of the suffering Servant of Isaiah 53. In Daniel 11:33, we read, 'And those among the people who are wise shall make the many understand . . .' While in 12:3 we read, 'And those who are wise shall shine like the brightness of the firmament, and those who turn the many to righteousness, like the stars for ever and ever.' Those two verses echo very clearly what is said of the Servant in Isaiah 53:11: 'by his knowledge shall the righteous one, my servant, make the many to be accounted righteous . . .' Those who have suffered and died, therefore, will know that their 'labour was not in vain in the LORD', to coin a later phrase. Their suffering will prove to have had a vicarious effect, since, like the Servant of Isaiah 53, they will turn the careless and renegade 'many' to acknowledge and confess God. That is why I said that Isaiah 53 was a mainspring in the development of the idea of resurrection from death. It is part of this powerful Old Testament line of witness to the ultimate triumph of the will and purpose of the God who is righteous.

There have been many who have urged that the idea surfaces in the book of Daniel because of foreign influence, especially that of Persian Zoroastrianism. I would not wish in any way to deny that religion is influenced by the atmosphere of its social, cultural and political context. Our own church life today shows how pervasive is the influence from the world in which we are set. Nor should we by any means always think such influence is bad. There *is* a wrong kind of 'worldliness' to which we are always tempted to succumb. But a church, or any religious group, that managed to seal itself hermetically in total isolation from its world would be of precious little use to its generation. It is often said that the church which marries the spirit of its age will be a widow in the next. This is true. But if the church never even talks to its age it will remain an unwanted and uninfluential old maid in every age. For all this, however, I am not convinced that the emergence of the concept of resurrection in the book of Daniel was due to foreign influence. I have tried to show that there is sufficient evidence that it draws on a persistent strain within the Old Testament itself, and that the concept was born of a long-held conviction in the sovereign power and goodness of God rather than in a sudden blinding light of revelation from Zoroastrianism.

It is fitting that we should speak of 'resurrection' when speaking of Old Testament concepts, since, with their view of human beings as a unified 'body/soul', the 'resurrection of the body' was a natural development. 'Immortality' is, strictly, the product more of a Greek, dualistic view of human nature as eternal soul imprisoned within a temporary body. Such a concept does emerge late in the Jewish Wisdom literature. Like the apocalyptic writers, with whom we connect the writer of the book of Daniel for convenience here, the Wisdom writers wrestled with the problem of evil and, especially, the suffering of the good and the apparent prosperity of the wicked. Again, it was, no doubt, the increasing severity of the nation's sufferings drove them to face this issue, and also the fact that they too faced the theological problems monotheism brings. The earliest Wisdom literature simply asserted that there is a link between 'fear' of God and prosperity. Such confidence foundered on the very facts of human existence. We see it beginning to totter in the probings of the books of Job and Koheleth. Ultimately, the resolution of the problem was found in the idea of a life beyond death. *The Wisdom of Solomon* written, probably, somewhere round about 100 BCE, is the first to make explicit reference to immortality. The foolish, he says,

> did not know the secret purposes of God, nor hoped for the wages of holiness, nor discerned the prize for blameless souls; for God created us for incorruption and made us in the image of his own eternity . . . the souls of the righteous are in the hand of God, and no torment will ever touch them. In the eyes of the foolish they seem to have died and their departure was thought to be a disaster, and their going from us to be their destruction; but they are at peace. For though in the sight of others they were punished, their hope is full of immortality.
> (2:22–3, 3:1–4)

Canning, Foreign Secretary in the period after the Napoleonic wars, sought to repair the damaged balance of power in Europe with an alliance with America. To the Commons he reported, 'I have called in the New World to redress the balance of the old.' That is what the writer of Wisdom has done. Thus we should see his work as the flowering of the Old Testament line of thought which remained convinced, in spite of all temptation to believe the contrary, that there would be an ultimate victory of the God of righteousness. He uses a Greek concept to do it, but stands within a truly Old Testament line.

But there is another path along which I believe the Old Testament writers advanced to a concept of life after death. And this is a path they found themselves walking in the company of God. *The presence of God*, his unfailing companionship through all the vicissitudes of life, *becomes the bedrock of their hope*, not only for all that lies in wait for them in this life, but in all that must follow it. For it finally becomes unthinkable to them that the God who has proved so faithful to them now could ever let them arrive at a point on their pilgrimage where he says he is now leaving them and allowing them to fend for themselves. It is no surprise, therefore, that this represents some of the finest writing in the Old Testament. I have already referred to Psalm 139. Let us hear its magnificent poetry again:

> Where can I go from your spirit?
> Or where can I flee from your presence?
> If I ascend to heaven, you are there;
> If I make my bed in Sheol, you are there . . .
> If I say, 'Surely the darkness shall cover me,
> And the light around me become night',
> Even the darkness is not dark to you;
> The night is as bright as the day,
> For darkness is as light to you.
> (Ps. 139:7–8, 11–12)

That is poetry, but it is also the expression of a great person of God who is convinced that such a God as has accompanied the pilgrim through all the ordeals of the way, cannot abandon him now. There is no height nor depth inaccessible to the love and power of this God. Now, it may be, that this is still metaphor. But what power such a metaphor must have, especially with its language of 'light' and 'darkness', eventually to awaken the sense of a presence that will not abandon even those who go down to Sheol, the place thought of above all as the domain of 'darkness'.

Another psalmist seems to have become convinced that this is more than metaphor; it is reality. In Psalm 49:5 the psalmist asks:

> Why should I fear in times of trouble,
> When the iniquity of my persecutors surrounds me . . . ?

The end of such powerful tyrants who trust in their wealth and the power they give is death, and a death that brings no hope:

> Their graves are their homes for ever,
> Their dwelling-places to all generations,
> Though they named lands their own . . .
> Like sheep they are appointed for Sheol;
> Death shall be their shepherd . . .
> (vv. 11, 14)

But he has another confidence:

But God will ransom my soul from the power of Sheol,
For he will receive me.
(v. 15)

Not only does the reference to the death and burial of the wicked make this seem a quite literal reference to death and resurrection, the word translated 'he will *receive* me' (לקח) is the very word used of the assumption of Enoch, where in Genesis 5:24 it is said, 'Enoch walked with God; then he was no more, because God *took* him' (my emphasis). It is used again of the 'taking' up of Elijah in 2 Kings 2:3, 5, 9, 10. Indeed, must we not see these two instances of the assumption of two heroes of the faith, Enoch and Elijah, as belonging to this strain of thought and experience? The closeness of their walk with God was such that it was natural for God to 'take' them to continue that fellowship. And the psalmist of Psalm 49 sees himself, by a great daring leap of faith, to be destined to follow them, not by avoiding the experience of death and burial as they did, but as being assured of the continuing presence and power of God to 'receive' him from the power of Sheol back into a relationship that cannot be broken by the fact of death. The same is true of the psalmist of Psalm 73. He had been tormented by the prosperity of the wicked, by their arrogant complacency and utter disregard of God. The acuteness of the issue for him led almost to an abandonment of faith. Yet, significantly, it was in the sanctuary that a true perspective was restored to him. There he saw their 'end'. But he contrasts their lot with his:

Nevertheless I am continually with you;
You hold my right hand.
You guide me with your counsel,
And afterwards you will receive me with honour [or 'to glory'].
Whom have I in heaven but you?
And there is nothing on earth that I desire other than you.
My flesh and my heart may fail,
But God is the strength of my heart
And my portion for ever.
(vv. 23–26)

Here too, it might just possibly be that 'afterwards' refers to the end of his period of suffering and doubt. But again, the contrast with the fate of those who come to an 'end' and the use of the word 'receive' must surely mean that here is another whose experience of God now inspires the confidence that death cannot be strong enough to break such a relationship.

Might we therefore use the language of faith for a moment and say that perhaps it was in the economy of the divine plan that his people learned first what joy a life lived in relationship with such a God brings here and now, before they advanced, tremblingly but ultimately confidently, to the belief that such a relationship would continue after death? That advance was made because they found in experience that God is a God, the power of whose love and the dependability of whose word are such that it is impossible that the realm of death and Sheol should prove itself stronger. Christian Aid have an advertising slogan that has always greatly impressed me: 'We believe in life *before* death'. That is what the Israelites believed and rejoiced in, and thus they learned that it is the quality of life lived with God, rather than just its durability, that is at the heart of the good news about God. No one has put that more expressively than R. Martin-Achard:

> For all of them [i.e. the great people of faith among the Israelites], the heart of the matter is not so much the question of everlasting life, as that of life with God; they are less concerned about the length of their days than about the relationship that should unite them with Him; they are more preoccupied with belonging to God than with their existence.[6]

And is that not also the lesson of the New Testament? How often have we been told, and said in our own preaching, that 'eternal life' is not just life that goes on for ever? To tell some people that life, as they know it now, is going on for ever and ever would be to provoke the response 'But that would be hell.' Precisely! 'Eternal life' is life of the new age, the new realm of God's kingdom, known through the constant fellowship of the risen, living Christ. And, incidentally, life lived with the risen Christ cannot be quashed by the small incident of the death of our bodies.

I said that the passing of the years brings new perspectives. Once someone has retired he or she begins to look at their life's work in a new perspective. One is grateful for all that was good and enjoyable in it, and sorry for the many mistakes and omissions that marred it. But some of the things that seemed most important at the time now begin to fade. Coups of organisation, even perhaps the building up of some churches, the achieving of some reputation, the publication of a few books and articles, begin to look less sensational than they appeared at the time. What continues to count are the relationships that were formed with people, some of which became carrier waves for the love and power and the Spirit of God. The people one stood with in the hour of need, when illness struck or death made bereft; those whom one saw find even a little of the light of Christ in the darkness of despair or something of his strength to remake in the hour of guilt and failure; these are what seem to matter most. One begins to realise more and more as life progresses that the most important thing about being human is found in relationships. The deep love between two, the family ties, the bonds of friendship that keep us linked to those with whom we now no longer have the common interest of shared work, these are what seem 'eternal'.

As one begins to feel more and more acutely that such relationships, such love, are stronger than all the vicissitudes of life, then the question arises, 'So why should they not be stronger than death?' Above all, the love of God seen ultimately to have been following one all the way, and never closer than in those dark passages where the sight and assurance of it were clouded, cannot be destined to end with the mere incident of death, especially as it has been known through relationship with the Lord of life who was raised from the dead by the power of that same God. To turn to that other Old Testament track we have been following, when one sees the persistence of so much human cruelty, of sheer viciousness, of criminal folly, of bigotry – all of which seem indefinitely to postpone the building of the new Jerusalem here on earth – how can one believe that a God, whose ways are those of justice and righteousness and who has implanted in us some of his own passion for the righting of wrongs, is ultimately helpless before the waywardness of his own creation?

Such glimpses, born on the wings of faith, conceived in the depths of human love, and nurtured by the unfailing presence of the God who journeys with us all our days, bring an assurance of the truth of the gospel that neither death nor life can separate us from the love of God in Christ Jesus our Lord. When we tread that path of faith and discovery, we are treading a path whose trail was blazed, even before the fullness of the revelation that came with Jesus Christ, by the great men and women of vision of the Old Testament, who, by their faith, in the words of the writer of the letter to the Hebrews, saw what was promised and 'greeted it from afar'.

Notes

1 Delivered at Spurgeon's College on 6 November 1997.

2 H. H. Rowley, *The Faith of Israel* (London: SCM Press, 1961).

3 J. Barton and D. J. Reimer (eds.), *After the Exile: Essays in Honour of Rex Mason* (Macon: Macon University Press, 1996).

4 *The Vitality of the Individual in the Thought of Ancient Israel* (Cardiff: University of Wales Press, 1964[2]), 3–22.

5 Hosea uses the Pi'ēl of the verb חיה, to 'make alive'.

6 R. Martin-Achard, *From Death to Life*, trans. J. Penney-Smith (Edinburgh: Oliver and Boyd, 1960), 180.

Part 2
Historical Perspectives

6

Death and the Life Thereafter in the Thinking of William Tyndale*

B. R. White

In their thinking about death and the life thereafter, the English Reformers of the sixteenth century faced questions which in many cases still puzzle believing men and women, especially those who hold to the more traditional evangelical understanding of the Scriptures and of the Christian life. At the same time, the Reformers were concerned with questions which many ministers and theologians of the mainstream Christian churches today do not show much enthusiasm for asking. Perhaps the chilly philosophical climate that has been evident in many places in the western world has had its effect in producing frozen theology. Nonetheless, the questions will continue to be asked. For, like it or not, death is the one inescapable reality. It faces and often seems to threaten us all.

What, then, were the questions with which the Reformers struggled? They were questions thrown up by a combination of biblical theology and a particular socio-religious context, and we must recognise them as such. But they were also questions which have something for us: they are not merely academic questions belonging to the past. For example, since the Reformers believed, on the basis of Scripture, that death was not merely a matter of physical breakdown but the consequence of God's judgment upon sinful humanity, they had to ask what the relationship was between the physical event and divine judgment. In the same way, since they believed that at death the physical body and the soul were separated, they felt compelled to ask what part both body and soul played in God's ongoing purposes for the one who died. Similarly, they asked what happened after death. They believed that the Roman Catholic doctrine of purgatory had no basis in Scripture and that it was tied to a burdensome penitential cycle.[1] They opposed what they believed was a theology of a treasury of merit controlled by the pope. But if purgatory did not prepare a soul for heaven, where and how was it prepared? Or was it miraculously transformed at some crucial moment in time? These were questions that were being widely raised.

This study will concentrate on one English Reformer, William Tyndale (c. 1492–1536), now chiefly known as a translator of the Bible into English.[2] The question to which William Tyndale gave attention was: how did the doctrine of the general resurrection tie in with the view held by many Protestants from that day to this, that men and women were immediately translated at death to heaven or to hell? After all, there was a promise from the crucified Lord to the thief beside him on the cross: 'Today you shall be with me in Paradise.' For many that settled the matter – and for many it still does. Another issue, closely linked with this question and dependent upon the reply given to it, was: if people were not at once brought to their reward at death what happened to their souls in the meantime between death and the general resurrection? That death, preparation for death, and an explanation of how it was to be understood were important topics both pastorally and apologetically to the English Reformers is very clear from the fact that Miles Coverdale, another early English translator, took the trouble to translate a Lutheran treatise on the subject.[3]

Although William Tyndale is remembered today mainly for his work as a pioneer Bible translator, he was also, at the very least, a competent populariser of other people's theology and an effective Protestant controversialist. He certainly owed a considerable debt to the writings of Martin Luther.[4] But he also seems to have learned from others, and, inevitably given his work of translation, he did some thinking of his own. His importance for us is not only that he was the earliest of the English Reformers to have left a considerable corpus of writings behind him, but also because he seems to have given some significant thought to the doctrine of death. At all events, his writings raise most of the central questions and attempt some answers. In this article we consider his arguments. I will also make some comments on what I believe to be some of the significant aspects of the subject for us today.

It is important, first, to grasp what William Tyndale had to say about the nature of the Christian life so that we may remind ourselves of the rather different perspective of his generation as compared with ours. For Tyndale, this life was a preparation for eternity, whereas for most Christian people today, even for many evangelical Christians, this life (and its good things) is infinitely more important than the next. It was because death was so near and was felt to be so that Tyndale's theology of the Christian life was intimately bound up with his idea of death. Keith Thomas has pointed out that 'it is beyond dispute that Tudor and Stuart Englishmen were by our standards, exceedingly liable to pain, sickness and premature death'.[5] Even toward the end of the seventeenth century it has been calculated that about a third of the boy children born into the homes of the English nobility died before they reached the age of five – and, presumably, they had a far better chance than had other children born in poorer circumstances.

How then did William Tyndale see the Christian life? Like the apostle Paul and Martin Luther, Tyndale saw the law as a means to 'drive us to Christ'. He described the law as that which 'pulleth from a man the trust and confidence that he hath in himself and in his own works, merits, deservings and ceremonies . . . For it is not possible that Christ should come to a man, as long as he trusteth in himself.' After the preaching of the law comes the preaching of the Gospel: 'God's gift together with the Spirit of God who looseth the bonds of Satan and coupleth us to God and his will through strong faith and fervent love'. The consequence of this is that the believer comes to the assurance 'that it is not possible that God should forsake him or withdraw his mercy and love from him'.[6] Strong faith and fervent love issue in a deep and constant obedience to God. Loving obedience is not the root of our salvation but its fruit, for the root is faith. Changing the metaphor a little Tyndale comments that

> we say, Summer is nigh for the trees blossom. Now is the blossoming of the trees not the cause that summer draweth nigh, but the drawing nigh of summer is the cause of the blossoms, and the blossoms put us in remembrance that summer is at hand.

Hence, seeing the fervour of love blossom in outward deeds of obedience we may be assured of 'a strong faith within'.[7]

When Tyndale turns to baptism, he sees it as intimately bound up with the covenant God makes with humanity.[8] Furthermore, a Baptist may recognise this view as being especially valuable for the way it fits into a baptismal theology geared to the baptism of believers. For the Protestant Reformers the sacraments were sermons made visible and tangible. Hence Tyndale can argue that 'as a preacher, in preaching the word of God, saveth the hearers that believe, so doth the washing'. The washing of baptism saves because it proclaims the all-sufficient sacrifice of Christ effective for all who repent and believe. 'The plunging into the water', affirms Tyndale,

> signifieth that we die and are buried with Christ as concerning the old life of sin . . . And the pulling out again signifieth that we rise again with Christ in a new life, full of the Holy Ghost, which shall teach us and guide us, and work the will of God in us.[9]

In support of this he quotes, as we would expect, Romans 6, and lays stress on the work of the Holy Spirit in the baptised which could be easily justified from Romans 8. However, unlike the apostle Paul but in a way that is very similar to Luther, Tyndale lays little stress on any notion of a once-for-all union with

Christ effected in baptism for the believer. What Tyndale stresses alongside the idea of baptism as the promise of God's mercy in Christ is the concept of baptism as signifying a constantly renewed commitment of the believer to his Lord.

This is where Tyndale's special understanding of death, which he closely shared with Luther, begins to emerge. Tyndale argues that while it is true that from the point of view of our Christian profession we are now dead and risen in Christ, from the point of view of the continuing rebellion of our flesh 'we do but begin to die and to be baptised'. The truth baptism proclaims, of union with the crucified and risen Lord, is only partially true, true in anticipation in this life. The drowning of the rebellious desires of our flesh begins at our baptism as, by 'the working of the Spirit, we begin to live, and grow every day more and more both in knowledge and also in godly living'. But the fullness of what baptism proclaims and promises, the fulfilment to which baptism is a testimony and a promise, only comes about, says Tyndale, 'at the last moment of death'.[10] Hence, because Tyndale reckons that as long as we live 'we are yet partly carnal and fleshly', even though in Christ, we are committed to a daily wrestling which finds final victory only in death. In another place he sums up his understanding of the matter when he writes:

> We have enough to do all our lives long, to tame our bodies, and to compel the members to obey the Spirit and not the appetites; that thereby we might be like unto Christ's death and resurrection, and might fulfil our baptism which signifieth the mortifying of sins and the new life of grace. For this battle ceaseth not in us until the last breath and until that sin be utterly slain by the death of the body.[11]

William Tyndale also follows biblical teaching and Martin Luther when he recognises that human beings must die not merely because of physical decomposition of bodily powers but because they are sinners. He stresses that physical death exhausts the effect of the curse which lies on men and women as sinners and completes the purging of the sinful nature. Hence he has a positive view of the idea of purgatory, though it is very different from the ideas of the 'Old Church', which were explicitly rejected by English Reformers such as John Frith (1503–33).[12] For Tyndale, purgatory is now, and is twofold. The divine process of purging the sinner (that is the believing sinner) is first accomplished by the preaching of the word and secondly by the sufferings through which he passes. Thus Tyndale can say that the apostles 'knew no other ways to purge, but, through preaching God's word, which word only is that purgeth the heart',[13] citing John 15:3. Seeing this necessary purging of the believer as a process, he can tell the student of the Scriptures to

> seek ensamples, first of comfort, how God purgeth all them that submit themselves to walk in his ways, in the purgatory of tribulation, delivering them yet at the latter end and never suffering any of them to perish that cleave fast to his promises.[14]

'Tribulation', for Tyndale, is a word which covers all the suffering of a Christian but often especially appears in contexts where he is speaking of persecution. The life of the Christian is to be one of purgation, both through the sufferings which come directly as the result of discipleship and also from other sufferings through which all men and women must pass.

In fact Tyndale's argument with the Old Church's teaching about purgatory was carried on at more than one level. At their most serious, his arguments meant that he was seeking to do the job of every Christian theologian: it was his task to seek to ensure that his theology set out a more adequate description of what it meant to encounter the God and Father who had disclosed himself in Jesus Christ. Hence Tyndale took opportunity to lay considerable stress on the fact that the God with whom we have to do is our 'most kind Father', and he demanded that the theology of the Christian believer's experience after death should match up to such an understanding of God.[15] At the same time, and perhaps also in the interests of a more adequate theology, he launched a biting attack on the thinking he had inherited. For example, after hearing the argument that the teaching about the cleansing fires of purgatory was intended to reduce people to a godly fear, he sarcastically asks his famous Catholic opponent, Thomas More (1478–1535), how much fear his learned enemy believed could really be induced by 'that terrible fire which thou mayest quench almost for three halfpence'. He also asked – in the light of the claim that the treasury of merits which the pope dispensed was ultimately drawn from the merits of Christ – who had given the pope the ability 'to buy and sell Christ's merits'.[16] The last reference to the traditional doctrine of purgatory shows Tyndale's humour at its driest. The pope, he said:

> taketh authority also to bind and loose in purgatory. That permit I unto him for it is a creature of his own making. He also bindeth the angels: for we read of popes who have commended angels to fetch divers out of purgatory; howbeit I am not yet certified whether they obeyed or no.[17]

But I quoted Tyndale's conviction that God would never allow any of those to perish who 'cleave fast to his promises'. That anticipation of later Calvinist teaching about the final perseverance of the elect person was published several years before John Calvin's *Institutes of the Christian Religion* appeared. The point is clarified and underlined elsewhere in Tyndale's writings. Like Calvin, he is insistent that salvation lies entirely in the mercy of God and more than that, within the electing grace of God. Of predestination and election Tyndale had this to say: our justifying and salvation are clean taken out of our hands, and put in the hands of God only; which thing is most necessary of all. For we are so weak and so uncertain, that if it stood in us, there would of a truth be no man saved . . . But now is God sure . . . and therefore have we hope and trust against sin.

On the other hand, he warns his readers against speculating about predestination. Only those who had suffered much dare ponder it. He said that unless 'thou have borne the cross of adversity and temptation and hast felt thyself brought unto the very brim of desperation' it would be impossible to think about the subject 'without thine own harm and without secret wrath and grudging inwardly against God'. By this he seems to have meant that only those who had to grasp the doctrine to save their souls dare let their minds play upon it. Nevertheless, Tyndale was sure that God gives his Spirit to the elect to provide strength 'every day more and more, according as he is diligent to ask of God for Christ's sake'.[18] In his *Answer* to Thomas More he stressed the dynamic for daily discipleship which lay in the conviction that the believer was saved for eternity. It is worth noting this 'Calvinism' in an English Reformer before Calvin. There is sometimes a tendency too readily to attribute aspects of English Protestant theology in the sixteenth century to the influence of Calvin.

For Tyndale it is clear that the life of the Christian believer is to be a daily struggle towards heaven. Hence he could say that the fullness of Christ was not known by a man in his earthly life: such fullness would not come 'till the body be slain by death'. For this reason he also expected the believer to look forward to death with joy. He wrote:

> The perfecter a man is, the clearer is his sight and seeth a thousand things which displease him and also perfectness which cannot be obtained in this life; and therefore desireth to be with Christ, where is no more sin.[19]

This picture of a man so much in earnest about his sanctification that he becomes more and more sensitive to his own failings and comes to long for the completeness which Christ alone can perfectly give beyond death is crucial. Tyndale's vision is of the Christian life as a struggle crowned at last with perfection. It is hardly a popular vision in contemporary society.

In common with other English Reformers, Tyndale held a theology of martyrdom and suffering with Christ. The word 'tribulation' is often used by him to refer to 'persecution', even though he clearly recognises that there is a great deal of additional suffering, not related directly to persecution, which is to be sustained by the Christian. He insists, however, that '(w)e are called . . . to die with Christ, that we may live with him and to suffer with him, that we may reign with him'. That is fundamental, but so is his conviction that the Christian is never called upon to suffer in his own strength alone. Just because, he says, God himself values nothing so much for 'the mortifying of the flesh, as the cross and tribulation, he comforteth us in our passions and afflictions by the assistance of the Spirit', so it is the Spirit of God who 'through tribulation purgeth us and killeth our fleshly with our worldly understanding and belly wisdom and filleth us full of the wisdom of God'. It is because of this that Tyndale can speak of our 'right baptism' signified 'by plunging into the water'. More generally he emphasises that prosperity is a 'right curse and a thing that God giveth to his enemies' while tribulation for righteousness' sake is not merely a blessing 'but also a gift that God giveth unto none save his special friends'.[20] I am not sure how well such teaching would go down in some evangelical circles today, especially among those who stress the material blessings which are said to accrue because of faithful tithing!

In fact the theology of suffering, in the particular sense of that suffering which may lead to martyrdom, is of special importance to the first generation of English Reformers. Of course the theology of martyrdom is, in itself, nothing new: there is, as they themselves readily discovered, much material in the New Testament, from the earliest section of the Sermon on the Mount on to the Revelation given to John on Patmos. Furthermore, a theology of martyrdom rapidly developed among the Christians of the earliest Christian centuries as they faced the angry might of the Roman state.[21] From the Donatists onwards, Christian dissenters also faced the anger of Mother Church. Tyndale's own argument, and he (like so many of his friends in the first generation of the English Reformers) was himself to come at last to the fire, was tied up very closely with his doctrine of assurance. In one place he puts his position both positively and negatively: 'By suffering art thou sure; but by persecuting canst thou never be sure.' He argued from the example of Stephen, the first Christian martyr, to prove his conviction that 'a Christian perceiveth righteousness if he love his enemy, even when he suffereth persecution and torment of him and the pains of death, and mourneth more for his adversary's blindness than for his own pain'.[22] In speaking of the Christian 'perceiving righteousness' Tyndale is referring to the Christian becoming aware of and becoming assured of his righteousness by faith. This righteousness is God's gift within the heart of the believer and is that from which his loving response, even to those who torture him, will flow.

Indeed Tyndale goes further: the willingness to suffer for the sake of the Gospel is an evidence that those who thus suffer are 'the children of God' whose status among the elect is sealed by the Spirit of God. On the other hand, those who 'in adversity flee from Christ' show themselves to be the children of darkness. Tyndale was deeply conscious that just as the true servants of God whose lives were recorded in Scripture suffered at the hands both of false brethren and the secular power of princes 'so shall it be with us until the end of the world'. Following a similar thought, in another place Tyndale stressed that both the world and the pope tended to turn a blind eye to ordinary wickedness but they both actively persecuted doctrinal nonconformity. However, he affirmed, 'God persecuteth us because that . . . when we know the truth, we follow it not.'[23] It is not surprising, therefore, that Tyndale is concerned to insist that God has called believers not to soft living and peace in this world but to war, and the only peace that the Christian should (in his view) be concerned to seek is peace of conscience before God. This teaching was undergirded by a deep conviction that death was but a doorway to more of Christ and that this life was primarily a preparation for the world to come. Such a conviction has the almost automatic effect of loosening the believer's attachment to the good things of this life and of freeing him for sacrificial obedience to Christ. Of course, Tyndale is too sensible a writer and too deeply aware of New Testament teaching to fail to warn that Christian believers should take great care to make sure that they suffer because of the offence of the Gospel and not because of their own misdeeds. At the same time, those really suffering for Christ are suffering *with* him and can comfort themselves with the hope of the blessing of an inheritance in heaven.

It is Tyndale who, significantly, plumbs the depths of the possible misery of the martyr for Christ persecuted by the authorities of the Church. Not only may such a person be condemned to death; he will also have to go through the misery of being excommunicated from the earthly fellowship of the Church, of being told that he has no part nor lot in the salvation gained by the blood of Christ, of being falsely accused of doings and sayings of which he is not guilty and of feeling himself abandoned by all the world. Even the reason for his martyrdom will be misrepresented for 'all the world is persuaded and brought in belief that thou hast said and done that thou never thoughtest and that thou diest for that thou art as guiltless of as the child that is unborn'.[24] Such isolation and misrepresentation might make the boldest martyrs fear their sacrifice has been utterly wasted or they themselves utterly mistaken! Yet Tyndale warned that preaching the truth as he and his friends believed it 'is a salting that stirreth up persecution', and that therefore the office of preacher should not be sought by any but those who have all their hopes set on God and none on the rewards this world can supply.[25]

Turning now to what Tyndale believed about life beyond death, the first thing to note is that biblical references to death and what follows thereafter were understood by Tyndale in the light of his primary conviction – that the next great event after death was the general resurrection. He believed that to teach that men and women were immediately at death translated into heaven or hell or purgatory made nonsense of the great apostolic conviction that we must all appear before the judgment seat of Christ at the resurrection of the just and the unjust. Hence he tells Thomas More, just as he is prepared to tell his

Protestant associate George Joye, that 'in putting them in heaven, hell and purgatory [you] destroy the arguments wherewith Christ and Paul prove the resurrection'.[26] For Tyndale this was an important theological principle and one that had profound practical implications.

Thus he challenges More to explain where, if the souls of those recognised as saints by the Old Church are in heaven now 'in as great glory as the angels, after your doctrine, shew me what cause should be of the resurrection'. The believer has no fear about the judgment for the works done in life since his good works are nothing but the fruits of that love which had been kindled in him when he came to know himself saved by God's infinite love. So Tyndale looked forward with confidence to the return of Christ when people would be judged and receive their rewards. In passing he also, in commenting on the will of a Gloucestershire gentleman, William Tracy, commended the example of that Particular Protestant in avoiding any grand arrangements for carrying his corpse to the grave. Nevertheless he believed that burials should be undertaken with due regard for 'the honour and hope of resurrection'.[27] In consequence of his view that the final disposal of people in heaven and hell follows the last judgment (and Tyndale seems to have been sure that 'hell', which he sees as 'everlasting death', was where 'the wicked and ungodly shall be tormented, both soul and body after the general judgement')[28] he asks what becomes of the souls of believers and unbelievers, or, perhaps more exactly, of the elect and the non-elect, between death and the Last Judgment.

Tyndale's answer seems clear – at least about the elect. He admits that Scripture makes no mention of the details of what happens to the souls of men and women when their bodies die. They 'rest in the Lord and in their faith' is his description. To talk or write further of their condition is to be guilty of 'the presumptuous imagination of his own brain'. Tyndale insists that this is a secret known only to God and with that answer people should be content,

> being certified of the Scripture, that they which die in the faith are at rest, and ought no more to search that secret, than to search the hour of the resurrection, which God hath put only in his own power.[29]

It is the idea of being at rest that lies behind the concept of what was sometimes known as 'soul sleep'.

It was a controversial concept. Thomas More was only one of those who believed that through his teaching in this area Tyndale was virtually inciting people to sin. As a Roman Catholic, of course, More not only considered that the belief in the reality of hell encouraged people to live moral lives on earth but that the doctrine of purgatory also helped. As he wrote: 'What shall he care how long he live in sin that believeth Luther, that he shall after this life neither feel well nor ill in body nor soul till the day of doom?'[30] But Tyndale, less predictably, was also attacked for his beliefs by his own old friend and fellow Protestant exile George Joye (c. 1495–1553). Although Joye was active in printing the Bible in English, he was an intemperate character who irritated most of those with whom he worked.[31]

Yet Tyndale had those who held similar views to his own. In 1531 John Frith published his *Disputation of Purgatory* in which he denied that the Old Church's doctrine of purgatory could be found in or justified from Scripture. Like Tyndale, he believed that there were only two means by which God purged the sin of men: by the Word of God received by faith and by the cross of Christ borne through 'adversity, tribulation, worldly depression' which 'is called the rodde or scourge of God wherewith he scourgeth euery sonne that he receaueth'.[32] When a Roman Catholic critic asked how evil deeds could be restrained unless good works either avoided or shortened the soul's purgatorial pilgrimage, Frith again followed Luther and Tyndale. He insisted that good works were the fruit and proof of saving faith and were not the root of the soul's justification before God. Like Luther and Tyndale he was seeking to test the Church's doctrine by the gospel; people could be encouraged into a new relationship with God rather than pressurised by the stick of purgatory or the carrot of heaven.

Meanwhile, for one reason and another, Tyndale had failed to publish a revised edition of his New Testament as he had long promised. Although his revision was nearly complete and George Joye and others seem to have known about it, neither this nor Joye's earlier friendship with Tyndale prevented Joye from producing an edition of his own. Tyndale's major complaint about this, however, was not that his own edition had been pirated and a new edition had been put out by Joye, but that the latter, without any reference to Tyndale (and without explaining that a significant change to the text was made without either Tyndale's consent or knowledge), had changed the word 'resurrection' throughout the translation to refer directly to the 'life after death'; this he did by replacing resurrection with the words 'life' or 'very life'.

When at last Tyndale brought out his own 1534 revision, he complained bitterly (and with justification) in a preface of Joye's misuse of his translation. Joye had believed, Tyndale affirmed, that the word 'resurrection' in the New Testament described the immediate state of believers' souls after their death. Apparently there had been some private disputes about this issue among the English Reformers. Tyndale affirmed that we shall all

> both good and bad, rise both flesh and body, and appear together before the judgment seat of Christ, to receive every man according to his deeds. And that the bodies of all that believe and continue in the true faith of Christ, shall be endued with like immortality and glory as is the body of Christ.

He went on to assert that he believed the souls of those who had departed this life 'in the faith of Christ and love of the law of God, to be in no worse case that the soul of Christ was, from the time he delivered his spirit into the hands of his father, until the resurrection of his body in glory and immortality'.[33]

George Joye, unabashed, replied to this by saying that the belief that at death the true believer's soul was removed at once to the final bliss of the presence of Christ was both the truth and was also of great encouragement to 'the poor, afflicted, persecuted and troubled in this world for Christ's sake'. He also claimed that many of the wicked were encouraged by Tyndale's teaching to continue in their sin since doomsday (whose reality they doubted anyway) was thought to be a long way off.[34] As Norman Burns has pointed out, the belief that spirit is incorruptible seemed to most an obvious and necessary consequence of being a Christian.[35] The greatest of all the continental Protestant Confessions, the *Second Helvetic Confession* (1566), echoed the views of John Calvin in stating that 'we believe that the faithful after bodily death, go directly to Christ . . . Likewise we believe that unbelievers are immediately cast into hell . . .'[36]

The future was not to lie with Tyndale's ideas but with the position taken by such statements. We may say that Tyndale's position makes quite good sense of Paul's teaching about the future fate of the individual. Yet it has a weakness. Tyndale lays great stress, as we have seen, on the point that the final resurrection has little significance if the saved and lost are separated before then. However, while he is clear that the elect, when they die, rest or sleep 'in Christ', nothing seems to be said about where those 'sleep' who are not elect. The implication is that their position must be less blessed. In that case in some sense the sifting and separation of the elect and the non-elect has already taken place. On the other hand, Tyndale was surely right to complain that in what became virtually official Reformed teaching the Last Judgment has no element of surprise – its findings are prejudged.

The usefulness of the discussion in this study may lie less in an attempt to reach a conclusion about what happens at death and more in a consideration of the way we should regard this life: for the Reformers such as Tyndale this life was an antechamber to eternity. In the light of the teaching of Tyndale, two things may be said. First, this present life, for the believer, is one that involves sanctification through self-sacrifice. It is a life energised by the Holy Spirit and the essence of this life is signified in baptism. Secondly, the ultimate sacrifice of death for the sake of Christ, martyrdom itself (which was the sacrifice made by Tyndale and others of his time), is not a waste of a life but is, rather, a high privilege.

Notes

* Original manuscript edited and slightly amended by I. M. Randall with the authors permission.

1 E. Cameron, *The European Reformation* (Oxford: Clarendon Press, 1991), 79–83.

2 For Tyndale see D. Daniell, *William Tyndale: A Biography* (New Haven and London: Yale University Press, 1994).

3 For an introductory perspective on the background of the English Reformation see C. Haigh, *English Reformations* (Oxford: Clarendon Press, 1993).

4 C. R. Trueman, *Luther's Legacy: Salvation and English Reformers, 1525–1556* (Oxford: Clarendon Press, 1994).

5 K. Thomas, *Religion and the Decline of Magic* (Harmondsworth: Penguin, 1971), 5.

6 Parker Society [hereafter PS], I, 416, 22 (William Tyndale, *Doctrinal Treatises* . . . [1848]; *Expositions* . . . and *The Practice of Prelates* [1849]; *Answer to More* . . . [1850], edited for the Parker Society by Henry Walter [Cambridge: Cambridge University Press]).

7 PS, I, 83–4.

8 Trueman, *Luther's Legacy*, 112ff.

9 PS, I, 253.

10 Ibid., 255.

11 Ibid., 500.

12 J. Frith, *Disputation of Purgatory* (Antwerp, 1531); Trueman, *Luther's Legacy*, ch. 5.

13 PS, I, 321.

14 Ibid., 399.

15 PS, III, 282.

16 Ibid., 28, 143. For Tyndale and More see P. Ackroyd, *The Life of Thomas More* (London: Chatto & Windus, 1998), 299–304.

17 PS, I, 269.

18 Ibid., 505, 113.

19 Ibid., 75, 114.

20 For quotations from Tyndale in this paragraph see PS, I, 137–8, 504.

21 W. H. C. Frend, *Martyrdom and Persecution in the Early Church* (Oxford: Blackwell, 1965).

22 PS, I, 139, 74.

23 Ibid., 140, 404–5, 412.

24 PS, II, 29.

25 Ibid., 32.

26 PS, III, 180.

27 Ibid., 280; Daniell, *William Tyndale*, 222.

28 PS, I, 64, 531.

29 PS, II, 185.

30 N. T. Burns, *Christian Moralism from Tyndale to Milton* (Cambridge, Mass.: Harvard University Press, 1972), 99.

31 Daniell, *William Tyndale*, 322–6.

32 Cited by W. A. Clebsch, *England's Earliest Protestants, 1520–1535* (New Haven: Yale University Press, 1964), 91.

33 G. E. Duffield (ed.), *The Work of William Tyndale* (Appleford: Sutton Courtenay Press, 1964), 312–13.

34 Ibid., 315–16.

35 Burns, *Christian Moralism*, 19.

36 A. Cochrane, *Reformed Confessions of the Sixteenth Century* (London: SCM, 1966), 295.

7

Do Princes Dread Their Coronation Days?

Teaching about 'the life to come' in the period of nonconformist persecution (1662–89)

Raymond Brown

The terms of this annual lectureship, instituted at the initiative of a leading London Congregationalist, John Drew, require that our attention be directed to some aspects of Christian teaching concerning the future – immortality, resurrection, life to come, heaven. Within the inevitably narrow compass of this lecture let us go back to a crucial period in the history of English Dissent – to those three costly decades in the later half of the seventeenth century, and the experience of intense persecution found in them, and from which the name 'Nonconformist' is derived. I briefly remind you of the historical context. Shortly after the accession of Charles II an attempt was made to regularise Christian worship and ensure that local meeting houses did not become semi-secret, religio-political subversive societies. A series of parliamentary statutes were passed which imposed severe restrictions on people whose consciences would not allow them to confine their worship to the Book of Common Prayer. An Act of Uniformity compelled all local incumbents to use the Liturgy of the Prayer Book and those who could not do so were ejected from their livings. For at least two centuries afterwards dissenters recalled the date, 24 August, as the occasion of 'Black Bartholomew' and reminded successive generations of the courage and heroism of about 1,800 ministers who relinquished their homes, security and all financial remuneration for conscience sake. Although subsequent legislation made it illegal for them to hold public services as such, they continued to gather devout believers together in homes, barns, fields and forests as well as meeting houses, always at risk of being discovered and arrested, usually with the aid of an informer who was paid for his work; part of the fine was always diverted to the informer for services rendered. Spying on dissenters became a lucrative part-time occupation.

In the period of almost thirty years while this 'Clarendon Code' was on the Statute Book (only briefly relieved by a short period of toleration) life was exceptionally hard for these people and quite naturally the subject of the 'life to come' secured a firm place in Nonconformist teaching. Here I want to focus on their thinking about heaven – first, the *relevance* of the doctrine, then look briefly at its *source* and give the remainder of our time to its *application*.

The Relevance of Their Teaching

Death was a stark, inescapable reality in seventeenth-century England. The average expectation of life in this period has been estimated at about thirty-two years. For one thing, the economic stability of the country was, to say the least, precarious. Poverty was the first step on the road to death. Prosperity rose or fell with good or bad harvests and the life of many thousands of people was little other than a grim struggle for survival. A succession of poor harvests would mean that thousands of people would be buried. Underfed people were natural victims for disease and while most of us know something about London's Great Plague of 1665 and the Great Fire of the following year it needs to be remembered that the plague was a fairly common phenomenon in England and elsewhere long before 1665 and that it made its most severe impact on poor people. A variety of other severe illnesses remained as constant hazards, whatever the social composition of the community – typhus, dysentery, measles, influenza claimed their victims in all parts of the land. Less dangerous, but still incurable, sicknesses made suffering Christian believers naturally wistful about the prospect of a better life. The saintly Richard Baxter scarcely knew a day free from pain. Other Nonconformist leaders like John Howe and Thomas Goodwin were courageous invalids for years on end and they were certainly not alone. No wonder they sighed for heaven. Whenever and wherever Nonconformist people gathered for their meetings someone in the congregation would have had recent contact with a bereaved person and the message of 'the life to come' brought reassurance, comfort and hope in a desperately uncertain society. Some of the most sensitive Nonconformist expositions on heaven were preached in London itself during the devastating Plague year of 1665.

Throughout those grim months it was unnecessary to remind anybody of the reality of death. It is reckoned that nearly 100,000 people died in London. Carried initially by fleas on rats, the disease spread rapidly from April onwards. The scenario was terrifying: the houses of sick people clearly marked with a black cross, men and women who could afford to leave the city doing so in a vast and fearful exodus, the death cart rumbling through the streets night after night ('bring out your dead'), the unthankful task of the Plague watchman making his grim report of infected homes, and that sad reminder of human greed: nurses who made sure that they spread the infection within a family so that they could steal everything from a house when all its occupants had been carried away. By the summer months deaths were recorded of three, four or five thousand a week, once rising to eight thousand. Edmund Calamy preserved the heroic story of men like Thomas Vincent who, Calamy said,

> Had the Zeal and Courage to abide in the City amidst all the Fury of the Pestilence in 1665, and pursu'd his Ministerial Work in that needful but dangerous Season with all Diligence . . . both in public and private . . . He thought it was absolutely necessary that such vast Numbers of dying People should have some Spiritual Assistance, so He constantly preach'd every Lord's Day through the whole Visitation in some Parish Church or other. His Subjects were the most moving and important.

The awfulness of the judgment, then everywhere obvious, gave a peculiar edge to the preacher and his auditors:

> It was a general Inquiry through the preceding Week where he was to preach: Multitudes follow'd him wherever he went; and he preach'd not a sermon by which there were not several people awaken'd. He visited all that sent for him without fear, and did the best Offices he could for them in their last Extremities; Being in Season and out of Season to save souls from Death . . . But God was pleased to take a particular care of this good man.[1]

London's Plague year was followed by its Great Fire. Richard Baxter was not alone in regarding the successive calamities as an expression of God's wrath and it certainly presented the Dissenting Ministers with a renewed challenge to expound God's Word with compassion, relevance and urgency. Baxter's autobiography says that the 'Churches being burnt and the Parish Ministers gone' the 'Nonconformists were now more resolved than ever, to preach till they were imprisoned'.[2]

Courageous men of this calibre knew only too well how to address themselves to the central themes of Scripture, and the radiant certainty of 'the life to come' frequently recurred in their biblical exposition. But in addition to a precarious economic situation, widespread poverty, the prevalence of disease and the risk of fire (by no means confined to London) there was another reason why Dissenters were glad to be reminded of heaven. For many of them death became the price they were compelled to pay for their spiritual convictions. Each of the main Dissenting denominations – Presbyterians, Independents, Baptists and Quakers – have their prison martyrs, though the number of Quakers who died either in prison, or as a direct result of serious deprivation because of a prison sentence, far outweighs all others. Yet for these prisoners, doubtless the worst of afflictions was not their own physical suffering but the thought that being locked up they could do nothing to help their families. Bunyan wanted to be at home with his blind daughter. How agonising for the Baptist minister, Joseph Davis, when his desperately sick wife dragged herself to prison to see him, her 'affections carrying her', as he lovingly put it, 'beyond her ability': so worn with illness and so physically frail that when she arrived at prison he had to carry her in his arms because she was far too weak to get up the flight of stairs herself. When she was dying he was allowed to go to her in 1665 'to see her last End, and dispose of my House and Shop-Goods, and put my (three) Children out to Nurse. After which I returned again to Prison as ordered . . .'[3]

In such dark times Bunyan personified persecution as 'that hunter without pity' and in their natural grief many hundreds of Nonconformist people were given fresh hope as they were reminded of the joy, security and peace of a promised heaven.

The Source of Their Teaching

Naturally (and primarily) they drew their basic convictions from the pages of the *Bible* itself, as these courageous people treasured Scripture. In such uncertain times many of them, the preachers especially, made sure that they memorised vast sections of it, so that if imprisoned and denied access to a Bible they would be able to recall the teaching of whole books. Thomas Vincent knew the entire New Testament and all the psalms by heart for, as Calamy explains, he 'took pains as not knowing but they (as he has often said) who took from him his Pulpit . . . might in time demand his Bible also'.[4] These expositors were spiritual giants as far as their knowledge of Scripture was concerned but it is important for us to note that this almost encyclopaedic grasp of biblical teaching was not peculiar to preachers. Even in an age of high illiteracy the average Christian believer had a firm grasp of God's Word and was certainly familiar with its key passages and main lines of teaching. For many of them the process of memorisation was aided by their commitment to meditation, a recurrent theme in seventeenth-century Nonconformist spirituality. They did not hurriedly read Scripture. They knew that if it was to be of any lasting benefit to them, they must certainly spend time with it, and did so by constantly turning it over in their minds.

Preaching also helped in the process of memorisation and during these hazardous years of persecution the message of heaven was often heard in their exposition. Within a few months of Richard Baxter's death, Edmund Calamy was recalling the persuasiveness with which Baxter spoke about heaven: 'He talked in the pulpit with great freedom about another world, like one that had been there, and was come as a sort of an express from thence to make a report concerning it.'[5]

Naturally a huge number of these sermons found their way into print. Preachers who had been silenced by their enemies reached an infinitely greater audience through the printed message for, as Baxter put it typically, 'The Press hath a louder voice then mine.'[6] In one such book which brought an immense comfort to suffering people during these years, *The Mute Christian under the Smarting Rod*, Thomas Brooks compared and contrasted spoken and printed sermons and pointed out that 'The pen is an artificial tongue . . . it speaks to many thousands at once; it speaks not only to the present age but also to succeeding ages . . . Few men, if any, have iron memories. How soon is a sermon preached forgotten, when a sermon written remains.'[7]

And other books, besides published sermons, spoke of heaven and did so with possibly even greater popular appeal. Bunyan beguiled his natural sorrows and the discomfort of prison-years writing not only about the life to come but how one reaches it and of the *cost* of getting there as well as the pleasure of arriving safely. His *Heavenly Footman* puts it with unmistakable clarity:

> If thou wouldst so run as to obtain the kingdom of heaven, then be sure that thou get into the way . . . If thou now say, which is the way? I tell thee it is CHRIST . . . be much exercised about Christ which is the way; what he is, what he hath done . . . why 'he took upon him the form of a servant', why he 'was made in the likeness of men'; why he cried; why he died; why he bear the sin of the world; why he was made sin, and why he was made righteousness; why he is in heaven in the nature of man, and what he doth there?

Then from the sublime Christology directly to the use of simple vivid imagery, the homely unforgettable illustrations – how can a man or woman run to heaven if encumbered with bad footwear, weighed down by heavy clothes, and useless belongings:

> Thou must strip thyself of those things that may hang upon thee to the hindering of thee in the way to the Kingdom of heaven as covetousness, pride, lust or whatever else . . . which may hinder thee in this heavenly race . . . would you not say that such a man would be in danger of losing, though he run if he fill his pocket with stones, hang heavy garments on his shoulders and great lumpish shoes on his feet . . . if thou intendest to win . . . then thou must lay aside every weight.[8]

Not only new books like Bunyan's *Pilgrim's Progress* and *The Holy War*, Baxter's *The Saint's Everlasting Rest* and scores of others lured these people on to a better country, but older books as well. Hundreds of literate Nonconformist homes treasured, alongside the Bible, their own copy of John Foxe's famous book from the previous century and Samuel Clarke's more recent *General*

Martyrologie with their stories of courage and heroism in time of cruel persecution. Even the illiterates could see the woodcuts and remember that those who died had first passed on a faith which had made them strong and renewed their confidence in God's heaven. It is hardly surprising that in such dark days the brave tales of martyrs sustained them, nor that they found special help in the letter to the *Hebrews* particularly in what Richard Sibbes described as its 'little book of martyrs' in chapter 11, and its assurance that they too were seeking a better country 'that is a heavenly one and that God was not ashamed to be called their God for he had prepared for them a city'.

Moreover their assurance and inspiration about heaven was conveyed to them not simply through spoken and published sermons, and printed books, older and modern, but also through even more personal and greatly treasured documents, those pastoral letters written from the heart by imprisoned pastors who wanted to keep in touch with congregations suddenly bereft of spiritual leadership. By the third day of his imprisonment, Thomas Hardcastle had written a letter for his Bristol congregation. There was to be no time to lose if specially vulnerable members were to be saved from drifting. Like Hardcastle and Bunyan, other imprisoned pastors had equal opportunity to reflect on the glories of heaven and reaffirm that the life to come is incomparably better than this one. When Thomas Browning wrote to his congregation from Northampton Jail he told them:

> I long after you much in the Lord, yet rejoicingly stay His good Pleasure. I would not come out a Moment before his time; I would not take a Step without his Direction. I am wonderfully well; better and better. The Cup of Afflictions for the Gospel is sweeter, the deeper; a stronger Cordial, the nearer the Bottom; I mean death itself. Oh the joy unspeakable and glorious, the dying Martyrs of Jesus have had! . . . I tell you, if you knew what Christ's Prisoners, some of them, enjoyed in their gaols, you would not fear their Condition, but long for it.[9]

The Application of Their Teaching

They believed in heaven and often talked about it, but what difference did it make to their lives on earth? First, for these dissenting leaders the doctrine of heaven *encouraged their endurance*. In the appalling physical conditions of seventeenth-century jails these believers patiently longed for heaven. Its assured beauty, tranquillity and permanence all stood in marked contrast to the ugliness, discomfort and squalor of their crowded cells, dark and damp hovels where many hundreds of them sat, month after month, with little to cheer them but the recollection of all that God had said to them so persuasively in Scripture, and the privilege of daily communion with Christ. From such a jail

Thomas Browning wrote passionately to his people urging them to be faithful to Christ:

> Come, the worst is Death, and that is the best of all. What, do we stick at dying for him, who stuck not at it for us? Do we find Difficulty in that which will be our Entrance into Glory? Do Princes dread their Coronation Days? Are brides and bridegrooms reluctant to come to their weddings? Oh love the Lord, ye his Saints! My Brethren, do not budge. Keep your ground; the Scripture is your Law; God is your King . . . Fear nothing of Events till they come; only fear offending God with a Neglect of your duty. There is no Shadow like the Shadow of God's Wings, keep therefore close to God.[10]

In 1665 George Hughes was sentenced to imprisonment on St Nicholas Island off Plymouth, and his son, Obadiah, was locked in another dungeon on the same island. The cruel authorities deliberately kept them apart and refused to allow them any opportunity to meet. He wrote letters to his son reminding him that although there was no access to his father, the way of prayer was open, and that courage was the greatest thing:

> I am the mark aimed at; and how far God may suffer men to proceed, I know not: But free communion with God in prison is worth a thousand Liberties gain'd with the Loss of Liberty of Spirit. The Lord keep us his Freemen . . . The will of the Lord be done, either for Liberty, or Restraint, for Life or Death. I wait for the Lord, and rejoice in him; to which Stronghold alone, I commend you; the Lord strengthen Faith, and lengthen Patience: We shall then do well, and inherit the Promise.[11]

Second, their teaching about heaven not only made them brave; it *kept them holy*. In their bewildering adversity heaven became more of an immediate experience than a distant prospect. Their doctrine of an eternal inheritance inspired their holiness. The presence of Christ was so real to these prisoners that they made a serene heaven in an earthly hell. Even in the loneliness of St Nicholas Island George Hughes can write to his son, 'I am well, and best of all in Heaven; and satisfied with the will of God, which will bring us to glory.'[12]

Baxter maintained that 'man is no more a Christian indeed than he is heavenly'. His greatest ambition was to 'live and die in the joy which beseemeth an Heir of Heaven'.[13] But these valiant men and women did not merely sigh for heaven; they anticipated it. If there is to be *praise* in heaven, then it must begin now. Joseph Alleine testified from prison: 'Never did my soul know the *heaven* of a believer's life, till I learnt to live a life of praise.'[14] If there is to be purity in heaven, then we cannot possibly treasure sin now. If there is to be reconciliation in heaven, how can we bear to make enemies on earth? Bunyan's final pastoral work on earth (like Luther's) was to reconcile two estranged people, and the last sermon he preached, returned to the theme 'Dost thou see a soul that has the image of God in him? Love him, love him; say This man and I must go to *heaven* one day; serve one another, do good for one another . . . that you may look your Father in the face, with comfort, another day.'[15]

The quest by these brave people for a higher and better life needs to be seen, of course, against the background of the selfishness and moral corruption of the Restoration period where the principal theme of its theatre is sexual intrigue, either for its own sake or for money. The playwrights of the day came under heavy attack from their contemporaries for blasphemy and frivolity but dramatists simply insisted that their works were a mirror of the age. Those who adopted such lifestyles scarcely gave a thought to the meaning and purpose of this life let alone the one that is to come. But these dissenting preachers insisted that people are not likely to enjoy the privileges of an eternal inheritance if they cannot begin the life of heaven while they are on earth. This became one of the main aspects of their holiness teaching. John Howe said that 'It can never be well, till our own Souls be an Heaven to us . . . Bear yourself as the inhabitant of another country,'[16] and Matthew Henry delighted in quoting his father Philip's saying that 'all who would go to heaven when they die, must begin their heaven while they live'.[17]

Third, their doctrine of the life to come not only encouraged their endurance and inspired their holiness; it *motivated their evangelism*. It would be a mistake to infer that these good people simply prepared *themselves* for a fuller and better life just beyond the immediate horizon of this world. Confident that they would reach that other country they longed that others would travel with them. Men and women must be won for Christ in this life if they are to enter heaven. The note of persuasive appeal sounds time and again through their best literature. They used every possible literary device to make people *think* about eternity. In a homely book significantly entitled *The Heavenly Trade* the West Country preacher, Bartholomew Ashwood, likened human experience in this life to the narrow compass of one single day. Some of its best hours had passed and perhaps the reader had not yet trusted Christ and night must fall:

> There are but twelve hours in the day, and how many of them have been slept and sinned away, and how few of them may be before you, who knows? What if your Sun should set at noonday? or a summons meet you in the midst of your work . . . What will you then do? Some of you are in your afternoon, and what time is that to set forth such a long journey as the way to Heaven is ... others of you are in your morning (the best time to put forth in your travel towards glory). O lose not your season for eternity: Make much of time . . . 'Tis now or never, while the Light shines, the Lord knocks, the Angel moves on the waters, while the Lord delays His coming: Salvation-work is quick work . . . Souls, 'tis for your lives, make all possible haste about the work of your Salvation.[18]

Richard Baxter's *Call to the Unconverted* states the same issues with unmistakable clarity:

> If you be not willing to turn today, you are not willing to do it at all. Remember you are all this while . . . under the guilt of many thousand sins . . . and you stand at the very brink of hell; there is but a step between you and death . . . Up therefore presently, and fly as for your lives: as you would be gone out of your house if it were all on fire over your head. O if you did but know what continual danger you live in, and what unspeakable loss you sustain and what a safer and sweeter life you might live, you would not stand trifling . . . Your lives are short and uncertain: and what a case are you in, if you die before you thoroughly turn . . . Stand not wavering, as if you were yet uncertain, whether God, or the flesh be the better Master; or whether Heaven or Hell be the better end; or whether sin or holiness be the better way . . . Now while you are reading or hearing this, Resolve . . . Before Satan have time to take you off, Resolve . . . and that with a firm unchangeable Resolution.[19]

These preachers made sure their congregations or readers were presented with the stark alternatives; they refused to allow people to rest in a comfortable but dangerous neutrality. In Joseph Alleine's *Alarm to the Unconverted* he pleads with his readers to consider their destiny: 'And were it not better you should be a joy to angels than a laughing stock and sport for devils.' Along with their strong convictions about God's sovereignty and the doctrine of election there is this sustained emphasis on our immediate opportunity to trust Christ. That is what pleases God most of all. The angels leap for joy when someone is converted:

> Verily, if you would but come in, the heavenly hosts would take up their anthems and sing 'Glory to God in the highest'; the morning stars would sing together, and all the sons of God shout for joy, and celebrate this new creation as they did the first. Your repentance would, as it were, make a holiday in heaven, and the glorious spirits would rejoice, in that there is a new brother added to their society, another heir, born to the Lord, and a lost son received safe and sound.[20]

These alternating notes of serious warning and tender evangelistic appeal are rarely expressed to greater effect than in *Pilgrim's Progress*. Christian asks Hopeful what it was that brought his sins to mind and made him feel his need of God. The future life is a crucial factor. The fear of death has a prominent place. Hopeful says that his sense of sin returned, 'If I heard the bell Toull for some that were dead; If I thought of dying my self or, if I heard that sudden death happened to others; But especially when I thought of my self that I must quickly come to Judgement.'

But Bunyan made sure that those who were troubled about their sins and, like him, were smarting under the pain of a wounded conscience, heard the message of forgiveness and peace. The penalty of sin was only part of the message. The prospect of heaven was presented with alluring appeal. Christian and Hopeful passed from this uncertain life, and, Pilgrim says:

> Now I saw in my dream, that these two men went in at the Gate; and loe, as they entered, they were transfigured, and they had Raiment put on that shone like Gold . . . Now just as the gates were opened to let in the men, I looked in after them; and behold, the City shone like the Sun . . . And after that they shut up the Gates: which when I had seen, I wished my self among them.[21]

There is everything there the persuasive evangelist could wish for – the testimony of transformed lives, the open gates of assured salvation, the bright sunlight of a better future luring the seeker on, even the wistful longing at the closed gates as a necessary warning that not all will enter because, like Pilgrim's earlier friends, some will think it folly to venture on such a costly journey.

Finally, their doctrine of heaven *enriched their hope*. It brought them comfort and peace in times of loneliness, suffering and bereavement. Naturally grieved over the loss of his treasured wife, Margaret, Richard Baxter said: 'Death will quickly draw the veil and make us see how near we were to God and one another and did not sufficiently know it.' His partner had often shared her 'hopeful perswasions' that they 'should live together in heaven'[22] and those who had suffered parting on earth recalled with gratitude that heaven is but seconds away.

Baxter was comforted in his loneliness with the assurance that Jesus himself had passed triumphantly through the experience of death and was waiting for us on the other side. Death was simply the process by which we went out of one room into another:

> Christ leads me through no darker Rooms
> Than He went through before;
> And he that to God's kingdom comes
> Must enter by this door.
>
> My knowledge of that life is small
> The Eye of Faith is dim
> But 'tis enough that Christ knows all
> And I shall be with him.[23]

This thought of the *nearness* of heaven was so dear to the Nonconformist people that they refused to make a sharp distinction between this life and the next. They frequently emphasise that the undivided people of God belong to one family; some members lived in fairly modest rooms on earth while others have been given the privilege of superior accommodation in heaven. With typical sensitivity Bunyan likens the Lord's people to those who live in the stately home of (say) Bedfordshire nobility. Some are merely domestic servants living 'below stairs' but others have graduated from lowly service to the dignity of high nobility; they are 'above stairs'. Only a few months before he died Bunyan published his *Solomon's Temple Spiritualised* in which he expressed the truth with memorable clarity:

> They above, and we below, are yet one and the self-same house of God . . . the difference then betwixt us and them, is, not that we are really two, but one body in Christ, in divers places. True we are below stairs, and they above; they in their holiday and we in our working day clothes: they in harbour, but we in the storm; they at rest, and ie In the wilderness; they singing as crowned with joy; we crying, as crowned with thorns. But I say, we are all of one house, one family, and are all children of one Father.[24]

I want to end this lecture by looking in closer detail at one example from a strata of relevant literature not yet mentioned – the personal letter of condolence written within a believing family. The letter I want to use is, in my view, a remarkable example of the biblical knowledge, theological convictions, and spiritual insight of a late seventeenth-century dissenting layman, and a young one at that.[25] Nathaniel Pinney lives and works in London. His father, John Pinney is Presbyterian Minister at Bettiscombe, Dorset. His eldest son had died suddenly at the end of December 1679 and the younger brother, away from home, writes to comfort his grief-stricken parents. The letter quotes thirteen different texts or passages of Scripture, and they are almost equally divided between Old and New Testaments. It reveals an astonishing grasp of scriptural knowledge and no mean skill in their relevant pastoral interpretation for a young man who has just reached his twentieth birthday.

He first reminds his parents that in their tragic bereavement there are three voices to which they should pay particular attention. First of all, *heaven itself* speaks to them in their sorrow. Writing about his elder brother's passing Nathaniel says:

> I confess the subject is astonishing and very terrible, and may I say with the prophet Jeremiah, Oh that my head were waters, and my eyes a fountain of tears that I might weep day and night for the loss of this my dearest brother. But alas, why should we sorrow since heaven itself proclaims such blessed who die in the Lord [Revelation 14:13], 'And I heard a voice *from heaven* saying, Blessed are the dead . . .' And should not we on earth then hear?

A voice speaking from the very place where Nathaniel's brother now lives must surely bring comfort and hope. The voice describes the people who are there and assures us on earth that all is wonderfully well with them. It is almost as if, in his 'holiday-clothes', he is sending an attractive postcard: 'This is a glorious place to be. Wish you were here.'

Second, the *Holy Spirit* speaks. Nathaniel goes on to quote from Revelation 14:13, which continues 'Yea, saith the Spirit, that they may rest from their labours.' It is the Holy Spirit's voice as well as heaven's voice that addresses the bereaved parents. The Spirit of truth confirms the reliability of the heavenly voice. Heaven is truly a real place and not the figment of distressed human imagination. It is an authentic place ('Yes, says the Spirit') and it is a restful place: 'Oh happy rest where he is gone, dear Father and Mother.' Those who have forged on ahead of us, now released from all strain and tension, are in perfect peace.

But, third, says Nathaniel, *the departed one also speaks*:

> Methinks I hear him who being dead, yet speaking in our Saviour's language [Luke 23:28], Daughters of Jerusalem, *weep not for me* – For my part I have ease for pain, joy for sorrow, I feel no aching bones nor fear evil times, but have rest for labour, and would you weep for me?

There are additionally a series of great spiritual principles of which the young Pinney reminds his godly parents. The truths must have been part of the Dissenters' rich theology of bereavement and they are just as significant now as they were three hundred years ago. At the risk of robbing them of the warm, intimate manner in which they flow from young Nathaniel's mind I venture to enumerate them, if only to demonstrate the wide range of his thinking and the pastoral sensitivity with which he applies biblical truth.

1 *All those dear people we love in life are God's choice gift to us but it is all too easy to idolise the gift rather than adore the giver*:

> I know he was dear unto you but, O, alas, we are too apt to settle our affections on wrong objects and to scatter those great excellencies on earthly things . . . was he not the gift of God? The Lord giveth and the Lord taketh away, blessed be the name of the Lord. O let us centre all our cares, fears, sorrows, affections in Him, for He is, and will be a satisfying portion, to all that seek Him.

2 *Their son's appointed ministry on earth must have been completed or the Lord would not have allowed him to be taken*: 'Since He had no more work for him to do on earth, be content that God hath taken him to heaven.'

3 *As Christian believers we are all going to heaven one day so it is only the timing of his brother's departure that is their source of grief*: 'Alas dearest soul, where he has gone we all must come and we are now posting after, for here we have no continuing city but we look for one that is to come.'

4 *It is infinitely better there than it is here*:

Undoubtedly he is happy and therefore let us be found admiring God's mercy to him in taking him to Himself, and away from the evil to come. We live in most sad and woeful times, our days are very gloomy and dismal, but he doubtless is now beholding that beauty of holiness with a perfect aspect, that he saw but through a glass before ... As for me, I look upon it as a peculiar mercy of God towards him, in removing him from those fiery trials we have just cause to suspect are approaching ... therefore dear Father and Mother, comfort your hearts in this, for why should you sorrow, when your dear son has only left a wicked and troublesome world, where there is nothing but sinnings, sufferings, murmurings and prayings, to inhabit a glorious heaven where is nothing but rejoicing and praising and the full enjoyment of a blessed God to all eternity.

5 *In every human grief there is some deep lesson or other God can teach us which we cannot fully discern without the dimension of sorrow*: 'Pray God sanctify it unto us, and let us glorify Him in all things, that we may now gain some good to our souls in his death, as well as much comfort in this life.'

6 *Always be sure to acknowledge God's sovereignty in everything*:

Oh dear Father and Mother, let me advise, desire and earnestly beg you would endure this hard stroke with much patience and submission to the will of Almighty God, for we find God commanding it and commending it [Luke 21:19] 'In your patience possess your souls' and the Apostle adds in *James* 'My brethren, count it all joy, when you fall into divers temptations knowing that the trial of your faith worketh patience . . . Oh doubtless, a patient and submissive frame of spirit in all cases wherein the immediate hand of God is acting is mighty well-pleasing to Him and much becoming a Christian.

7 *God is no one's debtor and He has both the desire and the resources lovingly to compensate in measure for every single deprivation in human life*:

O pray be not so much dejected nor cast down. God is all-sufficient to make up this loss to you, and it may be will give you far greater comforts, otherways. Job was a man that endured much loss and sorrow, yea so much that he desired rather to die than to live and least of all expected any more comfort on earth and yet . . . the Lord gave Job twice as much as he had before. He doubtless is able and will comfort you who is richly able to give us all things to enjoy.

8 *God is still with you and will never disappoint you*:

Dearest father and mother I have much fear still of your too much grief, which much troubles me. Oh let me pray and entreat you to resolve with the Psalmist 'We will fear no evil' we will not be troubled nor moved, for God will be with us. Thy staff and thy rod shall comfort us.

9 *How wonderful that his brother loved Christ*: 'And pray God, grant we make as good a choice as our dear relation hath made before us . . . Oh I say, let your

very souls rejoice, and let it be your comfort that God hath thought you worthy to be the parents of so gracious a child.'

10 *The most important thing by far is for mourners to make sure that they too are destined for a happy eternity.* Nathaniel imagines his brother's present message to his family: 'Rejoice and be exceeding glad, for I am now in heaven, embracing my dearest Saviour, where all my joys are fully completed, and now let your concernment be, in an earnest desire, and a strict endeavour to follow me.'

What undergirds the letter is its firm Trinitarian theology. God has prepared the *security* of heaven for those who love Him. The Saviour has entered the *realm* of heaven and waits to welcome all who have trusted in His redeeming work. The Spirit has confirmed the *reality* of heaven: 'Yes, indeed, says the Spirit – they certainly rest from their labours and their deeds follow them.' Yet vital and comforting as sound theology is to bereft mourners, Nathaniel Pinney is too good a Christian to imagine that words alone can meet his parents' need. If it is humanly possible he must do something more than write. Is there not some way he can get to them? At the end of his choice letter 'their most obedient and distressed son' adds a postscript: 'Pray God support and comfort you . . . Farewell. *I shall endeavour to persuade my master tomorrow to let me come down to you.*' Young as he was he knew that we best minister to bereaved people not only by what we say but by what we are – thoughtful, understanding, supportive, practically helpful, not over-talkative, but perhaps even best in silence by just being there when we are wanted most.

The certainty and prospect of heaven sustained these Nonconformist people through the dark decades of the late seventeenth century and stirred them to courageous endurance, practical holiness, urgent evangelism and sustained hope. We who have been spared their sufferings must not ignore their priorities. It is not other-worldly escapism to insist that heaven is preferable to earth; it is but another way of saying that, now and always, Christ is better than things.

Notes

1 Edmund Calamy, *A Continuation of the Account of the Ministers ... who were Ejected or Silenced* ... 1727, 1:31–4, *An Account of the Ministers ... who were Ejected or Silenced* ... 1713, 2:32. Baxter also refers to Vincent's preaching at this time: 'The Face of Death did so awaken both the Preachers and the Hearers, that Preachers exceeded themselves in lively, fervent Preaching, and the People crowded constantly to hear them.' Cf. Richard Baxter, *Reliquiae Baxterianae*, ed. Matthew Sylvester, 1696, 3:6.

2 Baxter, *Reliquiae Baxterianae*, 3:39.
3 Joseph Davis, *The Last Legacy of Mr. Joseph Davis Senr*, 1720, 27–8.
4 Edmund Calamy, *An Account*, 2:32.
5 Edmund Calamy, *Historical Account of my own Life*, ed. J. T. Rutt, 1829, 1:220–21.
6 Richard Baxter, *True Christianity*, 1655, Epistle Dedicatory A4v.
7 Thomas Brooks, *The Mute Christian under the Smarting Rod*, 1684, The Epistle Dedicatory.
8 John Bunyan, *The Heavenly Footman*, The First, Second and Third Direction, ed. G. Offor, *The Works of John Bunyan*, 1853, 3:383–4.
9 Matthias Maurice, *Monuments of Mercy*, 1729, 52–3.
10 Ibid, 53–4.
11 Edmund Calamy, *An Account*, 2:232–4.
12 Ibid, 2:233.
13 Richard Baxter, *Dying Thoughts*, 1683, 187–8.
14 Charles Stanford, *Joseph Alleine: His Companions and Times*, 1861, 304.
15 Offor, *Works of John Bunyan*, 2:758; John Brown, *John Bunyan: His Life, Times and Work*, 1928, 371–2.
16 John Howe, *The Blessedness of the Righteous*, 1673, 399; *A Treatise of Delighting in God*, in *Works*, 1862–63 edn., 2:217.
17 J. B. Williams (ed.), *Memoirs of the Life, Character and Writings of the Rev. Matthew Henry*, 1828, 1974 edn., 212.
18 Bartholomew Ashwood, *The Heavenly Trade*, 1687, 124–5.
19 Richard Baxter, *A Call to the Unconverted*, 1658, concluding Directions 8 and 10, 279–80, 282–3.
20 Joseph Alleine, *Alarm to the Unconverted*, 1959 edn., 95–6.
21 John Bunyan, *The Pilgrim's Progress*, ed. J. B. Wharey and R. Sharrock, 2nd rev. edn., 1960, 138–9, 161–2.
22 J. T. Wilkinson (ed.), *A Breviate of the Life of Margaret Baxter*, abridged, 1928, 160, 128.
23 Richard Baxter, *Poetical Fragments*, 1689, 62.
24 Offor, *Works of John Bunyan*, 3:497.
25 G. F. Nuttall (ed.), *Letters of John Pinney 1679–1699*, 1939, 6–11 (spelling modernised).

8

The Glory of God's Justice and the Glory of God's Grace

Contemporary reflections on the doctrine of hell in the teaching of Jonathan Edwards[1]

John E. Colwell

There can surely be little doubt that, when John Drew inaugurated this annual lectureship on the theme of 'immortality', the 'instruction, assurance and inspiration' concerning the 'Soul's destiny' which he had in mind were intended to relate to the glories of heaven rather than to the horrors of hell. I certainly cannot claim to have read every lecture delivered under this benefice but, judging from the list of titles, the intentions of John Drew have been so interpreted by most if not all of those who have been granted the honour of addressing this theme. Rev. Dr. N. Micklem spoke in 1951 on 'The Hope *and Menace* of Immortality' (my emphasis). Rev. Dr. Norman Snaith spoke on 'Justice and Immortality' in 1963. In 1966 Rev. Dr. H. Cunliffe-Jones spoke on 'God's Judgment of the Individual after Death' while Prof. I. Howard Marshall addressed the theme of 'Universalism' in 1987.[2] But only in 1960 do we find any mention of 'hell' in the heading of a Drew Lecture when Archbishop A.M. Ramsey spoke on the theme of 'Heaven and Hell'.

This apparent concentration on the hope of heaven is to be expected. Who but a captive audience, obliged to attend such a lecture, would gladly endure a forty-five minute exposition of eternal torments? The theme of hell is not only thoroughly disagreeable, but is also profoundly painful and disturbing. As the writer of *Hebrews* states: 'It is a dreadful thing to fall into the hands of the living God' (Heb. 10:31).[3] The prospect of a 'raging fire that will consume the enemies of God' is truly 'fearful' (Heb. 10:27) but the possibility that such torment is unending is an unspeakable horror beyond contemplation.

Consequently it is hardly surprising that some have resolutely refused to contemplate it, either denying the prospect of divine punishment by proposing that all men and women will ultimately be saved, or denying the unending duration of that punishment by questioning what is perceived to be the traditional teaching of the church concerning the soul's immortality. While the terms 'conditionalism' and 'annihilationism' may not be quite synonymous the ideas represented by these labels arrive at a similar conclusion: that men and women are created with the possibility of being immortal but that the fulfilment of this potential remains dependent upon God's grace operating through faith; that those who finally lack this gift of eternal life are therefore under threat, not of unending punishment, but of the termination of their existence. It is at this point, where a traditional understanding of God's judgment is perceived to depend upon a traditional understanding of immortality, that the theme of hell impinges directly upon the purposes of this lectureship.

Neither has this questioning of a traditional conception of God's judgment been restricted to those who (deservedly or otherwise) have gained a reputation for challenging other aspects of the Church's tradition and teaching. In a paper read at Rutherford House in the summer of 1991 no less a pillar of evangelical orthodoxy than John Wenham offered a spirited and characteristically irenic defence of his belief in 'conditional immortality', tracing this commitment to the influence of Basil Atkinson.[4] Previously L. E. Froom had presented the 'conditionalist' case in his book *The Conditionalist Faith of Our Fathers*,[5] and Edward Fudge had argued the issue more concisely in his work *The Fire that Consumes*.[6] Moreover, John Stott, Philip Hughes and Michael Green have each written in support of the 'annihilationist' or 'conditionalist' view, albeit with differing degrees of tentativeness.[7] Confronted by such prominent and influential challengers a reappraisal of the theme of hell as unending punishment cannot be wholly out of place in any contemporary consideration of the soul's immortality.

In the course of his debate with John Stott under the title *Essentials* David Edwards refers to the 'notorious sermon' on the theme of 'Sinners in the Hands of an Angry God' preached by Jonathan Edwards in 1741 and promoting what he considers to be an 'unchristian picture of God as the Eternal Torturer'.[8] Inasmuch as Jonathan Edwards has become the *bête noire* for so many of those who would challenge a traditional conception of hell there is arguably a case for focusing a reappraisal of the theme on the manner in which it is expounded within his writings. If the traditional understanding of hell as unending punishment can be defended here it can probably be defended anywhere.

It is certainly not difficult to understand why modern readers find cause for offence in Edwards' language. In the course of this 'notorious sermon' on the fate of the wicked Edwards writes:

> The wrath of God burns against them, their damnation does not slumber; the pit is prepared, the fire is made ready, the furnace is now hot, ready to receive them; the flames do now rage and glow. The glittering sword is whet, and held over them, and the pit hath opened its mouth under them.[9]

Neither does Edwards leave any room for doubt that the horror of this torment is unending: '. . . justice calls aloud for an infinite punishment of their sins'.[10] But the manner in which Edwards graphically portrays this unrelenting prospect is truly terrifying:

> When you look forward, you shall see a long forever, a boundless duration before you, which will swallow up your thoughts, and amaze your soul; and you will absolutely despair of ever having any deliverance, any end, any mitigation, any rest at all. You will know certainly that you must wear out long ages, millions of millions of ages, in wrestling and conflicting with this almighty merciless vengeance; and then when you have so done, when so many ages have actually been spent by you in this manner, you will know that all is but a point to what remains. So that your punishment will indeed be infinite.[11]

Again in a sermon preached on the text of Romans 2:8–9 Edwards re-enforces the utter hopelessness of the reprobate:

> In this condition they shall remain throughout the never-ending ages of eternity ... They will dwell in a fire that shall never be quenched, and here they must wear out eternity. Here they must wear out one thousand years after another, and that without end. There is no reckoning up the millions of years or millions of ages; all arithmetic here fails, no rules of multiplication can reach the amount, for there is no end. They shall have nothing to do to pass away their eternity, but to conflict with those torments; this will be their work for ever and ever; God shall have no other use or employment for them; this is the way that they must answer the end of their being ... Time will seem long to them, every moment shall seem long to them, but they shall never have done with the ages of their torment.[12]

But notwithstanding the desperate hopelessness conveyed by Edwards' language one must ask whether, in essence, he is describing anything more horrific than that which we find in the Synoptic Gospels on the lips of Jesus himself. Moreover one must recognise that, both in his conception of hell and in his expression of its torments, Edwards was no more than an imaginative and eloquent representative of the common view of his time, which itself had been the common conception of hell in the major expressions of the Christian church and was certainly the characteristic view of the Puritan tradition. Prof. J. I. Packer refers to Edwards as a 'Puritan born out of due time'[13] and, if this assessment is valid, then the glib dismissal of Edwards as a fanatical 'bogey man', frightening children with threatenings of hell fire, is simply inadequate. Any balanced appreciation of Jonathan Edwards must recognise him not only as typical of the Puritan tradition but also as an extraordinarily able and thoughtful exponent of that tradition. Indeed the irony of the common caricature of Edwards is that it runs parallel with what can only be described as a renaissance of interest in Edwards both as a philosopher and as a theologian of remarkable perception.

Born in East Windsor, Connecticut, on 5 October 1703, Jonathan Edwards was brought up as the son of a Christian pastor and, in the autumn of 1716, enrolled as a student at what was to become Yale. Following a period as a supply preacher in New York he was finally awarded his Master's Degree in 1723 and was elected tutor at Yale in May 1724. In 1727 he joined Solomon Stoddard, his maternal grandfather, as co-pastor of the flourishing Church at Northampton, Massachusetts, where he remained until, in 1750, after an unhappy period of dispute with certain prominent families in the town concerning matters of church discipline, he was dismissed from the pastorate. His removal to what was then the frontier mission station of Stockbridge enabled him to embark on what was perhaps his most effective period of writing, resulting in 1754 with the publication in Boston of *A Careful and Strict Inquiry into the Modern Prevailing Notions of that Freedom of Will, which Is Supposed to Be Essential to Moral Agency, Virtue and Vice, Reward and Punishment, Praise and Blame,*[14] and four years later with the publication (also in Boston) of *The Great Christian Doctrine of Original Sin Defended; Evidences of its Truth Produced, and Arguments to the Contrary Answered . . .*[15] Invited in 1757 to become President of the newly formed Princeton College he was inoculated against smallpox, contracted a severe fever, and died on 22 March 1758, leaving behind merely in volumes of notes and memoirs the elements of that which, had it not been for his untimely death, would have issued in publications that would have established him as unquestionably a leading thinker of his generation. With reference to this tragedy the Lutheran theologian Prof. Robert Jenson remarks, 'It is as if America had been given its Hegel and had not noticed.'[16]

There is a discernable tendency even among the most admiring of Jonathan Edwards' commentators either to be embarrassed by Edwards the Calvinist and impressed by Edwards the student of the Enlightenment and interpreter of Newton and Locke or, contrariwise, to be impressed by the former and embarrassed by the latter.[17] But, as Robert Jenson persuasively argues and demonstrates, Edwards' thought cannot be so conveniently divided: 'Edwards himself did not think he was doing aesthetics, metaphysics, speculative science, moral philosophy or psychology, as these disciplines are now known. He intended all his thinking as one unified project of specifically believing reflection . . .'[18] The totality of Edwards' diverse interests and writings, his essays in 'Natural Philosophy', his sermons, his accounts and analyses of the phenomena of religious experience, his theological treatises, spring from his inner and overwhelming sense of awe before the personal reality of God and the sheer beauty, harmony and majesty of all his ways and works. It is this all dominating preoccupation with the majesty and glory of God that underlies his expositions of the horrors of eternal punishment and the latter ought not to be considered other than in the context of the former.

The ambiguity inherent in the subtitle of this lecture may not have passed unnoticed. Is the reference to 'reflections' that were 'contemporary' to Edwards or 'contemporary' to ourselves? In a sermon dated April 1739 on the text from Matthew 25:46 'These shall go away into everlasting punishment', and headed 'The Eternity of Hell Torments', Edwards states that his aim is to respond to two opinions: the first being that '. . . the eternal death with which wicked men are threatened in Scripture, signifies no more than eternal annihilation; that God will punish their wickedness by eternally abolishing their being', and the second being that '. . . though the punishment of the wicked shall consist in sensible misery, yet it shall not be absolutely eternal; but only of a very long continuance'.[19] With characteristic perception the 'Preacher' observes:

> What has been will be again,
> What has been done will be done again;
> There is nothing new under the sun.
> (Ecc. 1:9)

There would seem to be only one issue of apparent substance raised by modern 'annihilationists' that is not anticipated by Edwards in the course of this single sermon, namely this central question regarding the nature of immortality. Maybe we ought not to be surprised that Edwards fails to address this question since it would appear to arise from a misunderstanding concerning the traditional teaching of the church on this matter. When John Wenham speaks of immortality 'being inherent in God alone'[20] he seems to be implying that the church has traditionally taught otherwise. Yet Augustine himself distinguishes between the soul's immortality and that of God himself 'who alone is immortal' (1 Tim. 6:16).[21] Similarly Calvin, in his *Treatise on Free Will against Pighius*, argues that the soul is not immortal of itself, yet neither is it 'mortal by its nature' since the nature of the soul derives, not from 'the primary faculty' of its 'essence' but from that with which God has endowed it.[22] Commenting on this passage François Wendel observes:

> Not only is the soul created, but its immortality is a gift of God which he could withdraw from the soul if he wished; and the soul deprived of the divine support would perish just like the body and return to nothing.[23]

The mainstream of Christian thought has considered the soul to be immortal, not necessarily or independently, but contingently and dependently. Consequently, while Edwards is prepared to support his arguments for the soul's immortality with references from Socrates, Plato and Cicero, he nonetheless concedes that the life of the soul could cease through its 'abolition' by God. Edwards' central vision of creation as continually dependent upon God would render any 'independent' or 'necessary' understanding of the soul's immortality quite inconceivable.[24] But if this is the case, if the soul's immortality is contingent rather than necessary, then the soul's continuing punishment in hell is the outcome, not of God's passive acquiescence, but of God's active determination, continually maintaining the existence of the soul in judgment. Accordingly the distinction between the traditional teaching of the church and the opinions of modern 'conditionalists' is not that the former perceives the soul to be independently immortal and therefore insusceptible to annihilation while the latter do not, but rather that both hold the soul's immortality to be dependent upon the positive and continuing determination of God, the former accepting that God actively maintains the soul in judgment, the latter recoiling from such a thought as obscene if not blasphemous. That is to say, any distinction between these two opinions concerning the nature of immortality is more apparent than real. There is a distinction between concepts of 'contingent immortality' and 'conditional immortality', but it is less a distinction related to the nature of immortality itself than it is a distinction related to the perceived purposes and character of God. The truly substantial distinctions between the two opinions concern the interpretation of biblical metaphors of judgment, the morality of a punishment that is unending, and the nature of God himself.

During the course of his sermon on Matthew 25:46 Edwards ponders the possibility that the word here translated 'everlasting' might mean something less than an unending punishment of the wicked. But for Edwards, as previously for Augustine, such a possibility is excluded by the juxtaposition of 'eternal punishment' and 'eternal life'.[25] In this respect Philip Hughes seems to evade the issue by conveniently changing the contrast from one between everlasting life and everlasting punishment to one between everlasting life and everlasting death.[26] Edward Fudge is somewhat more convincing in his contention that it is the result of the punishment, rather than the punishment itself, which is eternal: what is intended is eternal *punishment* rather than eternal *punishing*.[27] Yet while this may appear to be an attractive possibility in relation to this particular text one must ask whether it is sufficient as an interpretation of the various and horrific metaphors of final judgment that are specified within the New Testament. In the course of the same sermon, but referring to the text of Mark 9:44, Edwards comments:

> Now, it will not do to say, that the meaning is, Their worm shall live a *great while*, or that it shall be a great while before their fire is quenched. If ever the time comes that their worm shall die; if ever there shall be a *quenching* of the fire at all, then it is not true that their worm *dieth not*, and that the fire is *not quenched*. For if there be a dying of the worm, and a quenching of the fire, let it be at what time it will, nearer or further off, it is equally contrary to such a negation – *it dieth not, it is not quenched.*[28]

In a sermon preached on the text of Luke 17:32 and entitled 'The Folly of Looking Back in Fleeing out of Sodom' Edwards comments more generally on the biblical metaphors of judgment and notes that the 'reason why so many similitudes are used, is because none of them are sufficient. Any one does but partly and very imperfectly represent the truth, and therefore God makes use of many.'[29]

In fairness, Fudge, Wenham and others painstakingly grapple with other possible references for such metaphors. I can only confess that I find their alternative interpretations ultimately unsatisfactory and unconvincing. Metaphors may be only metaphors but they must be significant of something and, when taken together, would seem to be indicative of a prospect unspeakably dreadful and unrelenting, a prospect vastly more terrifying than that of the oblivion which would be the consequence of annihilation. It is not that such metaphors must be taken literally but that the underlying sense of that which is unrelenting cannot be evaded. It is not to deny that there are many texts which admit to an annihilationist interpretation, but it is to recognise that there are some texts, albeit few texts, in which the element of unending duration cannot be denied without extreme hermeneutical contortions. Again in his sermon on 'The Eternity of Hell Torments' and commenting upon Jesus' words concerning Judas, 'It would be better for him if he had not been born' (Mt. 26:24), Edwards observes that this would seem 'plainly to teach us, that the punishment of the wicked is such that their existence, upon the whole, is worse than non-existence'. But this would not be the case if the punishment of the wicked consisted merely in their annihilation. In addition the 'wicked, in their punishment, are said to *weep, and wail, and gnash their teeth*'. This would seem to imply 'not only real existence, but life, knowledge, and activity'. The wicked are both 'sensible' of their punishment and 'affected' by it.[30] Edwards continues:

> Annihilation is not so great a calamity but that some men have undoubtedly chosen it, rather than a state of suffering even in this life. This was the case of Job, a good man. But if a good man in this world may suffer that which is worse than annihilation, doubtless the proper punishment of the wicked, in which God means to manifest his peculiar abhorrence of their wickedness, will be a calamity vastly greater still; and therefore cannot be annihilation. That must be a very mean and contemptible testimony of God's wrath towards those who have rebelled against his crown and

> dignity – broken his laws, and despised both his vengeance and his grace – which is not so great a calamity as some of his true children have suffered in life.[31]

But the underlying question for those who would seek to interpret the biblical metaphors of judgment in terms of ultimate annihilation is whether the concept of a punishment that is unending can be considered as a just response to human sin. However grave human sinfulness may be, is not such unrelenting punishment out of all proportion to the crime? John Wenham writes:

> In my book *The Enigma of Evil* I try to grapple with all the moral difficulties of the Bible and many of the difficulties of Providence. My main theme is to show how God's judgments reflect the goodness of the God we adore. The one point at which I am so seriously perplexed that I have to devote a whole chapter to it is the subject of hell. My problem is, not that God punishes, but that the punishment traditionally ascribed to God seems neither to square with Scripture nor to be *just* . . . I know that no sinner is competent to judge the heinousness of sin, but I cannot see that endless punishment is either loving or just.[32]

With greater hesitation but to similar purpose John Stott also comments that, while not wishing to 'minimise the gravity of sin', he must question 'whether "eternal conscious torment" is compatible with the biblical revelation of divine justice'. The only means in which this could perhaps be comprehended would be if 'the impenitence of the lost also continues throughout eternity'.[33]

Yet, as both writers admit, we simply are not in a position to assess either the utter purity of divine holiness or the utter depravity of human sinfulness. We therefore ought not to pontificate on what is or what is not just. Seeking to demonstrate that such a punishment need not be considered as inconsistent with God's justice Edwards reasons that

> If the evil of sin be infinite, as the punishment is, then it is manifest that the punishment is no more than proportionable to the sin punished, and is no more than sin deserves. And if the obligation to love, honour, and obey God be infinite, then sin which is the violation of this obligation, is a violation of infinite obligation, and so is an infinite evil. Again, if God be infinitely worthy of love, honour, and obedience, then our obligation to love, and honour, and obey him is infinitely great. – So that God being infinitely glorious, or infinitely worthy of our love, honour, and obedience; our obligation to love, honour, and obey him, and so to avoid all sin, is infinitely great. Again, our obligation to love, honour, and obey God being infinitely great, sin is the violation of infinite obligation, and so is an infinite evil. Once more, sin being an infinite evil, deserves an infinite punishment, an infinite punishment is no more than it deserves: therefore such punishment is just . . .[34]

Similarly in a sermon entitled 'The Future Punishment of the Wicked Unavoidable and Intolerable', preached on the text of Ezekiel 22:14, he argues that God does not see as we see with our 'polluted eyes'; in his sight our sins are 'infinitely abominable'. We ought not therefore to think it 'strange' that 'God should deal so severely' with us or that the wrath which we shall suffer 'should be so great'. As great as this wrath may be 'it is no greater than that love of God' which we have 'despised'.[35]

It is this infinite nature of human sinfulness before God's infinite holiness that seems to be overlooked by those who would question the justice of an infinite punishment. It is not that the gravity of human sin is so great that it requires countless ages of punishment for God's justice to be satisfied. It is rather that the gravity of human sinfulness is so great that God's justice can never be satisfied: '. . . there never will come that particular moment, when it can be said that now justice is satisfied'.[36] Even in endless torment the sinner '. . . *shall not suffer beyond what strict justice requires* . . .'[37] In the final paragraph of his sermon on 'The Eternity of Hell Torments' Edwards observes:

> Those who are sent to hell never will have paid the whole of the debt which they owe to God, nor indeed a part which bears any proportion to the whole. They never will have paid a part which bears so great a proportion to the whole, as one mite to ten thousand talents. Justice therefore never can be actually satisfied in your damnation; but it is actually satisfied in Christ. Therefore he is accepted of the Father, and therefore all who believe are accepted and justified in him.[38]

Thus when John Wenham, arguing against the possibility of hell as endless punishment, notes that, even in the 'utter dereliction' of the cross, Jesus 'did not suffer endless pain',[39] he merely confuses the issue. The sacrifice of Christ on the cross, by whatever metaphors we seek to comprehend it, is sufficient as an atonement for the sin of the world, not by virtue of its duration, nor by virtue of the physical torture endured, but rather by virtue of the perfection of the one who there suffered. The infinite punishment of the sinner will never atone for infinite sin. The death of the one who is infinitely pure can and does.

However, Wenham raises a far more compelling issue when, with reference to God's ultimate reconciliation of all things to himself in Christ, he asks how it can be 'conceivable that there can be a section or realm of creation that does not belong to this fulness and by its very presence contradicts it'.[40] The same point is made by John Stott who, commenting on the texts which speak of this final restoration, states:

> These texts do not lead me to universalism, because of the many others which speak of the terrible and eternal reality of hell. But they do lead me to ask how God can in any meaningful sense be called 'everything to everybody' while an unspecified number of people still continue in rebellion against him and under his judgment. It would be easier to hold together the awful reality of hell and the universal reign of God if hell means destruction and the impenitent are no more.[41]

Such comments, when referred to the writings of Jonathan Edwards, bring us to the very heart of his understanding of the character and glory of God as expressed in the title of this lecture. For Edwards the God of the Bible is glorified as much in manifestations of his justice as in manifestations of his grace:

> The glory of God is the greatest good; it is that which is the chief end of the creation; it is of greater importance than any thing else. But this is one way wherein God will glorify himself, as in the eternal destruction of ungodly men he will glorify his justice.[42]

In Edwards' view the justice of God, in the same measure as the mercy of God, is a 'glorious attribute' which is fulfilled and made apparent in the 'everlasting destruction and ruin of the barren and unfruitful'.[43] The everlasting punishment of the wicked therefore, far from conflicting with the ultimate triumph of Christ, is actually an outcome and outworking of that triumph.[44] Again in the sermon entitled 'The Future Punishment of the Wicked Unavoidable and Intolerable' Edwards states:

> God will before all these get himself honour in your destruction; you shall be tormented in the presence of them all. Then all will see that God is a great God indeed; then all will see how dreadful a thing it is to sin against such a God, and to reject such a Saviour, such love and grace, as you have rejected and despised. All will be filled with awe at the great sight, and all the saints and angels will look upon you, and adore that majesty, that mighty power, and that holiness and justice of God, which shall appear in your ineffable destruction and misery.[45]

Here we arrive at the most painful aspect of Edwards' thought, namely that the everlasting punishment of the wicked will be the cause of praise to God by saints and angels. It is God's purpose to demonstrate to 'angels and men, both how excellent his love is, and also how terrible his wrath is'.[46] In a discourse entitled 'The End of the Wicked Contemplated by the Righteous' and published posthumously in March 1773 Edwards clarifies that this rejoicing of the righteous over the fate of the wicked will not issue from gloating or any 'ill disposition'. Yet any form of grief on the part of the saints would be inconsistent with their state of perfect happiness. Here and now the saints have a duty to love the wicked and to seek their salvation. Here and now God deals with the wicked in patience and mercy. But it will not always be thus. In eternity God will have neither pity nor mercy for the damned and neither will the saints, who will then see and feel as he sees and feels. They will know then that 'God has no love' to the wicked and they themselves will then 'love what God loves, and only that'. They will therefore join the angels who rejoice in the glorification of God's justice together with his power and majesty. Moreover, in seeing the misery of the wicked there will be increased within them a 'joyful sense of the *grace and love of God to them*'.[47]

Similarly in the sermon entitled 'Wicked Men Useful in their Destruction Only' Edwards writes:

> The glory of divine justice in the perdition of ungodly men, appears wonderful and glorious in the eyes of the saints and angels in heaven . . . The destruction of the unfruitful is of use, to give the saints a greater sense of their happiness, and of God's grace to them . . . When the saints in heaven shall look upon the damned in hell, it will serve to give them a greater sense of their own happiness. When they shall see how dreadful the anger of God is, it will make them the more prize his love . . . When they shall look upon the damned, and see their misery, how will heaven ring with the praises of God's justice towards the wicked, and his grace towards the saints![48]

The theme is central to Edwards' understanding of hell and recurs in his sermon on Matthew 25:46:

> Hereby the saints will be made the more sensible how great their salvation is. When they shall see how great the misery is from which God hath saved them, and how great a difference he hath made between their state, and the state of others, who were by nature, and perhaps for a time by practice, no more sinful and ill-deserving than any, it will give them a greater sense of the wonderfulness of God's grace to them. Every time they look upon the damned, it will excite in them a lively and admiring sense of the grace of God, in making them so to differ.[49]

How can we continue with such language or contemplate such an obscene prospect? When we speak of the reprobate we are not merely contemplating a nameless mass who have committed horrendous crimes. We are thinking of friends, of family, of those who here and now we love, of those we long to lead to a knowledge of God's mercy. How can we possibly contemplate rejoicing before God when such as these suffer this relentless and horrific fate? Of course we cannot now tell how, in the light of glory, we will see and feel. Certainly we will then love what God loves and feel as he feels. But this only raises the question 'Is this truly how God will then see and feel?'

We may not agree with John Hick when he comments that '. . . either we reject the doctrine that any creatures are doomed to hell, or we revise the doctrine of God'[50] but we must recognise that the ultimate issue here is not that of the nature of immortality, nor even that of the nature of hell; it is rather that of the nature of God himself. Can it be appropriate, in the light of the testimony of Scripture as a whole, and in the light of the cross of Jesus in particular, to juxtapose the glory of God's justice and the glory of God's grace in quite this manner? In this matter also Edwards is representative of a Puritan tradition which, comprehending the cross of Christ within a substitutionary model, tended in some respects to consider God's justice as primary. By understanding the dynamic of the Atonement in terms of the person of Christ rather than in terms of the degree of his sufferings Jonathan Edwards qualifies this tradition. But we must question whether he has qualified it radically enough. While the cross of Jesus is certainly the outworking in human history both of God's justice and his mercy it is so in such a manner that the former is overwhelmed by the latter.

If God is in himself who he is in the gospel narrative, then in eternity and in human history his mercy overwhelms his justice. Ultimately in all God's dealings with men and women 'Mercy triumphs over judgment!' (Jas. 2:13). In the shadow of the cross we are committed to wrestle with that which the apostle Paul concludes in Romans 11:32: '. . . God has bound all men over to disobedience so that he may have mercy on them all'. This need not lead us to embrace universalism though perhaps we ought not to be surprised that Kenneth Morris, writing in the *Scottish Journal of Theology* in 1991, can trace the 'Puritan roots of American Universalism', especially as represented in the teachings of John Murray (1741–1815), Elhanan Winchester (1751–97) and Hosea Ballou (1771–1852).[51]

At various points in the course of his *Church Dogmatics* Karl Barth speaks in terms of the 'No' of God's judgment and the 'Yes' of his grace. At no point is it his desire to lessen the dreadful gravity of this 'No', but it is a 'No' that has been totally overwhelmed by God's 'Yes'. The terrifying threat of the divine 'No' remains but it can never be an equal and opposing force to the divine 'Yes'. The authentic 'Yes' of the gospel can never be heard apart from the 'No', but the 'No' can certainly not be heard apart from the 'Yes' which overwhelms it.[52]

I certainly do not intend to imply a form of universalism. As I have argued elsewhere, I personally do not accept that Karl Barth was any more a universalist than was the apostle Paul;[53] the very real threat of the divine 'No' remains. Mercy that can be counted upon in advance is no longer mercy. The Triune God remains the free Lord in all his ways and works. It is *his* mercy that overwhelms the 'No' of his judgment. In this we must concur with Jonathan Edwards when he states that it is 'the glory of the divine attribute of mercy, that it is free and sovereign in its exercises', and that it would be an 'unscriptural notion of the mercy of God, that he is merciful in such a sense that he cannot bear that penal justice should be executed'.[54] God has 'laid himself under *no obligation*, by any promise, to keep any natural man out of hell one moment . . .';[55] there is 'nothing that keeps wicked men at any one moment out of hell, but the mere pleasure of God'.[56] In an undated sermon on the text of Romans 9:18 Edwards observes that:

> Sinners are sometimes ready to flatter themselves, that though it may not be contrary to the justice of God to condemn them, yet it will not consist with the glory of

> his mercy. They think it will be dishonourable to God's mercy to cast them into hell, and have no pity or compassion upon them. They think it will be very hard and severe, and not becoming a God of infinite grace and tender compassion. But God can deny salvation to any natural person without any disparagement to his mercy and goodness. That, which is not contrary to God's justice, is not contrary to his mercy. If damnation be justice, then mercy may choose its own object. They mistake the nature of the mercy of God, who think that it is an attribute, which, in some cases, is contrary to justice.[57]

However, later in the same sermon he also concludes:

> . . . God can bestow mercy upon you without the least prejudice to the honour of his holiness, which you have offended, or to the honour of his majesty, which you have insulted, or of his justice, which you have made your enemy, or of his truth, or of any of his attributes. Let you be what sinner you may, God can, if he pleases, greatly glorify himself in your salvation.[58]

God is never obliged to be merciful. Mercy remains his free prerogative. Consequently the threat of an eternal punishment remains a real threat. The ultimate salvation of all men and women cannot be counted upon as either necessary or assured. But God's mercy and God's justice do not stand in an unresolved and equal tension and, for this reason, the ultimate salvation of all men and women cannot be finally discounted but can remain the goal of our prayers and our hopes. Universalism in its various forms maintains that all men and women must necessarily be saved, that if this were not so God would not be truly loving or merciful. But the Triune God is bound by no such necessity. As Father, Son and Holy Spirit God is loving in himself without having to love, create, or save anyone. In response to the dreadful warnings of Scripture I cannot discount the possibility that there will be men and women, maybe even 'multitudes' of men and women as Edwards suggests, who will fall into this fearsome fate. But neither, in the light of the gospel, am I permitted to discount the possibility that God could have mercy upon all if he so chose.

At this point Edwards objects that it would be impossible for God to declare 'that any thing *will* be, which he at the same time knows *will not be*'; that God has not only *threatened* an everlasting punishment of the wicked, he has actually *predicted* the same. To the counter-objection that God, through Jonah, threatened the destruction of Nineveh and later relented in mercy Edwards replies that this threat was '*conditional*', having the nature of a '*warning*' and not an 'absolute denunciation'. But of course there was no explicit conditionality in Jonah's threatenings against Nineveh (even though he himself suspected that such might be the case). Jonah's message sounds remarkably like a 'prediction' (Jon. 3:4), but it was a prediction that remained unfulfilled; it was a prediction that finally was qualified by the 'compassion' of God (Jon. 3:10). A threat is no threat at all without the possibility of its fulfilment. Mercy which can be presumed upon is no longer mercy. God's mercy remains his mercy. But equally his threatenings remain his threatenings.[59]

Moreover, if God's justice and God's grace do not coexist in eternal equilibrium then we cannot presume with Jonathan Edwards to ponder the righteous rejoicing with the angels concerning the fate of the reprobate. If any man or woman should ultimately fall into the fire of God's 'No' then even here that 'No' cannot be validly considered other than in the context of the 'Yes'. To use Karl Barth's words: '. . . it is the fire of His wrathful love and not His wrathful hate'.[60] In the light of the love of God in Christ I cannot comprehend how the fate of the lost could ever be anything other than a matter of grief, a grief which, along with the wounds of Christ, stands in eternity as testimony to the unrelenting love of God even for those who finally and fatally reject him.

All this is not to diminish the desperate gravity of the 'No' of God's judgment. It is rather to magnify the glory of the 'Yes' of his grace. It is to seek a valid means of accommodating the so-called 'universalistic' texts of the New Testament without lapsing into either universalism or annihilationism. Universalism assumes the 'No' to be abolished. Annihilationism assumes the 'No' to be diminished. Barth assumes the 'Yes' to be magnified without abolishing or even diminishing the 'No'.

With justification John Wenham observes that 'whichever side you are on, it is a dreadful thing to be on the wrong side in this issue'.[61] If the biblical metaphors of divine judgment can validly be understood in terms of the ultimate annihilation of the reprobate then to persist in speaking of hell as unending punishment is offensive, obscene and blasphemous. However, if these metaphors cannot, without 'special pleading' be understood in this way (and I for one remain unconvinced that they can be), then to belittle the fearsome gravity of this threatened divine 'No', albeit a 'No' that can only be heard in the context of the divine 'Yes' which overwhelms it, would be an inexcusable (though not unforgivable) breach of a grave responsibility. It is fitting, for the purposes of this lecture, to allow a final word to Jonathan Edwards, though the truly final word on this issue will neither be spoken by Jonathan Edwards, nor by any of his detractors:

> If there be really a hell of such dreadful and never-ending torments, as is generally supposed, of which multitudes are in great danger . . . then why is it not proper for those who have the care of souls to take great pains to make men sensible of it?[62]

Notes

1 The following paper was prepared at the invitation of the Trustees of the Drew Lecture on Immortality and was delivered on the 12 November 1992 at Spurgeon's College, London.

2 Published as 'Does the New Testament Teach Universal Salvation?', in T. A. Hart and D. P. Thimell (eds.), *Christ in Our Place: The Humanity of God in Christ for the Reconciliation of the World. Essays Presented to Professor James Torrance* (Exeter: Paternoster/Allison Park: Pickwick, 1989, 313–28).

3 With the exception of direct quotations from Jonathan Edwards all biblical quotations are taken from the New International Version.

4 John W. Wenham, 'The Case for Conditional Immortality', in Nigel M. de S. Cameron (ed.), *Universalism and the Doctrine of Hell: Papers Presented at the Fourth Edinburgh Conference in Christian Dogmatics, 1991* (Grand Rapids: Baker Book House, 1993), 161–91. Wenham had previously outlined this view in his book *The Enigma of Evil* (Leicester: IVP, 1983) and refers to two unpublished works on the theme by B.F.C. Atkinson, 'Life' and 'Immortality' (privately printed and undated), and H. E. Guillebaud, 'The Righteous Judge' (privately printed, 1964). Photocopies of both these works are obtainable from B. L. Bateson, 26 Summershard, South Petherton, Somerset, TA13 5DP.

5 L. E. Froom, *The Conditionalist Faith of Our Fathers* (Washington, D.C.: Review and Herald Publishing Ass., 1966).

6 Edward Fudge, *The Fire that Consumes: The Biblical Case for Conditional Immortality*, revising editor, Peter Cousins (Carlisle: Paternoster Press, rev. edn., 1994) (Original edn., Houston: Providential Press, 1982).

7 D. L. Edwards and J. R. W. Stott, *Essentials: A Liberal-Evangelical Dialogue* (London: Hodder & Stoughton, 1988), 313ff.; P. E. Hughes, *The True Image* (Grand Rapids: Eerdmans, 1989); E. M. B. Green, *Evangelism Through the Local Church* (London: Hodder & Stoughton, 1990), 69–70.

8 Edwards and Stott, *Essentials*, 291–2.

9 Jonathan Edwards, 'Sinners in the Hands of an Angry God', *The Works of Jonathan Edwards* 2, ed. Edward Hickman (Edinburgh: Banner of Truth Trust, 1974), 8; cf. similar passages in the sermon 'Sinners in Zion Tenderly Warned', *Works* 2, 201ff.; and a sermon on Acts 16:29–30, *Works* 2, 817ff.

10 Edwards, 'Sinners in the Hands of an Angry God', *Works* 2, 8.

11 Ibid., 11.

12 Edwards, 'The Portion of the Wicked', *Works* 2, 883.

13 J. I. Packer, *Among God's Giants: Aspects of Puritan Christianity* (Eastbourne: Kingsway, 1991), 409.

14 Edward Hickman (ed.), *The Works of Jonathan Edwards* 1 (Edinburgh: Banner of Truth Trust, 1974), 1–93.

15 Edwards, *Works* 1, 143–233.

16 Robert W. Jenson, *America's Theologian: A Recommendation of Jonathan Edwards* (Oxford: Oxford University Press, 1988), 3.

[17] Compare Perry Miller's *Jonathan Edwards* (New York: W. Sloane, 1949) and Iain H. Murray's *Jonathan Edwards: A New Biography* (Edinburgh: Banner of Truth Trust, 1987).

[18] Jenson, *America's Theologian*, viii.

[19] Edwards, 'The Eternity of Hell Torments', *Works* 2, 83.

[20] Wenham, 'The Case', 162.

[21] Augustine, 'The Nature of the Good', in *Earlier Writings*, selected and trans. John H. S. Burleigh (Philadelphia: Westminster Press, 1953), 339.

[22] Quoted by François Wendel in *Calvin: The Origins and Development of his Thought*, trans. Philip Mairet (London: Collins, 1963), 175.

[23] Ibid.

[24] Edwards, 'Miscellaneous Observations', *Works* 2, 472, 477–8. For a full discussion of the concept of immortality in the New Testament see Murray J. Harris, *Raised Immortal: Resurrection and Immortality in the New Testament* (London: Marshall, Morgan & Scott, 1983). Harris maintains that, while the concept of immortality in the New Testament positively implies more than mere survival beyond death, its opposite is not necessarily 'non-existence' or 'the annihilation of the unrighteous by divine fiat' (198–9).

[25] Edwards, *Works* 2, 86; cf. Augustine, *City of God*, 21, 23.

[26] Hughes, *The True Image*, 403.

[27] Fudge, *The Fire that Consumes*, 120ff.; cf. 17, 153, 207.

[28] Edwards, 'The Eternity of Hell Torments', *Works* 2, 86.

[29] Edwards, 'The Folly of Looking Back in Fleeing out of Sodom', *Works* 2, 66.

[30] Edwards, 'The Eternity of Hell Torments', *Works* 2, 85.

[31] Ibid.

[32] Wenham, 'The Case', 185.

[33] Stott, *Essentials*, 318–19.

[34] Edwards, 'The Eternity of Hell Torments', *Works* 2, 83.

[35] Edwards, *Works* 2, 81.

[36] Edwards, 'The End for which God Created the World', *Works* 1, 121.

[37] Edwards, 'Sinners in the Hands of an Angry God', *Works* 2, 10.

[38] Edwards, 'The Eternity of Hell Torments', *Works* 2, 89.

[39] Wenham, 'The Case', 185.

[40] Wenham, 'The Case', 190.

[41] Stott, *Essentials*, 319.

[42] Edwards, 'The Eternity of Hell Torments', *Works* 2, 87.

[43] Edwards, 'Wicked Men Useful in their Destruction Only', *Works* 2, 127.

[44] Edwards, 'A History of the Work of Redemption', *Works* 1, 619.

[45] Edwards, 'The Future Punishment of the Wicked Unavoidable and Intolerable', *Works* 2, 82.

[46] Edwards, 'Sinners in the Hands of an Angry God', *Works* 2, 10.

[47] Edwards, 'The End of the Wicked Contemplated by the Righteous', *Works* 2, 207ff.

[48] Edwards, 'Wicked Men Useful in their Destruction Only', *Works* 2, 127.

[49] Edwards, 'The Eternity of Hell Torments', *Works* 2, 87; cf. similar comments in 'The Warnings of Scripture Are in the Best Manner Adapted to the Awakening and Conversion of Sinners', *Works* 2, 69; and 'The Portion of the Righteous', *Works* 2, 902.

[50] J. Hick, *Evil and the God of Love* (London: Macmillan, 1966), 378.

[51] K. R. Morris, 'The Puritan Roots of American Universalism', *Scottish Journal of Theology*, 44 (1991), 457–87.

[52] Karl Barth, *Church Dogmatics* I–IV, Eng. trans. eds. G. W. Bromiley and T. F. Torrance (Edinburgh: T. & T. Clark, 1956–75), II, 2, 13; IV, 1, 350, 591ff.; IV, 2, 237, 315ff., 349.

[53] John E. Colwell, *Actuality and Provisionality: Eternity and Election in the Theology of Karl Barth* (Edinburgh: Rutherford House, 1989), 264ff.; also 'Proclamation as Event: Barth's Supposed "Universalism" in the Context of his View of Mission', in Paul Beasley-Murray (ed.), *Mission to the World: Essays to celebrate the 50th anniversary of the ordination of George Raymond Beasley-Murray to the Christian Ministry* (Didcot: Baptist Historical Society, 1991), 42–6; 'The Contemporaneity of the Divine Decision: Reflections on Barth's Denial of "Universalism" ', in *Universalism and the Doctrine of Hell*, 139–60; cf. J. D. Bettis, 'Is Karl Barth a Universalist?', *Scottish Journal of Theology*, 20 (1967), 423–36.

[54] Edwards, 'The Eternity of Hell Torments', *Works* 2, 83.

[55] Edwards, 'Sinners in the Hands of an Angry God', *Works* 2, 9.

[56] Ibid., 7.

[57] Edwards, 'God's Sovereignty in the Salvation of Men', *Works* 2, 851.

[58] Ibid., 854.

[59] Edwards, 'The Eternity of Hell Torments', *Works* 2, 86–7.

[60] Barth, *Church Dogmatics*, III, 2, 609.

[61] Wenham, 'The Case', 190.

[62] Edwards, 'The Marks of a Work of the True Spirit', *Works* 2, 265.

Part 3
Doctrinal and Philosophical Perspectives

9

Immortality and Light

Thomas F. Torrance

To rise from the dead and live in the age to come is the appointed destiny of the children of God.[1] In that continuing personal life they are like angels and can no longer die, for as children of the resurrection they are children of God. He is the God, not of the dead, but of the living, for in him all are alive. That was the message of Jesus handed down to us through the Evangelists as an essential part of the Gospel. Jesus did not speak of an 'immortality' which depends on the natural force of the soul to resist the corruption of death, but spoke instead of a life-relation with God which cannot terminate, for it is anchored beyond our mortal existence in the ever-living God himself. He preferred to speak of this as 'eternal life' which is freely given by the heavenly Father to his children on earth and which, far from ending with death, results in a resurrection to a fullness of imperishable life in God.

Jesus Christ is presented to us in the gospel, however, not merely as a teacher about eternal life, but as the actual embodiment of the Life of God in our humanity. Hence he constitutes in his own life, death and resurrection the saving intervention of God which brings an end to the power of death and mediates a new resurrected existence for humankind. In St John's Gospel this is expressed by the teaching that just as God the Father has Life in himself, so he gives the Son to have Life in himself and thereby to be the fountain of the life for others. In the midst of our mortal existence Jesus Christ is himself the Resurrection and the Life. All who believe in him may share his divine Life and its resurrecting power, so that when they die they will not perish but pass from the darkness of death into the light of an unending personal life with Christ in God.

Throughout the New Testament there is a rich theology of eternal life, with various distinct but complementary emphases in the epistles of St Paul, St Peter and St John, and in the Apocalypse, in which the teaching given in the Gospels is developed in the light of the redeeming passion and resurrection of Christ. My concern in this lecture, however, is not to work that together into a coherent doctrinal form, but to discuss certain basic elements in it from a particular perspective to which attention is not usually given, except in some well-known Christian hymns, namely, the relation of immortality to light.

I propose to do this by taking as a basis for discussion two passages from St Paul's first and second letter to Timothy, and proceed by way of comment and elucidation of the relevant points. The first passage is from 1 Timothy 6:12–16.

> Fight the good fight of faith; take hold of eternal life to which you were called when you made the good confession in the presence of many witnesses. In the presence of God who gives life to all things, and of Christ Jesus who in his testimony before Pontius Pilate made the good confession, I charge you to keep the commandment unstained and free from reproach until the appearing of our Lord Jesus Christ; and this will be made manifest at the proper time by the blessed and only Sovereign, the King of kings and Lord of lords, who alone has immortality and dwells in unapproachable light, whom no man has ever seen or can see. To him be honour and eternal dominion. Amen.

The second passage is from 2 Timothy 1:8–10.

> Do not be ashamed then of testimony to our Lord, nor of me his prisoner, but take your share of suffering for the gospel in the power of God, who saved us and called us with a holy calling, not in virtue of our works but in virtue of his own purpose and grace which he gave us in Christ Jesus ages ago, and now has manifested through the appearing of our Saviour Christ Jesus, who abolished death and brought life and immortality to light through the Gospel.

The basic ideas, and of course the language, which the apostle deploys in these passages, are familiar to us from the whole range of the biblical tradition, from the Old Testament as well as the New Testament, in which life and light are brought closely together. We may point to the thirty-sixth Psalm as typical: 'With thee is the fountain of life; in thy light do we see light.' God himself is Life and Light in an absolute sense which infinitely surpasses our comprehension, but as such he is the ultimate creative Source of all life and light, making alive and enlightening what he has made in accordance with his purpose of love and grace. In this respect the distinctive feature of the gospel is that this divine Life and Light have become manifest to us in an incarnate form in Jesus Christ. As the living God himself among men he quickens and enlightens all whom he brings into relation to himself, and grounds their creaturely life and light in the uncreated Life and Light of God.

I

'God alone has immortality and dwells in unapproachable light.' This is the major premise, so to speak, of everything that must be said here. God alone is unceasing and self-sufficient in his power to live, eternally existing in himself in a way that is beyond all comparison and infinitely surpasses our power to comprehend. He is by nature underived, without beginning and without end. Immortality belongs to him, and to him only, as the natural or intrinsic property of his being. As the one and only God he is the transcendent Creator and Lord of all. Everything that is, in heaven or earth, owes its existence to him, for he freely created it out of nothing and sustains it in its existence by the power of his eternal being. The whole universe of visible and invisible realities is radically contingent in its existence and nature, for it need not have come into existence and has no inherent force to continue in existence: it depends entirely upon the beneficent will of God.

It is in the light of this doctrine of the eternal God and his creation of the universe out of nothing that the question of human immortality must be considered. If to be divine and uncreated is to be intrinsically immortal, then to be creaturely and human is to be intrinsically mortal. Quite evidently this applies to our physical existence, for our bodies come into being and then crumble away and cease to exist as such, but does this apply to what we call the 'soul' or the rational self? Does the human soul enjoy life and light in virtue of any natural power of its own which makes it eternally durable throughout all the changes and ravages of time and therefore finally impervious to the corruption of death? The Christian view, however, is that the soul is a creature no less than the body. It came into being out of nothing through the creative will of God, so that like everything else in the universe it is naturally contingent and perishable, liable to dissolve back into nothing. Considered in itself, the soul can only pass away: it is intrinsically mortal and not immortal.

The extant literature of the Early Church reveals that this Christian doctrine of God and his relation to the universe which he has created and continues to sustain out of nothing soon came into a head-on collision with Greek thought at two significant points which bear upon our theme. It was a general tenet of Hellenic thought that the world was not created by God but was the embodiment of divine reasons, the eternal forms which are the ground of its intelligibility. It was also assumed by Hellenic thought that there is a radical dualism between the intelligible and the sensible, or between form and matter. While the actual world was recognised as composed of form and matter, form was held to be the divine, intelligible element, the definable timeless essence of things which makes them what they really are, but matter was held to be no more than the sensible element which is only fleetingly and accidentally related to reality as its appearance. Greek thought identified the real with what is necessarily and timelessly true, and discounted the sensible or material as deficient in rationality or merely contingent and accidental. It was this combination of ideas which prevented the emergence of what we call empirical science, for in refusing to accept the full reality of matter or the rationality of the contingent, it restricted scientific knowledge to the realm of necessary truths of reason and changeless geometrical forms utterly detached from space and time. A genuine science in our sense could not have arisen until those fundamental tenets of Greek thought were destroyed, and that is precisely what happened with the Christian doctrine of God and his relation to the world. The doctrine that God has freely created the universe out of nothing and endowed it with a created rational order of its own, implied the full reality of matter and the rationality of the contingent. Matter and form are here regarded as equally created out of nothing and as inseparably unified in one contingent rational order pervading the whole universe. The creation of matter out of nothing meant that it had to be treated as contingent reality, and not as unreal; and the creation of form out of nothing meant that it had to be differentiated from God's uncreated rationality as contingent rationality. It is not surprising that this Christian doctrine of creation was attacked as 'impious' and 'atheistic', for within the framework of Greek thought about God and the world it could only mean that God, from whom all rational form and reality derive, was himself created out of nothing.

This was the context in which, following the teaching of the New Testament, the Christian Church had to think out the notion of human immortality. Christian and Greek thought alike operated with the basic idea that to be immortal is to be divine, and to be divine is to be immortal. But Greek thought identified the divine with the rational, i.e. with what is timelessly and necessarily true. And since the soul was held to be the rational part of man, it argued for the immortality or the divine incorruptibility of the human soul – and that idea was underpinned by the ancient Orphic religious idea which pervades Greek mythology that the soul is a spark of the divine temporarily imprisoned in the body. In that event death could only mean the happy release of the soul from its entanglement in the darkness and irrationality of matter or contingent existence.

That notion of immortality was not open to Christians, as early Christian theologians like Justin Martyr, Athenagoras, Theophilus and Irenaeus were not slow to point out, for the human soul is creaturely and not divine, and if it is rational that must be regarded as a creaturely rationality utterly different from God's eternal uncreated rationality. The decisive factor in the argument, however, lay not simply with the doctrine of creation out of nothing which Christianity shared with Judaism, but with the doctrine of the incarnation. On the one hand, the doctrine of the incarnation as the personal embodiment of God's eternal Logos (which at the moment we may think of as the divine Reason or Rationality) in a particular creaturely being, shattered the Greek idea that the divine Logos is immanently embodied in the universe as its necessary rational order, which demanded a radical distinction between the uncreated Rationality of God and the created rationalities of the cosmos. On the other hand, the fact that in Jesus Christ God's own eternal Logos had become man, assuming physical contingent matter into union with himself, implies that the physical creation far from being alien to God is actually accepted and affirmed by him as real even for God, which has the effect of obliging us to cherish the material world of space and time as God's good creation and to respect its created order as the realm in which he has purposed to manifest his divine love. The doctrine of the incarnation, together with the doctrine of creation out of nothing, implied a radical distinction between God and the creature, between uncreated and created rationality, but it also had the effect of unifying the sensible and intelligible, or material and rational elements, in created realities, which changed the understanding of human nature. Instead of the soul and the body being regarded as antithetical, they were regarded as complementary, so that, to borrow an expression from James Denney's 1910 Drew lecture, man was understood as the body of his soul and the soul of his body. That was bound to affect the whole notion of human immortality, and it did, for it meant that a Christian understanding of man's continuing personal life after death has to take the body into its basic equation.

Before we turn to that, however, let us note that while on the Christian view the soul like the body is intrinsically mortal this does not mean that it must die. The creaturely soul is utterly contingent, for it depends upon God for its existence and its creaturely continuity. If it is to survive human death that must depend likewise on the creative and sustaining power of God who only has immortality and who only is the source of life. That is to say, human immortality can be conceived only as a gift of God's grace within a relation between the creature and God which God will not terminate but brings to a fruition in what the New Testament calls 'eternal life'. The soul can be put to death, as Jesus said, and warned us that that is something to be feared much more than the death of the body; but Jesus himself came to set humanity's relation with God on a wholly new basis of grace and love in which eternal life will be the very order of human existence.

II

Let us return to the point that, as God made him and gave him life, man is at once body of his soul and soul of his body. It is in that unity and wholeness of his human nature that God sustains him in being as man, and, in spite of the fact that he is essentially creaturely and perishable, brings him into a relationship with himself in which man's life need not cease but may continue without end. In this case the Christian is bound to look upon death with a horror unknown to the Greek or Oriental who thinks of the end of his physical existence as the release of his spirit, for the death of the body threatens his dissolution and therefore his survival as a human person. Life after death for the Christian must involve a recreation of his whole human nature as soul of his body and body of his soul, that is, a resurrection of man in his ontological integrity as man.

The situation is seen to be much more serious, however, when we recognise that death as we human beings now experience it, is rather more than the kind of death we find in nature around us, when for example a living organism perishes and disintegrates in the dust. Death as we human beings know it is more than 'natural corruption', St Athanasius argued in the *De Incarnatione*, for there is lodged in the heart of it the threat of divine judgment upon human sin and evil, which intensifies the power of corruption in human death far beyond its natural force (3–5). As Georges Florovsky wrote in his Harvard essay on 'The "Immortality" of the Soul':

> The burden of sin consisted not only in self-accusations of human conscience, not only in the consciousness of guilt, but in an utter disintegration of the whole fabric of human nature. The fallen man was no man any more, he was existentially 'degraded'. And the sign of this 'degradation' was man's mortality, man's death. In separation from God human nature becomes unsettled, goes out of tune, as it were. The very structure of man becomes unstable. The 'union' of soul and the body becomes insecure. The soul loses its vital power, is no more able to quicken the body. The body is turned into the tomb and prison of the soul. And physical death becomes inevitable. The body and the soul are no longer, as it were, secured or adjusted to each other.
> (*Collected Works*, 111, 112)

In this event the resurrection of man to eternal life in his wholeness and integrity as man must involve the act of expiatory atonement which deals decisively with human guilt and its divine judgment, and thereby destroys death by taking away its fearful sting. But it must also be a positive act of salvation in the ontological depths of human existence in which man's very being and nature are recreated and established in a life-relation with God which can never perish.

That is precisely the theme of the second passage which I have chosen as a base for our discussion here, salvation by grace which God 'has manifested through the epiphany of our Saviour Christ Jesus, who abolished death and brought life and immortality to light through the Gospel'. In the incarnation of his Son God has laid hold of our disintegrated and decaying human existence in such a way as to penetrate into the inner core of its corruption in death and destroy its power and at the same time to regenerate and reintegrate the human race through a life-giving bond of union with himself. Patristic theology was surely right, therefore, in stressing the fact that he who became incarnate in Jesus Christ was none other than the Creator Word of God through whom all things were made and in whom all things visible and invisible subsist and are held together. That is to say, the incarnation of the Creator within the conditions and structures of our space and time existence had an ontological effect upon the whole creation, and in particular upon the whole structure and life of the human race which would otherwise have disintegrated into nothingness under its own corruption and the divine judgment upon its evil. That is the staggering significance of what the New Testament calls the *epiphaneia* or *parousia* for it involves a vast *palingennēsia* of humanity and ultimately a new heaven and a new earth. All this is not to detract in the slightest from the fact that in Jesus Christ God has come into our world in an acutely personal and personalising way which re-establishes and secures and intensifies individual personal relation with God, but in so far as we take seriously the fact that Jesus Christ is the Creator Word of God himself in indissoluble ontological union with creaturely human existence, we are bound to reckon with the fact that every man irrespective of who he is, what he does or believes, subsists and coheres as man in Jesus Christ the incarnate creative ground of his being. That is to say, we have to take seriously the fact that since the incarnation human nature has been set on a new basis in relation to God who only has immortality. That is the irreducible ontological ground for our hope of immortality, an immortality which is the gift of God's grace but which he has eternally secured for us in Jesus Christ. Let us explore this a little further, in three respects.

1 Central to his hope is the oneness between Jesus Christ the incarnate Son and God the Father. In technical theological terms what is at stake here is what the Nicene-Constantinopolitan creed called the *homoousial* or *consubstantial relation* between Jesus Christ and God or what the Chalcedonian Council spoke of as the *hypostatic union* between the divine and human natures in the one Person of Christ. If that bond does not ultimately hold, if Jesus Christ is not really one in being and agency with God the Father Almighty, the Maker of heaven and earth and of all things visible and invisible, if he is not himself God of God and Light of Light, then the Christian hope is finally and utterly empty – the message of the gospel has no substance to it. The forgiveness of Jesus is merely the transient word of a human creature without any ultimate validity, the deeds of Christ in life and death are merely transient episodes with no more than moral or symbolic significance at the most. But if Jesus Christ really is one in being and agency with God the Father, then everything he said and did for us and our salvation has ultimate validity and reality. Where has this been more concisely or clearly expressed than in the Fourth Gospel? 'My sheep hear my voice, and I know them and they follow me. And I give unto them eternal life,

and they shall never perish, and no one shall snatch them out of my hand. My Father who gave them to me, is greater than all, and no one is able to snatch them out of my Father's hand. I and my Father are one' (Jn. 10:27–30).

2 No less central to the Christian hope are the passion and resurrection of Christ, but they are the passion and resurrection of the incarnate Son and Word of God through whom all things were made. The whole incarnate penetration of God into our fallen and corrupt humanity which has brought upon itself the divine judgment presses toward its culmination in the crucifixion and resurrection of Jesus, for it is through the atoning sacrifice of Christ on the Cross that the fearful division between God and man and man and God is healed in what the Bible calls 'propitiation'. The gracious drawing near of God to man and the incredible assumption of man into union with God in the incarnation is brought to its consummation in the death of Christ when the consubstantial oneness or hypostatic union in Christ's relation with God the Father, far from disintegrating, asserts its power in the midst of the perdition and dereliction of death thereby vanquishing death and destroying its power, and issuing in the resurrection not only of Jesus Christ himself but of the whole human race ontologically subsisting and cohering in him, the Head of the new creation. Who can plumb the fearful depth of what took place in the passion of Christ, when God incarnate cried out in desperate anguish in his struggle with the powers of darkness made obdurate by his own righteous judgment against them? The Cross tells us that God is not a God who holds himself aloof from mankind in its self-inflicted agony of guilt and violence and ontological pain, but has come into the midst of all that we are in our state of perdition in order to bring healing and reconciliation and renewal. Our salvation derives from and depends on the unreserved *self*-giving of God for us on the Cross when through incarnate atonement he undid sin and guilt in the depths of human being, destroyed death and brought life and immortality to light in the resurrection of Jesus Christ from the grave, the First-Born from the dead, as St Paul called him.

Let St Peter summarise this gospel for us. 'Blessed be the God and Father of our Lord Jesus Christ, who according to his great mercy begot us again unto a living hope by the resurrection of Jesus Christ from the dead, unto an inheritance incorruptible and undefiled and that does not fade away, reserved in heaven for you, who are guarded by the power of God through faith unto a salvation ready to be revealed in the last time' (1 Pet. 1:3–5).

3 This brings us to the third point I wish to note: the future consummation of our hope in Christ. Both of the basic passages which I have adduced from St Paul's letters to Timothy speak of our salvation and participation in eternal life or immortality in connection with the *epiphany* of Christ, which, as I have already noted, is equivalent to the other New Testament term *parousia*. It is highly significant that both terms refer to what we call the first advent of Christ

and his second advent – the New Testament does not use either term in the plural, as though there were more than one *epiphaneia* or *parousia*, for the advent presence of God in Jesus Christ in whom our creaturely humanity and Deity are brought into hypostatic union once and for all reaches from the birth of Jesus to his coming again to judge the quick and the dead. That is to say, the incarnation is not a transient episode in the economy of salvation, for the Kingdom of Christ shall have no end, as the Creed expresses it. We live, as Justin Martyr once expressed it, *in the midst of Christ's parousia* (*Dialogue with Trypho*, 52). This has to do with the fact that the incarnate coming and presence of the Son of God affected, as we have seen, the whole structure and existence of the human race, and not simply isolated individuals. But it also means that individuals who believe in Christ and participate in the *palingennēsia* of what took place in him from his birth to his resurrection share that experience with others, and enter into its fullness only as the saving renewal of the incarnation, passion and resurrection of Christ are finally actualised in the human race as a whole, and all things are gathered up in Christ the Head of the new creation. Here we have to do with the tension between what some scholars have distinguished as the 'realised' and 'futurist' elements in the Christian hope.

Let me focus attention only on one particular aspect of this: the astonishing fact that within the one indivisible epiphany or advent of the incarnate Son of God, the 'moment' when each of us dies and goes to be with Christ is somehow identical with the 'moment' when he will come again to judge and renew his creation, for in a real ontological sense those who die in Christ are already risen with him. That is something we find very difficult to understand owing to the refraction of time as we experience it in the world which Christ has already redeemed but which is eschatologically in arrears, as it were, in the enjoyment of its inheritance in Christ. We have to reckon here, however, with something like a 'relativity of simultaneity' which relativity theory has brought to light and which seems to contradict the common sense notions which we generate within the split space and time of our everyday experience. Thus Einstein found he could maintain the constancy of light in all uniformly moving systems by the novel idea of assigning two different but equally real times to the same event. I do not wish to argue from relativity theory in physics or cosmology to a solution of the problem we have in Christian theology of understanding temporal experience in Christ when in him the age to come telescopes back into this present age in such a way that in Christ we live simultaneously in two ages or times, the ongoing present and the future which comes to meet us, but only to suggest that this analogy from our scientific understanding of the behaviour of light in the physical universe may help to make a very difficult notion a little more understandable for some people today. The primary theological point to get clear, however, is the ontologically and temporally indivisible nature of the one epiphany or advent of the incarnate Son of God in whom all men and all ages are held together, without any detraction from real differences between different individual experiences or times. It is because we are resurrected together with Christ, and are indeed already risen in Christ that at the return of Christ to judge the quick and the dead and make all things new we meet up with an event that has already overtaken us. It is the ontological bond in Christ who has taken up our space-time into himself through incarnation and resurrection which constitutes the indestructible ground of our life eternal with Christ in God. To be in Christ is to be in him who *is* the Resurrection and the Life.

III

There is one final point we must discuss, the place of Christian confession, testimony or witness to which both of our basic passages from 1 and 2 Timothy refer. Let me recall the words. From 1 Timothy:

> Fight the good fight of faith; take hold of eternal life to which you were called when you made the good confession in the presence of many witnesses. In the presence of God who gives life to all things, and of Christ Jesus who in his testimony before Pontius Pilate made a good confession, I charge you to keep the commandment unstained and free from reproach until the appearing of our Lord Jesus Christ . . .

From 2 Timothy:

> Do not be ashamed then of the testimony of the Lord, nor of me his prisoner, but take your share of suffering for the gospel in the power of God, who saved us and called us to a holy calling, not in virtue of our works but in virtue of his own purpose and grace which he gave us in Christ Jesus ages ago . . .

At an earlier point we noted that through the incarnation of the Creator Word of God all that Jesus Christ did in life, passion and resurrection affected the very existence and nature of the human race and indeed of the whole creation. In the incarnation all things are gathered up, reintegrated and restored to their true ground and reality in Christ who has the primacy over all things and in whom all things consist. In a fundamental sense, therefore, the ontological regeneration and restoration of humanity has already taken place in Christ, so that as Patristic theology could argue, the general resurrection of all men follows from the resurrection of Christ the Head of the new creation as surely as in the process of physical birth the body follows the head. How, then, are we to think of individual resurrection in relation to the general resurrection, or the resurrection of believers in relation to the resurrection of all men, the righteous and the wicked alike?

Athanasius reminds us that in his incarnation the Son of God had a twofold ministry to fulfil. He was sent both to minister the things of God to man and to minister the things of man to God. That is to say, Jesus Christ had a Godward task to fulfil as man, as well as a manward task to fulfil as God. Granted that the whole act of condescension and humiliation which the incarnation represents is a sheer act of God's love in which the *self*-giving of God must be accorded the primacy, nevertheless the role of the human Jesus within that was absolutely essential, for it was precisely *as man* that God came in Christ to work out our salvation. Quite fundamental to the human side of his activity was the good confession which Jesus Christ made before Pontius Pilate. His human testimony or witness before God as well as before man was intrinsic to the whole course of his vicarious obedience as the Servant of the Lord and as such belongs to the very substance of our salvation in him. To partake of that salvation is to share with Christ Jesus in the confession which he himself made, for it is to be yoked together with him in the very exigencies and conditions of our human life which he came to assume and in assuming to heal and save. Not to share in the good confession of Christ, not to take up his cross and follow him, to be ashamed of his testimony and to resile from the call to die with Christ, is to contradict the very salvation and resurrection in which we are all involved through Christ's incarnational assumption of us into himself. No rejection or unbelief on our part can undo what Christ has done on our behalf or can undo the all-decisive impact of his passion and resurrection on our human existence, so that we are quite unable to cut ourselves off from the resurrection of all men, the just and the unjust, at the last day. But neither does participation in the resurrection depend on any act of will or decision on our part or upon our own effort in fighting the good fight of faith. As we had nothing to do with our natural birth, we can do nothing to effect our rebirth in the Spirit. We are not saved or regenerated in virtue of any activity of our own, whether it be contrition, personal decision, witness or confession, for what saves and regenerates us is the activity of Jesus Christ in his vicarious life and obedience, in which we are called to share through the grace of God. Even when we are commanded to lay hold on eternal life, what counts is not our feeble grasp of God in Christ but his almighty grasp of us within which our grasp of faith is enclosed and faithfully sustained. That Jesus Christ really took our place in the human responses of knowing, believing and worshipping God, of repenting, obeying, laying hold of eternal life or bearing testimony, is something that many people find it extremely hard to accept, ready as they may be to accept that God acts on their behalf in Jesus Christ, for somehow they want to reserve what they conceive to be an element of their own independence or freedom for themselves. But are they not thereby substituting their own faith and their own personal response in the place of Christ's which he offered to the Father on our behalf, and is that not a way of finally setting the Man Christ Jesus in his saving mediation aside, and indeed of declining to let him take our place completely and unreservedly? All this, of course, is not to detract in any way from the freedom he gives us or the obedient response he demands of us as his children, but to give them their full value, for it is only within his all-embracing and undergirding faithfulness in giving himself unreservedly for us in the totality of our human being and life that we are genuinely and spontaneously free in our response, for then they are rendered unconditionally in answer to unconditional grace. We cannot forget the parable Jesus told to the effect that when we have done all that it is our duty to do, we are still unprofitable servants. In other words, we are saved or justified by grace alone and not by *any* works that we do.

In spite of the fact that in God's gracious assumption of our human nature in Jesus Christ all men without exception are involved, in spite of the fact that Jesus Christ bore all the sin of humankind, including the sin of unbelief, so that when he died all died, and in spite of the fact that all people are included in his vicarious resurrection, the New Testament tells us that at the last day a division will become manifest as people are separated from one another, much as sheep are separated by a shepherd from goats. And that final judgment, as Jesus insisted, will involve a discrimination that will take us all by surprise. While God's saving grace, and with it the gift of the resurrection, is extended equally to all irrespective of their worth in such a creative way that their human being is not allowed to lapse back into nothingness but is sustained and reinstated before God, nevertheless it seems clear that not all will enjoy the fruit of the resurrection or the blessedness of eternal life in God. In the last day, as Jesus taught, when the dead hear the voice of the Son of Man summoning them to go forth from the grave, for some people that will mean a resurrecting to judgment. Here we are confronted with something that is quite inexplicable, which surely has to do with the irrationality of evil. Whatever else evil may be it entails a radical discontinuity, a break in our relations with God, which cannot be rationalised away through the continuities of logical explanation. The fact that atoning reconciliation between man and God was accomplished as God himself became incarnate and penetrated into the fearful chasm of our death and its separation from God showed that the chasm of evil was quite abysmal or bottomless. Only the utter self-giving of God in the indescribable anguish of the dereliction of the Cross could save us – that is the measure with which God has measured the enormity of evil and its discontinuity. The gospel does not offer us at any point an explanation of evil, or therefore of the fact that when face to face with the unreserved love of God and its unconditional grace, there are evidently people who finally refuse what God has done on their behalf.

Let us look at the problem from the perspective of the fact that God *is* love, and that all he has done for us from creation to redemption and will do in the consummation of all things is his ceaseless and total self-giving in love. In his love God gives himself impartially, equably, unconditionally to all alike, to the just and the unjust, the believing and the unbelieving, the good and the wicked. It is precisely because he does not withhold his love from the unbelieving or the wicked that his love opposes their unbelief or their wickedness, and that the relation of love into which he gratuitously assumes them resists the strange will of the sinner to isolate himself from God. Thus it is precisely the love of God which judges the sinner, while the unconditional nature of the self-giving of God in love even to the wicked can only mean his unconditional judgment. Since God *is* love, he can no more cease to love than he can cease to be God, and since his unconditional love is his unconditional self-giving he can no more restrict that self-giving or withdraw it in any way, than he can diminish or contradict the love that he eternally is. Moreover, since the self-giving of God in Love to humankind has once and for all been enacted in the incarnation, passion and resurrection of his Son in Jesus Christ, he can no more withdraw from the final consummation of his purpose of love or therefore from actualising the final judgment of his love upon a recusant sinner than he can undo the incarnation or go back upon the atoning sacrifice upon the Cross. In the last resort, therefore, it is by this Man, Christ Jesus, that God will judge the quick and the dead, for all judgment, as the Fourth Gospel expresses it, has been committed to him. Part of what baffles us in this state of affairs is the fact that the unrelenting outpouring of God's love upon the sinner continually sustains him in being even in the midst of his ultimate refusal of that love and its judgment of him.

Now let us turn back once again to our chosen passages from St Paul's letters to Timothy, in which the relation between the immortal God and the human creature is spoken of in terms of *light*. Here we operate with a distinction between uncreated and created light and between uncreated and created immortality. Just as the uncreated Light of God enlightens us in Jesus Christ, so the Immortality of God immortalises those whom Jesus Christ through his incarnate epiphany brings into a saving relation with himself. Just as Immortality and transcendent Light are one in God, so for us to be enlightened by God in Jesus Christ is to be given life and immortality. This relation between life and light, as we have already had cause to note, is common to the whole biblical tradition. But let us now think of it especially in relation to Jesus Christ, the real Light whose coming into the world enlightens every man with the light that is the life of men. That is to say, Jesus Christ is not like John the Baptist only a reflection of or a witness to the Light, but is himself the actual Light of God embodied in humanity. As such he is the Light of the world, who certainly penetrates into our darkness, even into the fearful darkness of death, but far from being extinguished by it, he destroys death and brings life and immortality to light through the Gospel.

Let me restrict our consideration of this to two points which bear upon our immediate theme.

1. In Jesus Christ the eternal, uncreated, unapproachable Light of God which no man can see and live, has embodied itself amongst us in the form of a human life. It is not only that the human life of Jesus was so drenched with the Light of God that it was utterly translucent with divine purity and holiness, but that the life of Jesus was itself the form God's Light has graciously taken in order to enlighten humankind. In Jesus Christ the uncreated Light of God adapted itself, so to speak, to dwell with frail, mortal man without consuming him, but in Jesus frail, mortal human nature has been adapted to receive the Light, God dwelling in it in such a way that it was made alive with the very Life of God. This does not mean that in Jesus Christ the uncreated Light of God overwhelmed or replaced the created light with which he was endowed in his humanity, but that in him uncreated and created light were united in such a way that neither was impaired or diminished through relation to the other. Nor does it mean that in Jesus Christ the eternal Life of God substituted for his human life, but that in him divine and human life were united likewise in such a way that neither was impaired or diminished through relation to the other. It is as such that Jesus Christ is presented to us in the gospel as both the Light and the Life of the world, the life-giving Light and the enlightening Life of humankind.

2. It is as such that Jesus Christ will judge the quick and the dead in the consummation of his epiphany – and there is no other Judge, for God has committed all judgment to his Son. That is to say, there will be no final judgment behind the back of Jesus, for as the incarnate embodiment of the Light and Life of God he constitutes in his own life, passion and resurrection both the ultimate Judge and the ultimate criterion by which judgment will be carried out. It is precisely as Jesus, and only as Jesus, that God will judge humankind at the last day. Just as in all his providential dealings with humankind, God sends the rain and makes the sun shine upon the just and the unjust alike, so throughout the whole course of redemption and in its consummation in the last day God has shown and will show the same impartiality of his grace toward the just and the unjust, the believing and the unbelieving, as he bears upon them by his enlightening and quickening power. Then, we are told, the just will shine forth as the sun in the kingdom of their heavenly Father, but nothing like that is said of the unjust. Although there is no darkness in God somehow the Light of God mediated in and through Jesus Christ bears upon the unbelieving and the recalcitrant in such a way that darkness results. According to the Evangelists this is precisely what happened already in the earthly ministry of Jesus when the seeing were made blind by his Light. That is the strange paradoxical result to which Jesus once referred in the words, 'If the light that is in you is darkness, how great is that darkness.' That is how, I believe, we are to understand the final judgment when there will emerge into the open the division that takes place, in their interaction with the Light and the Life that are Jesus Christ, between the

children of light and the children of darkness. It seems that while we cannot contribute one iota to our salvation, we are able, not to undo the love of God or the unconditional gift of his light and life to us, but to become so locked up in ourselves that the Light of God in Jesus becomes the fire of a consuming judgment and even the ultimate Love of God a kind of hell to us.

Now by way of conclusion let us focus attention once more on the *epiphany* of our Lord and Saviour Jesus Christ, in which all our hope for eternal life is rooted and pledged. Far from being some sort of manifestation of God's presence timelessly and tangentially bearing upon the human race from outside, the epiphany is the actual personal presence of the living God with all the fullness of his eternal Light, Life and Love, intersecting the course of human history and penetrating into its ontological ground in such a way as to heal the breach between the creature and the Creator and reconcile man to God, anchoring our human existence in the ultimate Reality of God the Father Almighty. Utterly divine and transcendent though it is, therefore, the incarnate epiphany of God in the birth, life, crucifixion and resurrection of Jesus Christ is also space-time reality. It is a real historical event that does not crumble away into the dust of oblivion, for God has negatived within it the corrupting force of evil and death so that it persists throughout all space and time as live imperishable reality, pressing toward the ultimate point when God will creatively and redemptively gather up and bring to its final consummation the activity of his grace in the return of Jesus Christ to judge the quick and the dead and make all things new. As such the epiphany is yet to be unveiled in its fullness both as a transcendently divine event and as an essentially historical event, in what St Paul has called its 'proper time'. That is to say, everything that the Christian Gospel tells us about the hope for personal, immortal life is bound up with the final advent of Jesus Christ which must be given its full space-time reality as an event of basically the same nature as the resurrection of Jesus Christ from the grave. But what took place intensively there in Jerusalem will unfold in all its extensive reality, embracing the whole universe in a new heaven and a new earth. That is the divinely appointed destiny of the created universe, and it is within that destiny that each of us will enter upon the inheritance prepared for us, in Jesus Christ in God.

Notes

1 The Drew Lecture on Immortality delivered at Spurgeon's College, London, November 1980.

10

Immortality and the Gospel

D. Bruce A. Milne

I begin with a text which takes us immediately to the theme of our lecture. 'Our Saviour Jesus Christ has destroyed death and has brought life and immortality to light through the gospel' (2 Tim. 1:10). Here immortality (*aphtharsia*) is linked in the closest way to the gospel (*evangelion*) which Paul immediately asserts to be the message of which he was appointed a herald, apostle and teacher (v. 11). The 'good news' or *kerygma*, that revealed message which has been committed like a priceless treasure to Timothy and his historic successors right down to ourselves today (v. 14) is a message which has the effect of, 'bringing immortality to light'; the verb is *phōtizō* and something of its force comes across in another New Testament usage, 1 Corinthians 4:5: 'Judge nothing until the Lord comes; he will bring to light what is hidden and will expose the motives of men's hearts.' Thus the gospel has the effect of bringing right into the blaze of open vision the previously sometimes shadowy and hidden fact of man's immortality. It belongs therefore to the glory of Christian faith born and rooted in the revealed gospel that death has been destroyed and assurance of life after death held out to all who believe. Immortality, in general terms the continuation of personal self-consciousness in some new order beyond death, is therefore a real and central element in the Christian gospel as a consultation of other major New Testament kerygmatic formulae, such as 1 Corinthians 15:3–4; Acts 3:18–19; 10:38–39; 1 Thessalonians 1:9–10 immediately confirms. The promise of immortality is fundamental to the gospel.

Now it is my purpose here to explore and reaffirm this union of immortality and gospel which God has clearly joined together in the holy wedlock of his redemption, and to do so against the background of a discernible and perhaps increasingly influential trend within modern theological reflection to divorce these partners and offer us a version of the gospel in which personal, conscious survival after death is either virtually absent or even explicitly eliminated. When John Drew founded this lectureship in 1903 he was able to assume that the opponents of immortality lay essentially outside the church in the ranks of the sceptical scientific and rationalistic fraternity. Today, as I will indicate, the enemy is also within the gates, and it appears to me that at some point it is incumbent upon a lectureship dedicated to the defence of human immortality to take cognisance of this fact and address itself to it. To fail to do so will mean that we are in danger, if not of fighting the battles of yesterday, at least of failing to defend our position on flanks at which it is presently under direct assault.

In his book *Death in the Secular City*, published in 1972, Russel Aldwinckle looking out over the bleak landscape bequeathed by the radical theologies of the 1960s noted the surprising fact of the degree to which 'thinkers who claim to be Christian seek to interpret the gospel in purely this-wordly terms' (19–20).

The decade or so since these words were penned has happily not lacked evidences of a significant recovery of supernaturalist and eternal, other-worldly perspectives within the convictions and experience of many individual Christians and congregations, but on the whole the theologians remain largely impervious, and indeed are in some cases in danger of moving from a neglect of immortality to a positive antipathy. Let me justify that from two highly influential writers. First, the German theologian Jürgen Moltmann in a passage from his *The Crucified God*:

> The symbol of 'resurrection from the dead' means a qualitatively new life which no longer knows death and therefore cannot be a continuation of this mortal life ... [hence] 'resurrection of the dead' excludes any idea of a 'life after death' of which many religions speak, whether in the idea of the immortality of the soul or in the idea of the transmigration of souls. Resurrection life is not a further life after death, whether in the soul or the spirit, in children or in reputation; it means the annihilation of death in the victory of the new, eternal life . . . The expression 'resurrection of the dead' does not deny the fatality of death whether this death is the death of Jesus on the cross or death in general, with the help of ideas of a life after death in some shape or form. (169–70)

Now I imagine that like myself and others who have commented on this paragraph you find it rather puzzling at first blush. There are certainly things here which appear valid enough. Eternal life of which the New Testament speaks as the gift of God through Jesus Christ our Lord (Rom. 6:23) is certainly more than a mere second instalment of our present biological existence in space and time. Eternal life is an eschatological reality, the life of the new age begun now in the Holy Spirit. However Moltmann 'appears', and one can only use such a term since clarity of concept is not one of this writer's theological virtues, to wish to exclude any real individual future reference at all; and one is left with the clear impression that for all the stress in his theology on the dimension of hope, that 'hope' is merely a symbol for the triumph of God's purpose in some general sense, rather than the prospect, as in traditional interpretations, of the *parousia* as the invasion of our historical continuum at a datable point in the future and the inauguration from that moment of a new order, where some at least of the self-conscious agents who have lived and moved and had their being in this temporal scene will experience a new and extended order of life in sequential continuity to their historical existence here. And if Moltmann means to deny that, and along with other more competent interpreters of his theology I judge that he very probably does, then he stands in manifest contradiction to mainstream biblical Christianity. The important question, however, is why Moltmann appears to emit such antipathy to traditional notions of immortality. But before pursuing that question we turn to a second contemporary writer, Gustavo Gutiérrez, and his book *A Theology of Liberation*.

The heart of this writing lies in a section entitled 'From the quantitative to the qualitative', in which Gutiérrez argues for a redefinition, or reconception of the notion of salvation. The so-called 'quantitative' understanding of salvation which we are to abandon is:

> the salvation of the pagans, the extensive aspect of salvation; it is the problem of the number of persons saved, the possibility of being saved and the role which the Church plays in this process, . . . The notion of salvation implied in this view has two very well defined characteristics; it is a cure for sin in this life; and this cure is in virtue of a salvation to be obtained beyond this life. (151)

In place of this Gutiérrez proposes a so-called 'qualitative' understanding of salvation:

> salvation is not something other-worldly, in regard to which, the present life is merely a test. Salvation – the communion of men with God and the communion of men among themselves – is something which embraces all human reality, transforms it, and leads it to its fullness in Christ . . . To work, to transform this world, is to become a man and to build the human community, it is also to save. (151, 159)

There is in these sentences the obvious imprint of their author's setting in Iberian colonialist Catholicism; but for our purpose it is sufficient to note in this highly influential contribution to the theology of liberation a similar revulsion from the notion of personal immortality, and the attempt to reconceptualise the gospel without reference to it.

It would be a great mistake of course to make a simple identification between Moltmann and Gutiérrez, or even Moltmann and liberation theology in general; there are genuine differences. Nonetheless they are *united* in reflecting in the name of Christian theological construction a manifest unhappiness with the idea of personal immortality, or, in the terms of our Lecture title, a gospel without immortality; and, in this are representative of a wide and influential tendency within the thought and practices of the world Christian community today.

It is time now to ask the question why these and similarly orientated thinkers find personal immortality so uncongenial a notion. The straightforward, on-the-surface, answer is that they claim to detect in the concern for personal survival after death an evasion of immediate human reality, and in particular the struggle for justice in the face of injustice, and for meaning in the face of suffering. As Moltmann expressed it in his *Theology of Hope*, belief in a future life is to be questioned because it produces 'a resigned attitude to life here' (208), and Gutiérrez speaks similarly in criticism of a 'spiritual' interpretation of salvation which 'devalues and even eliminates earthly realities' (167). While such a claim may have a certain superficial attractiveness it does not in my judgment stand up to close examination. For one thing it is guilty of gross oversimplification. The springs of human action are complex and multifarious as any psychologist or psychoanalyst with any degree of analytical skill will document, to say nothing of the perceptive Christian pastor. The postulate that belief in personal immortality will, in general, produce social and moral quietism is, to say the least, an undemonstrated and I suspect in principle undemonstrable proposition. Which leads to the further difficulty, that in practice a belief in immortality has very commonly *not* had this effect. One need but glance across the history of Christian mission over the last hundred years to observe the manifest conjunction of active, sacrificial and compassionate response to human need *and* whole-hearted belief in the life to come; and we are all acquainted with a multitude of God's everyday saints who combine these factors with a cheerful naturalness which makes one wonder what kind of Christian company these thinkers move amongst to produce theories which are at such obvious variance with everyday congregational experience.

The truth is that this particular argument for the divorce of immortality from the gospel is largely a case of rationalisation, and we need to seek the real roots of this contemporary trend at a deeper level in three other contributory factors, and the full force of the case for this realignment of the gospel is not felt until they are uncovered.

1. The first is *the spirit of modern secularism*. In his book *What Kind of God?* Heinz Zahrnt alludes to John A. T. Robinson's account of a conversation the former bishop had late one night in Chicago with a Jewish student in the course of which the student admitted, 'If I could really think, like our fathers, of this life as a mere few seconds' preparation for eternity, it would make a lot of difference. But I can't. Can you?' Robinson admits, 'I had to agree. I couldn't,' and, Zahrnt goes on, 'for our part we must agree with the English bishop and

admit that none of us can either, if we are true contemporaries' (22). Now of course such an assertion has no logical force; it is simply subjective testimony. But as a contributory factor in modern theological disaffection with immortality it is highly significant. The process of secularisation, the gradual exclusion of explicit reference to God from area after area of human affairs and the corresponding extension of humanity's seeming mastery of, or at least manipulation of the environment and its natural powers – a process powerfully documented in some of Dietrich Bonhoeffer's *Letters and Papers from Prison* – has come to exercise a serious 'drag' upon the Christian hope; and indeed in some thinkers has come to assume the proportions of a millstone.

2. The second contributory factor in the this-worldly reconceptualisations of the gospel is *the impact of Marxist criticism.* Marx's attack upon religion, and Christianity in particular, whatever that attack's theoretical inadequacies, gains its essential purchase from its exposure of the failings of Christian social principles in practice, and many influential Christian writers have found themselves unable to dismiss the force of a passage such as the following from a paper Marx published in 1847:

> The social principles of Christianity have now had eighteen hundred years to develop, the social principles of Christianity justified the slavery of antiquity, glorified the serfdom of the middle ages, and equally know, when necessary, how to defend the oppression of the proletariat . . . the social principles of Christianity preach the necessity of a ruling and an oppressed class, and all they have for the latter is the pious wish that the former will be charitable. The social principles of Christianity transfer the bourgeois state's adjustments of all earthly infamies to heaven, and thus justify the further existence of these infamies on earth. The social principles of Christianity declare all vile acts of the oppressors against the oppressed to be either the just punishment of original sin and other sins, or trials that the Lord in his infinite wisdom imposes on those redeemed. The social principles of Christianity preach cowardice, self-contempt, abasement, submission, humility, whereas . . . the proletariat needs its courage, its self-esteem, its pride, and its sense of independence more than its bread. The social principles of Christianity are cringing, but the proletariat is revolutionary. So much for the social principles of Christianity.

One sometimes senses a certain loss of nerve among the theologians in the face of this penetrating criticism, with the result that the church's thinkers and spokespersons have become almost ashamed to refer to the transcendent dimension at all and try instead to play the game in terms of the rules and limits established by Marxist criticism, by devoting their energies to demonstrating, as effectively as they can, the profound social and political relevance of the Christian gospel and even its power as a revolutionary message which prompts revolutionary praxis.

While neither of the thinkers we took as our sounding board earlier could be accused of a simplistic sell-out to Marxism both make frequent reference to Marx in their work, and Marxism has certainly been one of the primary catalysts of the South American theology of liberation.

Nor can we lightly shrug our own shoulders and pass by unaffected on the other side, for the church's record is not blameless, and it is still only too easy for the priest and Levite to hurry past, busy about the Lord's service while the body of the oppressed and suffering lies broken and bleeding in the sun.

3. We come now to the third contributory factor to the this-worldly realignment of the gospel, and the one where perhaps the deepest influence is exercised and which therefore needs to be probed most fully, namely, the urgent contemporary *preoccupation with the problem of evil and suffering.* While of course this is closely linked with the two other factors we have noted it needs serious attention in its own right. This factor is reflected in the refocusing of recent theological discussion upon the question of theodicy (that is, the problem of evil, or the reconciling of the Christian understanding of God with the evil and suffering of his world).

Although the centuries since the Enlightenment have witnessed a damaging assault upon the great metaphysical arguments to which Christians of earlier generations frequently turned to verify their claims to a knowledge of God, theology over the last century has regularly continued to employ various residual forms of metaphysics to justify its claims about God, even if reduced at times to a phenomenology of religious faith and experience. This whole tradition even in its most attenuated forms was based upon the assumption of the fundamental rationality and orderliness of the world. The modern historical experience, however, stemming from the French Revolution and the Industrial Revolution and the shattering impact of two world wars, the horror of Naziism and Auschwitz and all the lesser Auschwitzes of more recent years have, for many moderns, called into question that framework of meaning which underlay traditional accounts of God and his relationship to the world. Thus, while these traditional expositions moved from the world to God, that very movement today becomes the trigger of atheism. Moltmann puts it in a question in his essay 'God and Resurrection':

> how can we believe today in a supernatural event such as the resurrection of the dead when we no longer know, feel or fear the almightiness of God, without being dishonest to our intelligence and alienated from the suffering of our contemporaries? (*Hope and Planning*, 31)

The primary text for this contemporary questioning is Dostoevsky's novel *The Brothers Karamazov*, where the story is told of a poor serf child who accidentally hit his master's hunting dog with a stone while he was playing. The master had him seized and the next morning he was taken out and torn to pieces by his master's hounds before his mother's eyes. Ivan Karamazov says:

> In heaven I do not want the mother to embrace the torturer who had her child torn to pieces by his dogs. She has no right to forgive him, and if that is so, what becomes of the eternal harmony of the future? I don't want harmony. I don't want it out of love I bear to mankind. I want to remain with my suffering unavenged. Besides too high a price is paid for harmony. We cannot afford to pay so much for admission. And therefore I hasten to return my ticket of admission. And indeed, if I am an honest man, I'm bound to hand it back as soon as possible. This I am doing. It is not God that I do not accept, Alyosha. I merely most respectfully return him the ticket. I accept God, understand that, but I cannot accept the world he has made.

The real issue therefore becomes not the existence of God in some abstract theoretical sense; in the face of this kind of question the existence or non-existence of God is almost a secondary issue; the issue rather is that of the justification of God in the face of the world. Or, as Ulrich Simon puts it in his deeply personal account *A Theology of Auschwitz*, it is the question of God's accountability to man. Those who operate on the basis of this kind of question patently talk of personal immortality, which appears diversionary and even irrelevant. The only God who is credible and the only gospel which can be embraced is a God and gospel which vindicate themselves in the face of the realities of present suffering in this world.

It is this issue which I believe to be the real waterspring of the disinterest in, and even dismissal of, the question of personal immortality in recent theology; and any relevant apology for immortality must at some point address itself to it. And it is at this point that the more traditional apologetic for immortality does not really meet the need, whether as the philosophical case for man's essential dualism, or the empirical argument which appeals to the fact of extrasensory perception and alleged telepathic communication through mediumship, or the historical approach in terms of the evidence for the resurrection of Jesus. While all these traditional arguments have their place and importance, simply to go on restating them will not, in my judgment, be enough *today* to fulfil John Drew's intention of 'removing doubt and strengthening faith upon the soul and its destiny in the interests of personal immortality'. What then are we to say to those today, both inside and outside the churches for whom the hope of life everlasting has become a secondary, even irrelevant issue in the face of the realities of human suffering in this world and this time?

We can begin our response, I believe, with *two* fairly obvious preliminary considerations.

First, these theologians and writers tend to have an unbalanced view of reality. While there are no doubt regrettable, even appalling, things in the world, it is not all like that. There are also beautiful, joyous, and even godlike things happening and being experienced by men and women all over the world and every day. That they are largely unheralded in contrast to the avalanche of the sordid and violent which daily appears to pour through the international media is not because they are any less real a feature of our world or less significant as evidence to be weighed before man calls in question the righteousness of his Maker.

Second, the problem of suffering and the presence of evil are not recent phenomena but have been with us since the Fall.

It may be that the scale of suffering is greater today, though one wonders how that could ever be proved, except perhaps on the assumption that the balance of pain and pleasure in individual human experience tilts in the majority of lives towards pain, and therefore that the sheer increase in total human population implies a corresponding increase in total suffering. But the vastness of the generalisations required in this kind of computation seriously undermine its validity. And further, the modern world has available to it, admittedly mainly in the developed world, the means of reducing and eliminating pain which our forefathers had no access to. One need but reflect, as C. S. Lewis suggests in one place, that Christianity emerged, grew and flourished in a world that, for example, knew nothing of chloroform to recognise both that the problem of suffering can hardly claim to be a distinctly modern phenomenon, and also that Christianity has at very least a viable, working solution to it.

Now, while both these preliminary considerations are in my judgment pertinent ones, we need, in making them, to beware of simply reflecting the attitudes of the contented, well-fed, well-educated, multi-privileged world of the 'North' to use the language of the Brandt Report. For those points to stick they need to be made to stick in the face of the reality of the so-called 'absolute poverty' of the 'South', a condition of life defined by the president of the World Bank as

> so limited as to prevent realisation of the potential of the genes with which one is born. A condition of life so degrading as to insult human dignity – and yet a condition of life so common as to be the lot of some 40% of the peoples of the developing countries.

Moving to the more formal level, one interesting response to the argument against immortality from human suffering is that made by John Hick. Hick's case which he describes as 'The basic religious argument for immortality' is that we should go all the way with those who stress the present agony of man as being the primary datum for theological reflection, but to use precisely this fact as itself an argument for immortality. Hick draws attention to the teleological thrust of human existence: man moves forward towards the realisation of his human potential. In practice, however, this potential is realised to any extent in only a few lives. The actual situation is that captured in two sentences of Erich Fromm: 'Living is a process of continuous birth. The tragedy in the life of most of us is that we die before we are fully born.' Hence, argues Hick,

> if the human potential is to be fulfilled in the lives of individual men and women, those lives must be prolonged far beyond the limits of our present bodily existence. The self that is to be perfected must transcend the brief and insecure career of an animal organism. There must, in short, be some form of continued personal life after death. (*Death and Eternal Life*, 156)

The attraction of this argument is immediately apparent. It carries the battle into the opposing camp by claiming that precisely the issues raised by these opponents of personal immortality in fact point directly to it. Nor is this approach without some value – and no full theodicy would wish to ignore it. However, Hick's case is not without its difficulties which quickly persuade us that any attempt to rehabilitate the notion of immortality and to defend an immortality-affirming gospel needs to attempt a more radical criticism. For one thing Hick's case has not persuaded in practice. No amount of promise of a better and fuller realisation of the human potential in another life will suffice for those for whom the present reality appears such a terrible denial of any kind of purpose, and of any notion that man was created for some form of self-realisation within a universal order, or effectively suppress the sentiments of Stendahl: 'the only excuse for God would be for him not to exist'. Putting it another way, Hick's case appears to leave too much for the future. The promise of self-fulfilment however genuine is drowned out by the seemingly interminable rumble of the rail trucks into Auschwitz to disgorge their pathetic human freight before they are fed like rats in their millions to the gas ovens; it is obliterated from hearing by the wail of the oppressed and the starving from every corner of the globe.

But Hick's argument has another weakness, and it is at this point that we can begin to develop our case for the rehabilitation of personal immortality and the reaffirmation of the God-sealed union of immortality and the gospel. This weakness concerns Hick's willingness to accept the view of the world presented by these critics of immortality, and in particular his unwillingness to bring to bear a *moral* evaluation of the human condition. The problem of man by Hick's view is essentially that of a frustrated potential, and his death is simply a physiological fact, the point at which the psychophysical nature of man reaches a condition in which its physical element (the body) can no longer maintain its precarious hold within its environment and collapses in death. But it is this whole amoral framework of interpretation which has its roots back in Enlightenment naturalism, which I believe needs to be called into question, and indeed until it is, there is no possibility of launching an adequate apologetic for personal immortality in the face of this particular cultural and theological form of its denial.

We move then to the heart of this lecture, and from what has inevitably been the criticism and evaluation of other viewpoints, to the exposition of what I judge to be the essential Christian and biblical case for immortality and its intrinsic place in the glorious gospel of the blessed God which is committed still to our trust. The essence of the case lies in the recognition of *the primacy of the moral dimension*. Only when reality is understood in fundamentally moral terms can we attain a true awareness of the meaning of existence and of death in particular.

Now in fact there is a clear pointer in this direction given in the very protest movement itself. For what sustains their protest is what can only be described as a moral indignation at the character of existence. Hence, for all that Dostoevsky's Ivan may dismiss any notion of an 'order' in things, some vision or recognition of, and respect for, order, is the necessary assumption of the protest he lodges against a world where abominable wickedness is possible. Ulrich Simon admits the same in his discussion of the implication of Auschwitz:

> The dust of Auschwitz (the dust that is of its innumerable nameless dead) posits the Law . . . the legacy of Auschwitz is a constant warning against relativity and tolerant judgments in matters of human conduct. It asserts the unpopular division into right and wrong, sheep and goats, actions to be approved and actions to be condemned. (96)

And Camus makes a similar concession in some provocative words in *The Rebel*:

> From the moment that man subjects God to a moral judgment he kills him. But what becomes of the basis of morality then? Man denies God in the name of righteousness, but can he understand the idea of righteousness without the idea of God?

Even Karl Marx's assault upon organised religion is, as Reinhold Niebuhr pointed out many years ago, 'sustained by a withering scorn which only the presupposition of moral responsibility could justify' (*An Interpretation of Christian Ethics*, 92). All of which leads Moltmann to speak perceptively of a 'piety of unbelief'.

Thus the entire force of this protest against 'otherworldliness' (for our purposes, personal immortality as a significant and legitimate religious concern) in the name of a concern for, and a solidarity with, the suffering of this present world, turns in the end on the fulcrum of the recognition of the sovereignty of the moral law. In other words, this whole modern philosophical and theological vogue is radically parasitic upon a vision of order and righteousness which has been substantially derived and nourished from the revelation of the God of righteousness and truth whom we meet in the pages of the Bible.

However, we cannot rest at this point, for the moment we admit the reality of the moral law as a reflection of the nature of existence, and of the God whose nature that law expresses, we are forced to rethink and revise our whole interpretation of the predicament of man. For man is not now merely the pitiable victim of his inhospitable environment, and his suffering is not an arbitrary brute fact which breaks uninvited into his dreaming innocence. For the man who suffers is the man who is already out of step with his Maker. According to Scripture God made man very good, to live before him in righteousness and bliss; to find himself and his fulfilment in his obedience, worship and service of his God. But tragically, appallingly, man has refused to be cast in that role. He has risen up against God, and in his folly identified with the enemy of God in resistance of and opposition to God; all of which Genesis 2 and 3 makes unambiguously plain. But man is not merely thereby 'out of step' with God, basically moving in the right direction though liable from time to time to put his foot in it, or at least in the wrong place. Rather he is in headlong flight in the opposite direction, swept willingly along on the tide of cosmic iniquity, a tide which must one day break and shatter upon the rock of God's unchangeable righteousness. That is the true character of the human predicament and the final context of all man's life, and not least his suffering. It is true of course, and Scripture itself freely concedes it, that individual suffering may at times, from the fragmentary perspective of this mortal life, seem to exceed the degree of culpability in the human objects of the suffering; and conversely, from the fragmentary perspective of this mortal life, the perpetrators of suffering on occasion appear to evade proper judgment. But that there is an intrinsic link between our sin and our suffering, our pride and our pain, our antagonisms and our agonies, *that* for the Bible is beyond dispute. Putting this another way, Auschwitz speaks not merely of God's permission but of man's perversity; it is evidence every bit as much of the abomination of man as of any alleged absence of God. The recognition of this moral perspective also brings into the open the pride, the *hubris* which tries to mask itself behind the call upon God to justify himself and which speaks of God's accountability to man. 'Let God be God and every man a liar'. Here man stands exposed not as the innocent, righteous sufferer subjected to the fearful and arbitrary assaults of an uncaring and even immoral heaven – rather he is seen for what he is, the rebel struggling against the claim of his Rightful Lord and Maker, and his purpose of love which summons man even in his rebellion and guilt to turn to him and find in taking his place as God's free servant and loving worshipper, his own deepest fulfilment and surpassing bliss and joy.

This moral dimension and its implications for interpretation is focused most sharply, however, when we turn again directly to the fact which supremely concerns us in this Lectureship, the fact of death, this indubitable universal reality. 'It is appointed to all men once to die', no biblical statement is more secure from challenge. But what *is* death? Paul puts it succinctly 'Death is the wages paid by sin.' That is the first thing which must be said; that is where we need to begin. In other words death is an essentially *moral* reality. It is never a merely physiological event; it is value-laden. In death man does not merely encounter his physical limitations or the threatening forces of his environment. In death he encounters God. In death the fundamental moral situation of man is exposed and laid bare. In death man is seen for what he is, 'Man *coram Deo*', man before God.

For Scripture, and the New Testament in particular, death is never a neutral, amoral phenomenon, a natural, even relatively friendly, fate. Such a view is not only conspicuous by its absence but basically alien. The New Testament establishes an unambiguous association of death with sin and guilt. 'Death is the wages paid by sin' (Rom. 6:23), 'sin leads to death' (Rom. 6:26), 'sin results in death' (6:21); it is the inevitable result of 'living according to the sinful nature' (8:13). Sin is 'the sting of death' (1 Cor. 15:56); death is the fruit produced by sin (7:5). Sin is, in James's vivid picture, the womb in which death is conceived and from which it emerges to haunt and finally slay man (Jas. 1:15). This line of teaching of course simply carries forward the prophetic witness of Jeremiah and Ezekiel 'that everyone will die for his own sin', and reaches behind that to the beginning in Genesis 2 and 3 where God's prohibition of Adam (2:17) carried the fatal warning 'when you eat of it you will surely die'. Thus 'sin entered the world and death through sin', and in this way death came to all men because all sinned. (Rom. 5:12). Hence death came through a man (1 Cor. 15:25), and 'sin reigned in death' (Rom. 6:21; cf. Heb. 2:14; Lk. 1:79; Rom. 7:29; 8:24; 1 Jn. 2:9). And this is in essential harmony with the teaching of Jesus in the Fourth Gospel, where to believe in him is also to pass from death to life (5:24; 8:51; 11:25), and with Jesus' observation recorded in Matthew 8:22, 'let the dead bury their dead'. It is not accidental that the Father of the prodigal can affirm, 'this my son was dead'.

For the Bible then, death is a profoundly moral reality. It is the witness to the claim upon man made by God and man's resistance of that claim. In his death man's sin becomes open and naked as the truth of his life. Death is therefore, to use Karl Rahner's vivid phrase, 'guilt made visible', or in James Denney's words, 'the sacrament of sin'.

And the terror of death is disclosed here, for in death we see ourselves as we are before God – as those who have lived throughout our allotted time in rebellion against him and in guilt before him, in rejection of his claim upon us and in repeated disobedience to his good will. Here in our death all the illusions are stripped away, all the pathetic rags and tatters with which we seek in life to cover ourselves from our exposure to that awful gaze, all are here torn aside and blown away, the sham religiosity, the so-called 'Christian' service, the frantic philanthropic activity, the prayers and cheery smiles, the devotions and sacrifices, the public displays and the private gestures . . . all fall away, swept aside and scattered to the winds by the tempest of divine judgment that falls upon us in death, 'the soul that sins . . . it must die'.

For this is the meaning of death – the judgment of God; and any other description is the merest tinkering with externals. Death is not a natural phenomenon in man which allows us to shrug our shoulders and mutter our 'ah well, we can't last for ever', for in truth man was created to do just that, he was destined for immortality, and as immortals made in the divine image we shall and must last forever. And in this light we see death for what it is, as the enemy, the intruder, the tumbril of the evil one bearing us away. But even in this the deepest and darkest thing is not said; for the true terror of death is not that in it we escape from God, but precisely that in it we meet him. Karl Barth says:

> Death, as it meets us, can only be understood as a sign of God's judgment. For when it meets us, as it undoubtedly does, it meets us as sinful and guilty men with whom God cannot finally do anything but whom he can only regret having made. For man has failed as his creature. He has not used the freedom in which he was privileged to exist before God. He has squandered it away in the most incredible manner. He can hope for nothing better than to be hewn down and cast into the fire. (*Church Dogmatics*, III/2, 597)

That is the meaning of death – of your death and mine. It is God's act of judgment which I have brought down upon my own ears by my identification in the whole tenor of my life as well as in countless myriads of specific acts with that foul malignant dimension of resistance and antipathy to God which Scripture refers to as the demonic, the anti-kingdom of bottomless iniquity.

Nor, however, is death the exhausting of the judgment. It is rather its foretaste and prelude. 'It is appointed unto all men once to die, and after this comes judgment' (Heb. 9:27). Our present death is the foretaste of the terrors of the second death (Rev. 21), for every one must appear before the judgment seat of Christ to give account; that judgment seat where books are to be opened and secrets uncovered and the thoughts of every heart revealed. (2 Cor. 5:10; Rev. 20:12; Rom. 14:12).

And no view of death which ignores or obscures this further dimension, which fails that is, to see it as judgment in anticipation of final judgment, can be accommodated to the teaching of Scripture as a whole, to say nothing of the plain teaching of Jesus himself. Such interpretation is moreover out of step with the character of the God whom both written and incarnate Words make manifest. For there is that in God which not only takes account of our sinning but which resists it and which moves in awful wrath against its foul momentum, a wrath which our death anticipates but does not exhaust. 'It is a fearful thing to fall into the hands of the living God.'

From this biblical perspective, therefore, to deny human survival is in effect to dismiss the whole revelation of Godhead given in Scripture and revealed in Jesus, and to replace it with an inevitably mythical, idolatrous projection born and conceived out of our fallen and fragmented desires.

But further, here we see why the hope of a blessed immortality is so basic and necessary an element in the Christian gospel, for the truest and deepest problem of humanity is the problem of God, the true God, the living God, whose 'wrath is revealed from heaven against all the ungodliness and unrighteousness of men', a wrath encountered and manifest in human mortality. And this problem dwarfs and drowns all others and renders the problems of his suffering, whether physical, emotional, political or social for all their reality and significance as essentially secondary. And therefore no message can even begin to be genuine 'good news', true 'gospel' except as it conveys an answer and declares a solution to this most fearful of predicaments. And it is here where Moltmann and Gutiérrez and all their variously related contemporary cousins stand exposed in their inadequacy. For the human need which they address, real enough as it is, is as nothing compared with the need of man in guilt before God. They are silent and tongue-tied just at the point where silence is betrayal. They have no word of hope just at the point where hope must be given if there is to be any ultimate hope at all. *'Good news' can only be good news if it can sustain its claim to be such in the face of God's holy wrath against our sin; and since that wrath is manifest in our death for a gospel to be such it must hold out to us as a central and basic element of its message the overcoming of death and the promise of immortality.*

Only therefore when we hear of the destroying of death and only when we hear of the bringing of immortality to light, then and only then do we hear true gospel, genuine, solid, and authentic 'good news' . . . but blessed be God, that we have heard, from the lips of God himself into whose hands we fall helpless in our dying . . . and we hear it still, over the mountains of our guilt and shame, across the dark, dread valleys of our sin . . . the voice, the Word of God, the great glad tidings of mercy, hope and life immortal gathered in a name, Emmanuel, God with us, Jesus Christ the Lord. 'For unto us a boy is born, unto us a Son is given . . . glory, glory to God in the highest.' It breaks upon us again in all its wonder, the eternal love and everlasting grace of the Almighty – Jesus has come, come to live among us, to share our life under the shadow of judgment, to face our temptations in all their malignance, to acknowledge the good claim of the law, to enter into solidarity with us in all our suffering and pain ... but all in order that he might at the last seize our cursed and suffering existence under judgment and raise it again to that life of holiness and joy from which it tumbled down at the beginning. And that meant death. It meant bearing in our place the divine punishment due us for our disobedience (Rom. 5:9); it meant taking upon his holy heart the divine wrath which burns against our unholiness (Rom. 3:25; Gal. 3:13); it meant grappling to the death with all the enslaving powers of wickedness which hold us in bondage (Col. 2:12; Heb. 4:12).

There in the darkness of Calvary shut in with the Father, God with God, he screamed out in his agony, 'My God, my God why hast thou forsaken me?' and that which had lain upon the heart of God from all eternity became real in the darkness of Golgotha. And the judgment of Godhead upon our sin and its implications was borne in his own being as the knife of judgment was plunged deep into his own holy heart . . . and he died . . . our death . . . in our place, for us, 'He died, the just for the unjust'. 'He made him to be sin for us, he who knew no sin'. 'The Son of God who loved me and gave himself for me.' Oh the wonder of it!

> Well might the sun in darkness hide
> And shut its glories in
> When God the mighty Maker died
> For man, the creature's sin.

But in that death, our need is met, our sin dealt with, God's wrath is borne, and our estrangement healed. And in that death our death is transformed. *Not* as by an act of sheer power expressed in the resurrection. That would be to revert once again to a merely non-moral and purely phenomenal understanding of our situation and our death. Death we recall is not the expression of human finitude but of human folly; not of our weakness but of our wickedness; it is sin's wages, sin's offspring, sin's sting. Our need is not an act of power but an act of propitiation, not the overwhelming of death but its overcoming by an act which meets the moral conditions under which death has won its power over us. The resurrection of Jesus is therefore not, as so many of the main New Testament passages make clear, the true basis of our hope of a glorious immortality. In itself the resurrection as an event does no more than demonstrate the possibility of life after death in some form. The true epicentre of that glorious hope, which has swung wide forever the gates of everlasting life to all believers, is the cross, where sin was overcome and with it the divine judgment which is the reason for our dying. The resurrection is therefore in essence the declaration, the public proclamation of the victory of Calvary, the manifestation that Christ has triumphed gloriously in the hell of Golgotha, that sin's reign is broken, its condemnation borne away, and so death's power is for evermore destroyed.

And this is precisely the insight expressed in the great New Testament doctrine of our union with Christ: 'I have been crucified with Christ', 'we died with him', and have been 'made one with him in his death'. Hence for all who believe, who have in the surrender of faith identified with Christ in his death, an identification which baptism focuses (Rom. 6), death has already been met and mastered and the grave lies behind us. And so are fulfilled the staggering words of Jesus 'I am the resurrection and the life; he who believes in me, though he die yet shall he live, and whoever lives and believes in me shall never die' (Jn. 11:35). And if there is still dying to be done, if our sin appears still to extort that final payment from us – it is no longer death in the terrible sense of divine judgment, the death in sin – it is rather the moment in which the child of God moves from one experienced level of his relationship to his Heavenly Father to another; a transition point in the ongoing existence of those who have died with Christ and are now one with him in his endless and indestructible life. A truth surely rarely better expressed than in the exultant words of Kohlbrugge:

> When I die – I do not die anymore, however – and someone finds my skull, let this skull still preach to him and say, 'I have no eyes, nevertheless I see Him; I have neither brain nor mind nevertheless I comprehend Him; though I have no lips, I kiss Him; I have no tongue yet I sing praise to Him with all who call upon His name. I am a hard skull, yet I am wholly softened and melted in His love; I lie here exposed on God's acre, yet I am there in paradise! All suffering is forgotten! His great love has done this for us, when for us He carried His cross and went out to Golgotha.

And it is here, I judge, that we confront the supreme argument for our personal immortality, and the argument for it which more than any other has sustained the people of God across the centuries, the recognition of the moral reality of death as the judgment of God, and the fact of Christ's dealing with that judgment by making it his own on the cross, and thereby opening the gates of eternal life to all believers.

That is of course why immortality belongs so fundamentally to the gospel and why a message which ignores or rejects it is in fact no gospel at all. Because it is in dealing with death that Christ gives token to his conquering of sin and his bearing of that divine judgment which is our greatest threat and the expression of our profoundest human predicament. And finally, to believe such things does not render us oblivious to the cry of the wretched, or the plight of the suffering – how could it? For it is precisely *this gospel* of immortality which is the supreme demonstration conceivable of the justice and holiness of God, of his everlasting passion for righteousness, and therefore the most massive confirmation of the validity of the struggle for a freer, juster, more compassionate, God-reflecting, and therefore God-honouring human society. And further, it is just this union of immortality and gospel which is the deepest vindication of the dignity and significance of humanity within God's world, and hence of the supreme value of the least privileged and most exploited man or woman or child on God's earth – as well as that of the most debased and evil exploiter ...

and which is creative, as nothing else could be, of that spirit of uncalculating, daring, self-sacrifice without which the pain and suffering of this broken world can never begin to be faced, let alone healed.

And now, finally, it is impossible merely to lecture on Immortality; for in handling such a theme I am faced inescapably with Richard Baxter's conviction, that I am myself a dying man addressing dying men and women. And so I need to ask as I close, what does all this mean for me, or for you, on the day we come to die – whether death meets us in a sudden, paralysing blaze of pain or in a long, slow dying into a drug-hazed unconsciousness – what does it mean then for you, for me, when the moment comes, as it surely must, when the dearly loved faces recede and the sights and sounds of the world which has been our life through all our years grow finally dim, and we fall helpless into the hands of God . . . what does it mean for then? It means that

On a hill far away stood an old rugged cross
The emblem of suffering and shame;
And I love that old Cross where the dearest and best
For a world of lost sinners was slain.

So I'll cherish the old rugged Cross,
Till my trophies at last I lay down;
I will cling to the old rugged Cross,
And exchange it some day for a crown.

Blessed be God, who has 'brought life and immortality to light through the gospel!'

11

Immortality

Human hope and Christian certainty

H. Dermot McDonald

I

The general theme for the Drew Lecture has been set for us by its Founder. Something on the subject of man's survival after death falls to be discussed each recurring year. But the present atmosphere of ideas; the prevailing climate of opinion of today differs radically from that when the Lectures were first delivered. It was then a period of transition. The age of belief was giving way the more readily to one of scepticism. But that scepticism had not as yet assailed the belief in man's existence beyond the grave, for even philosophers like McTaggart, who refused to affirm faith in God, considered post-mortem survival as undoubted. For the most part the belief in man's immortality was taken for granted by the generality of people; while philosophers and theologians of repute alike affirmed immortality as a self-evident truth. At the time of the Lecture's first delivery Bishop Butler's argument for revealed religion still compelled widespread assent. Yet even for Butler the idea of the soul's immortality was a premise to be assumed rather than a conclusion to be established. So was belief in man's immortality a constant theme of the poets for whom all nature was instinct with divinity. With such a view of reality it was to them incredible that man, as a spiritual microcosm of the spirit macrocosm should be terminated in nothingness at the tomb or snuffed out forever at the grave. They did not need the syllogisms of a masterful and scholastic logic to assure them of that. They saw in man a 'something' death could not destroy: and in the instinct for one's own survival an assurance of the fact of man's continuing life. On the subject of immortality they were content to affirm with Longfellow, who, in his *Auf Wiedersehen* declared that here, 'Faith overleaps the bounds of our reason.' Thus could Professor Butterfield observe:

> when all men in Christendom, year in and year out, for century after century, were continually being told that they were souls to be saved and that they were destined to life eternal, there was one point which it did not need any philosophy to understand, namely, that there is something in human beings which was to go marching on even after the whole globe should become a heap of dust drifting through space. This was not a theoretical valuation of personality, but something which was accepted as factual, as genuinely descriptive of people. The statement has reference to the very stuff that human beings were assumed to be made of, and it involved an assertion concerning the spiritual nature of personality itself.[1]

Such was it in those former times. But today it is otherwise. Now the situation is quite other than it then was. So radically different is it that believers in immortality of a past age would not easily comprehend the scepticism of the present. They would find it difficult to understand our contemporary mood and nomenclature which acts and speaks as though this life ends all. The one-world-at-a-time mentality of the common man; and this-world-only of the philosophical man would have been beyond them to appreciate. In their thought it would be hard to discern in the present outlook and attitude any motive for the pursuit of moral excellence if so be a man were no more than a mere accidental and ephemeral collocation of atoms.

And it must, of course, ever be a serious issue whether a utilitarian ethic is really moral. For by its advocacy the idea of the moral has itself no final reference point. There is here no absolute norm by which it may be judged. It may be granted – and there are case-histories enough to support the contention – that a denial of man's immortality does not foreclose the living of the good life. There are those who believe that their death ends their existence who find goodness to be good. But they would do well to consider the question, But why be good? And what is the good of goodness anyway? And even 'if disbelief in the soul's future did not arrest morality' the question posed by P. T. Forsyth must still be answered in the affirmative: Would not such disbelief 'lead to a lowered sense of that which is behind morality and is the condition of it – the value of personality?'[2]

It cannot be certainly otherwise at the end of the day than that the shortening of the soul's career must bring about the impoverishment of its interests and the narrowing of its initiatives. It is the hope of life immortal that gives the life that now is, its purpose and its poise. If there is indeed an eternal dimension to which our present experiences may be orientated then a sense of worthwhileness is brought into the business of living. But if all come to the same end, why then bother to follow, sometimes at cost and loss to oneself, the harder way of righteousness? In the case of there being no goal except the grave, why not let passion dictate our actions and what we want be what we acquire? If the good and the bad alike in the dust be equal made, must not the call to virtuous living be a hollow mockery and the maxims of justice, patience, goodwill, brotherhood, and every other particular of ethical conduct be so many empty words which lifestyle some may prefer to follow, but none need?

It is in the context of man's understanding of himself that the apologetic for the afterlife has been historically developed. There is the argument derived from man's instinctive belief in his own continued existence: and the argument derived from man's persistent estimate of his own high value.

From his first appearance man, it seems, thought of himself as somehow special. He felt himself to be other than the rest of the created order; to be other than a mere creature of passing time. He believed himself to carry eternity in his own being. He was not, he considered, made for death; and although death had come upon him it could not he felt finally annihilate his essential life. The idea of man as possessing something immortal is one of humanity's strongest convictions. And it was this instinctive belief that Plato sought to justify in his grand philosophy. The hope of immortality shone bright for Plato and is closely linked with his most sacred aspirations. He thus in the *Phaedo* and elsewhere set out to give a, 'Demonstration that the soul is immortal and indestructable.' In truth Plato's whole philosophy was designed to prove that there is that in man's make-up – the soul or mind; *psychē* or *nous*, for Plato seems to equate them – which by its nature is immortal. It is not a compounded entity like the body and is therefore not subject to separation into otherness and disintegration in nothingness. In Plato's reckoning the very essence of the soul is its essential *liveness*. To think of the soul as dying was for him an unbearable contradiction. Plato's several arguments for the soul's immortality are really variations on the one theme, the essential spirituality of the soul and therefore its eternal endurance. All natural phenomena are subject to change and decay. But the soul as uncompounded must forever remain. Plato was convinced that when his body lay mouldering in the grave his soul would continue on everlastingly. Thus did Plato make Socrates speak for him, 'Then beyond question the soul is immortal and will truly exist in another world.'

This conclusion of Plato that the soul is by nature spiritual and therefore the soul is by destiny immortal became the stock-in-trade argument of the church's apologetic throughout the long history of Western thought.

While, however, the argument of man's immortality as an instinctive belief in his own continued existence has its source in Platonic philosophy, that of the value of the human personality as a premise for the soul's everlastingness has a specific Christian origin. Celsus, that early opponent of Christianity, even while protesting his disdain for the gospel, at the same time is a witness to one of its supreme blessings to human society. 'The root of Christianity', he proclaims, 'is its excessive valuation of the human soul, and the absurd idea that God takes interest in man.' In the pagan world before the time of Christ, as in the pagan world since, however polluted or polished that world may be, the human person is regarded as having in himself no lasting worth. Aristotle, although himself a man of mind and heart, but more earthly than Plato, was not disposed to allow to the generality of human kind anything significant. It was his view that as a man is born, so he dies. Some are born savages and can no more be changed than the scavenger dogs of the streets. Artisans are but living machines incapable of virtue; while women are nature's failures in its attempts to make man. Such an unchristian origin of male chauvinism should make the men in our churches pause and consider how Jesus gave women equal status before God and in the gospel.

The canker at the heart of paganism was the absence of the certainty that life had any serious meaning or any permanent value. In Israel, even in the Judaism of Jesus' time, the strong desire for the continuity of the nation meant that the individual tended to be lost in the collectivity. The value of the individual was thus obscured. The scribes and Pharisees spoke disparagingly of 'the people of the land', and judged them accursed who sat loosely to their cherished traditions.

It is through Jesus that the recognition that men and women have value in their own person found revolutionising expression in human history. Here indeed is one of the distinctive universal and social contributions of Christianity to our civilisation. Jesus discovered the ordinary person and gave significance to the single individual. He saw beyond the distinctions of class, the externals of life, the disparities of conditions, and even the shame of corruption, to the priceless value of the human person. The principal effect of Christian faith on the general conditions of humanity has been the transcendent value it gives to the individual. In this regard the New Testament has been well called 'a treatise upon self-respect'. The central theme around which all its harmonies are compounded is the supreme worth, the spiritual nature, and the eternal possibilities of every man. From the perspective of the kingly rule of God, Jesus ascribed equal value to the Pharisee and the tax gatherer, the rich and the poor. And although he often spoke well on behalf of the poor, he did not deliberately avoid the rich. For he saw beyond the acquisitions of the Pharisee and the rich man – beyond the 'goodness' of the former and the 'goods' of the latter – to the real person. He insisted that it is not what a man has, but what he is that is of ethical consequence and eternal significance.

The conviction then that personality is a sacred thing has its seeds and sanction in the Christian gospel. To conceive of man as Nietzsche and Marx as the bearer of borrowed values, a sort of sandwich-board advertiser of goods to be had elsewhere than in his own spirit must lead to his degradation and dehumanisation. All such ideas conceive of man as without soul and affirm that man lives by bread alone. For man is what he eats. That is to assert that flesh is the essence of us, and that all our moral and intellectual life, like the peal of a bell, is a mere transient result of physical vibrations which stops when the cause which occasioned the sound has ceased. But truly to believe that at death my neighbour's personality, as my own, will disappear forever and that nothing of consequence will be lost, is really to exempt oneself from any present responsibility respecting him. How can we esteem our fellow man as possessing worth in his own right, and even more, treat him as such a being, if in a few years time his final goal is eternal non-existence? Even the pantheist's dream for absorption in the sea of universal life does not answer the demands of the situation; it merely robs the idea of immortality of meaning and motive. For here is a negation almost as complete as annihilation; the loss of all those determining factors and features which make life significant and personal.

It must be seriously doubted whether regard for human personality would have ever become a creative reality in society unless built on the powerful affirmation of life's value and the soul's immortality. For anyone who will trace to its cul-de-sac conclusions the hopes of a humanity in a world where death ends all will find himself turned back to assert that it cannot be the end of things that so precious a thing as personal human life be terminated at the sepulchre. The conviction arises in the soul awake to the reality at the heart of things that there must be more to life than to end in the dust of death. Man's belief in immortality comes almost unbidden to him. It is not a conclusion reached for him as a result of hard thinking. It derives rather from the fitness of things; from man's own feeling about himself as having in his own person qualities which are imperishable; qualities which need eternal scope for their fulfilment. Unless we can be sure of life's immortality, energy and zest must be drained out of living. And this must mean the self's loss of dignity, the mockery of its hidden wealth; and in the end the negation of all the things that are worthwhile. It was Aristotle who declared that God and nature do nothing in vain. It would seem then to be worse than nothing, and vanity, for human life, which has the power to transcend the present moment, to look before and after and sigh for what is not, to be obliterated into nothingness after so brief an appearance. Would life be worth the candle with its heartbreaks and its heartaches, with its sobs and its stabs, if all were to terminate in annihilation? To be thrown on the scrapheap after its few fleeting years have sped past. Can that really be the end of man's story?

These 'proofs' adduced for the soul's immortality are not, to be sure, of the scientific sort which can be set forth in easy comprehensive formulae such as that for the expanding power of heat or the solidifying action of excessive cold. But they are of such a nature nevertheless that arise from reflection upon the character and conditions of man's existence. There is that about man which compels the thoughtful person to admit the cogency of J. H. Holmes's judgment that the human individual has endowments which require for him a more than temporal sphere for their fulfilment. Man appears to carry more equipment than he needs for the adventure of his present life. In contrast with plants and animals which have only what is requisite for existence upon this planet, the outfit of man constitutes something like 'a vast over-provision' for his necessities. For the truth is, as Emile Brunner says,

> man does not die like other animals, any more than he lives like them. Human existence is an exception in the world of living beings; for man is the only living being who is a person . . . The more man is man, the more he realises the subjective nature of his being, realises that his personal life distinguishes him radically from all other living creatures.[3]

Man has that within him which suggests that he is destined for some further port than any on these shores. What he is in mind, heart and spirit, in the range of his interests and the lift of his soul, can only be explained on the supposition that he is preparing, and being prepared, for another and vaster life hereafter.

But to all such reflections on and reasonings for immortality the unbeliever and sceptic have raised their questions of objection. It is asked: Is not the hankering after immortality based on man's valuation of himself sheer egoism? And, is not the hope of immortality conceived as man's post-death self-survival sheer impossibility?

To court an immortality for one's self, it is argued, is but to inflate one's own feeling of self-importance. Far more credible is it to accept life's brevity with a sort of stoical heroism; and in the conviction that the species of which the single individual is but a passing phase is the only enduring entity, give himself to the betterment of humanity, to the welfare of the collectivity, to the progress of the race. Then when his task is finished must he lay down his life in the dust of death without repining having done for mankind what man should do. Man, the universal man, is the measure of all things; and the only immortality there is, is that of a humanity ever learning by hard struggle and its own efforts to guarantee its own survival and perfect its own existence.

The main supporting contention here adduced to buttress the objection that the desire for immortality is the quintessence of egoism is that humanity as such, and not the individual human being alone, is immortal.

Two responses may be made to this. One is, on whatever side of the debate between philosophical realism and pluralism one comes down, the remark of H. E. Fosdick is surely apposite: 'The race is not immortal if the individual is not. A limited succession of transient men does not make a permanent society.'[4] The other is this: a long look into the future does not show a triumphant humanity; and that for the single reason that there is a disease at the heart of it that it cannot, even if it ever willed it so, itself cure. However man may improve his environment or rearrange the economic forces of society, he cannot heal the soul. For the truth of the matter is, as Carl Jung declares, 'Man Suffers in spirit.' Put theologically, that is to say, the human species cannot redeem itself, however hard it tries; or perfect itself, however long it lasts.

But the specific objection that the wish for immortality is sheer egoism must have a fuller comment. There is, it must be allowed, an egoism false and true. There is, as Pierre Teilhard de Chardin grants, a self-centred idea of a future life which is the egotistical extremity of 'every man for himself.'[5] There are those who wish for their own life to go on and on after death but only with every pleasurable desire met and every sensual craving satisfied. That is indeed egoism: an interest in their immortality without concern for their morality; in their enduring life rather than in their ethical nature. There is a desire for life beyond, cherished on lines so individualistic and worldly that its effect on the life that now is, is merely to inflate one's native self-centredness. There is a dream of a future life so crass that it empties the present life of reality and vitality.

Yet there is an egoism which is proper. Christ himself allowed the rightness of such self-love. He called upon us to love our neighbour *as ourselves*. It is this self-love so purified by grace that the love of self becomes enriched in the love of God, to have not the hope for continuing life but the desire to glorify God and enjoy him forever. A wish for immortality based on any other consideration than that can rightly be charged as an overweaning self-esteem. For if 'the doctrine of immortality be held on subjective grounds, it is quite likely to end in religious egoism', says Forsyth.[6] Such a hope founded

> on the indestructable nature of soul substance, or upon an untamed passion for adventure, or upon endless curiosity, or upon the instinct and thirst for personal perfection, or upon our own native moral greatness, or even self-respect, is likely (if you go far enough to give scope for its gravitation) to end downward in a supreme care for *my* immortality, whatever becomes of yours. And that ends in people elbowing each other out of the way to get the elixir of life, or dip in the Bethesda pool for eternity.[7]

But to have the thought of an endless life of worship, praise, and service of the King Immortal and Eternal in the kingdom of just men made perfect is to render the charge of sheer egoism quite void.

II

There is the second question to be considered. Is not the hope of immortality conceived as man's post-death self-survival altogether incomprehensible? A number of objections spawned from the same logical root in empiricism have been advanced of late to sustain the thesis that the self's identity in an out-of-the-body existence is inconceivable. The classical dualistic view of the soul–body composition of the human person has become the subject of a severe and sustained criticism. In the light of modern theory and research, we are told, the notion of a material body inhabited by a non-material soul, or, as ridiculed by Professor Gilbert Ryle, the ghost-in-the-machine concept, is no longer viable or credible. It is not possible to regard the soul as another entity which exists apart from the body like the perpetual light of a lantern which continues to shine after the lantern has been shattered. Contemporary analytical philosophers have thought to strengthen the anti-survivalists' argument by declaring that the words used to describe psychical operations and characteristics do not in fact describe other than bodily motions. They have reference to the empirical individual, as such, as having actual observable existence and not to such illusory and illusive shadowy non-material as another self.

Two arguments here intertwine. There is the empirical argument that the soul's survival after death is not possible; and the linguistic argument that the self's identity after death is not credible.

As regards the first, the idea is that mind and brain, the psychical and the physical, are so intimately bound together that they cannot be conceived to exist apart. There is for the mind and the psychic an essential this-earthly basis. There is consequently an inseparable coexistence between body and personality. This theory goes by various names, the naturalistic, the monistic, the identity, the physicialist all of which boil down to the view that human consciousness could not survive the crisis of death, because its essential realities, self-awareness, memory, and the like, are bodily conditions only. Man is merely a somatic being existing only within the conditions of human interrelations. The idea that man is, or has, a spiritual essence distinct from a body is an illusion created by taking the subjective way of looking at things as expressive of a separate reality.

When Professors D. M. Armstrong, J. J. Smart, Antony Flew, and U. T. Place joined the chorus of philosophers and psychologists who peddle the tune that consciousness is not other than a process of brain activity it might be supposed that the refrain should end with a compelling climax. But an examination of the score will reveal that it runs out in broken notes in the minor key. For the truth of the matter is that its basic theme that the brain creates mind, and that there is an absolute identity between what William James calls brain-states and mind-states is not sound. All that observation and experiment can do is to establish a certain correlation between the two. Were the two to be identified then would they be subject to the same conditions. But they are obviously not; for while the brain is bound by the conditions of space and time, thoughts are not. Thoughts wander. For as the French philosopher Bergson has neatly declared, mind overflows brain. Thoughts are thus mental events and not just bodily motions. Therefore as Pascal remarked, 'Atheists ought to say what is perfectly evident; now it is not perfectly evident that the soul is material.'[8]

The linguistic argument that the self's identity after death is not credible has figured largely in the anti-survivalists' writings in recent days. A. J. Ayer made popular the dictum that only such propositions are true that can be empirically verified either actually or in principle. But the proposition that the soul exists apart from the body cannot be thus verified. Person words, as Antony Flew calls them, are words which refer to physical organisms and have meaning only in this context. Words such as 'you', 'I', 'McDonald', 'John Brown's body', and the like, indicate actual objects, 'which you can point at, touch, see and talk to.'[9] In a word, 'People are what you meet.' The only possible way to identify a person is to indicate some bodily features and criteria. Now at death the body really ceases to be; we thus have no way to identify a supposed post-mortem existent as being the same person.

The large subject of self-identity lies outside the terms of our present discussion. But in the context of our subject reference must be made to the word 'necessity' in the linguistic argument. We allow that bodily criteria are 'necessary' to personal identity; but only then as *contingently* necessary. They are 'necessary', that is to say, to existence and identification in the conditions of the world as we know it and in which we live. The case is different when these conditions no longer hold. What the anti-survivalists have not proved, and what they need to prove to make good their case is that bodily criteria are *absolutely* necessary: necessary, that is to say, when 'this-earthly' conditions are absent.

Believers in survival declare that the human individual will continue to 'exist' beyond the grave. It is against this concept 'exist' that the linguistic philosopher directs his objection. We know, he says, what it is to 'exist'; for *existence* there must be this, that, and the other. But you survivalists continue to use the word 'exist' without the necessary presence of the this, the that, and the other. The term has been emptied of all meaning and the idea of existence of all reality. The word, chants Professor Hepburn, has been 'stretched to breaking point'; it has been 'killed by inches, the death of a thousand qualifications', responds Professor Flew.

But why must we be compelled to play the language game according to their dictated rules? Philosophers who insist that a word must have a certain meaning, without specifying the context are, declares Professor D. Z. Phillips, 'guilty of arbitrary legislation'. The fact of the matter rather is that every assertion must find its verification in the context of the apprehension that gave it birth. The meaning of a word has its significance from the situation of its primary use. Thus the judgments of religious faith are, as Reinhold Niebuhr contends, 'verifiable on their own level'. This means that the judgment that I will survive death, and know myself, and shall be known for whom I am, can only be verified by a return to the convictions out of which they arose. In the context of faith in a personal God, of a transcendent world, and an eternal redemption, belief in immortality has its logic and its meaningfulness.

There are, of course, claims to alleged empirical verification of post-mortem survival adduced by the many societies for psychical research. But what *they* adduce as evidence is so crass and material – Oliver Lodge's son playing cricket in the great beyond! and the like – that we are not quite sure what is supposed to exist in the supramundane realm. The apparitions and the mediumistic communications picture their 'contacts' as following such human business that we are left wondering about the validity of their goings on. H. D. Lewis declares that were survival after death surely established in this way it must break through the barrier of doubt and enlist our interests more profoundly by its religious implications. But this is by no means the case. For if the awareness of immortality does not arise within religious faith itself, belief in an afterlife need be no more religious than that there is life on some other planet. Strange knockings and whispering voices in the unlit gloom of a West End lounge – even if the whole performance is not regarded as a devilish hoax – is not a sure foundation for faith in enduring existence beyond. Jesus rejected the challenge to him to provide sensory signs and worldly wonders to establish his high spiritual claims. Indeed, he made it quite clear that such demand for material evidences was a negation of faith's own reality. For if they believe not him who has spoken the truth of God neither shall they believe in any authentic Christian sense by the spell of the occult and the strangeness of the magical. As far as the gospel of Christ is concerned the frame of mind which desires evidences of mediumistic mumblings has missed the point and purpose of all that Christ has said and came to accomplish. The hope that seeks the ghosts' banalities is mocked by the trivialities which purport to come from a better life beyond. To believe in the life everlasting through the mediocre messages of spirits rather than through the moral victory of Christ is to put faith on an unsure footing. It is to prefer the gropings into the occult to the certainties of the gospel; and to make the medium more than the Mediator. It is, in a word, to have done with the finalities in preference to the tentative.

We are consequently compelled to conclude that all the arguments for immortality dressed up in whatever fashion, do no more than give the idea the sense of bare possibility. To base the soul's everlastingness on man's desires, hopes, equipment, or on his probings of the paranormal or the extension of his extrasensory perception can give no final certainty to life's continuity after the fold-up of our earthly tabernacle. The notion of survival beyond the grave as a deduction from man's estimate of himself is an empty thing. It lacks the vital sense of reality and validity. It is not because of the quality of his soul or of his disposition for immortality that the final assurance for man's continued existence rests. Indeed, as Helmut Thielicke says, 'We can speak of the infinite value of the human soul only because we are infinitely loved and have been dearly bought. God does not love us because we have value; we have value because God loves us.'[10] Such is, as Thielicke goes on to observe that 'alien dignity' with which we are invested. 'This is the only true meaning of the infinite value of the human soul.'[11]

In the last reckoning, therefore, the only firm assurance and sure argument for the soul's immortality must begin at the opposite end: it must, that is to say, be theological rather than anthropological. For it is a fact that it is only in the theological realm that all our idealisms about human personality, its sacredness, its autonomy, its power to transcend the present, and the like, have their significance. It is in relation to the absolute fact of God that man is understood. In the open possibility of a personal intercourse with God human personality gets its measure and its worth. We can therefore declare with Forsyth:

> It is a fundamental principle of all I say on the subject that a sure belief in immortality does not rest where philosophy puts it, but where religion puts it. It is not founded on the nature of the psychic organism, but on its relation to Another.[12]

It has consequently to be insisted with John Baillie that it is more in thinking of God than in thinking of ourselves that the certainty of immortality is likely to be born in us. It is on the reality of God that our claim to endure beyond the shock of death finally rests. Thus to attain a clearer hope and a stronger certainty of life everlasting we are not dependent so much upon the sharpening of our wits as on the deepening of our fellowship with God. All of which is to say that the assurance of immortality belongs to 'the depth grammar' of Christian commitment and biblical revelation. In this sense the idea of immortality is a derivative concept; it is derived, that is to say, from faith and disclosed to faith.

In a telling passage Emil Brunner contrasts the wavering of belief in immortality in the natural man with that of its certain hope in those who have experience of the redemptive action of Christ. He writes:

> The philosophical teaching about immortality rests on a dualistic teaching about man which divides him into a better and worse part, bisecting him into an upper mental and a lower sensual half. This attempt succeeds so so long as man is in a position to relegate the evil in himself to this lower nature, this 'not I myself'. The moment when his self-apology no longer succeeds, when he sees himself as responsible for evil; that is, in the moment when he recognises himself as a sinner, the idea of immortality cannot further be sustained. In that moment the alternative emerges clearly: either nothingness is the ultimate or eternal life is a gift of God. Since only through Christian faith is this self-recognition as a sinner possible, therefore only in a world where the Christian revelation has once taken place can nihilism develop itself to its full extent, i.e., it is a post-Christian possibility. Only in Christian faith are the two factors seen as a unity – death and sin. And therefore in it alone is the

> force which conquers sin also the force which conquers death; the redemptive action of Jesus Christ.[13]

Yet the affirmation that it is within the context of Christian faith that immortal life has its assurance does not leave the issue fully secured. For the question must be asked, In what way is the Christian belief in enduring life made finally certain? To answer this question two propositions will be advanced and amplified. The first is this: immortal life has its vindication in our life redeemed. And the second is this: immortal life has its verification in Christ's life resurrected.

For the Christian believer the essential nature of religious language, as Donald Evans says, is that of self-involvement. Consequently the affirmation of faith in the living God is at one with the testimony that God has become my life and my salvation. Thus to proclaim God as my life and my salvation is to affirm immortality as actualised and possessed in the immediate present. For what is 'now' in the reckoning of faith is but a 'shoot of everlastingness'. Therefore does faith as the creation of the Spirit of God partake of the energy of the eternal. Here and now for faith's apprehension, eternity has come into time. We are still indeed in time, but we are not its prisoners. Time measured by hours, by days, by months, by years, is not the yardstick of our existence. For in time we have come to partake of the timeless. By the indwelling of Christ, whose years fail not and who is alive for evermore, we are freed from time. Thus is eternity a reality *for* us, because a reality *in* us. The supernatural life that is presently ours speaks to us and within us the eloquence of the eternal. Immortality is thus a quality of the believing soul. Eternal life belongs, not firstly even if it does finally, to the end of our days; but to the heart of them. What the Christian believer hears is a word spoken to his inmost soul by One who has life in himself – because I live, you shall live also.

As a gift of God's love, Christ assures the future filled with regenerative power and rejuvenating glory. In the redemptive grace of God in Christ the soul is recreated for goodness: and the one who has experienced such regenerative action is not disposed to believe that God would make him good – for nothing! Not then in its created essence is the soul's survival assured; but in its new nature; in its source in that eternal life by which eternity has already commenced in the historic present of the life of faith.

For the Christian soul then the hope of immortality is not based on the permanence of its nature, but on the quality of its virtue. It is something he wants not just because there is a lot of it: but because in the reality of it he can live divinely in the 'now' of his existence. It is as holy the soul is eternal. And it is only God's salvation and Christ's redemption which gives duration to the soul's moral value, and to that holiness without which no man can see God.

The Christian thought of immortality does not then express a conclusion to which every man must come if he would only think clearly. It is rather a fact which some people experience in their faith in God. It is a sure inference from faith's discernment. For it is the reasoning of the man of faith that being embraced by the fatherly love of God in the redemption of Christ he cannot be destined to extinction in God's new world. The one who has tasted the love divine knows it can never die. It is in the nature of God that the soul finds its anchor both sure and steadfast. The deathlessness of the love divine, which has become his, is his guarantee. The love of God by which he has been redeemed in Christ will get him through and will not let him go. The ground of belief in immortality is not that life must go on and on; but that life in the living God, in the risen Christ, will abide.

Life in the Risen Christ – it is here the Christian believer finds the reality of his immortality made certain. The Christ who in the living present mediates to man the saving love of God in redemptive fellowship cannot now be in a grave on which the Syrian stars look down. Because he makes real to us the eternal life, he must be alive; and because in him God's everlasting love is made real, the hope of immortality has eternal sureness. This is the answer which will alone suffice to the question about a life beyond life. In the resurrection of Christ eternity has set foot in time. For he has conquered death to become the Victory over hell and the grave. As triumphant Lord he has inaugurated a new creation, a kingdom of redeemed spirits to reign with him forever. Thus says C. F. Evans, 'To a greater extent than in anything else, Christianity – at least the Christianity of the New Testament – is a religion of resurrection'.[14]

The resurrection is the affirmation of the atonement; and so, the divine guarantee that that which stood in the way of an eternity of bliss has been removed forever. In the death of Christ man is brought to God in the atonement of the Crucified Christ: and in the resurrection of Christ God is brought to man in the atonement of the Reigning Lord. The Crucified is revealed as the Saviour of the world in his resurrection from the dead, and in his resurrection as Son of God, Christ assures redemption to mankind. He reigns from the cross; he saves from the throne. Christ's atonement is historically absolute in the cross; and eternally actual in the resurrection.

Thus is the resurrection of Christ. as C. C. J. Webb says, that 'notable break' which marks off Christian faith from all others. For Christian faith is concerned not with survival beyond the tomb of the soul alone. It holds out the promise of 'new and glorious bodies' after these present ones have been broken in the dust; bodies fitted by their nature for the new conditions of their transformed existence. Herein is the distinctive Christian biblical commitment about the afterlife; the concept of the resurrection of the body. Entailed is the idea that God's redemptive activity is directed to the whole person, body, soul, affections, and his relationships with other persons.

The New Testament is consequently opposed to a naked spiritualism which regards some non-material element in man's make-up as alone immortal. By its declaration of the final unity of the total person in the kingdom immortal and eternal it accords well with that deeper philosophy which conceives of the body, not merely as the sheath or garment of the soul, but as part of the total person. It is the whole individual that is redeemed to eternal life. The New Testament is clear that Christ's resurrection, the pattern of those who are united to him, includes the body as well as the soul. And the indwelling of the Holy Spirit has put such honour on this frail tenement of flesh which he has made his temple, that we cannot believe that God would permit it wholly to perish. The faith that Christ has been raised was for the first Christians the starting-point of their conviction of their own resurrection to eternal life.

The case was not that their faith, any more than ours, rests on the incredible proposition that one man in some fifty thousand billion men, who, according to experts have lived before us, somehow managed to cheat death. The one who was raised from the dead is one who is known in Christian revelation, faith, and experience, to be redeemingly related to man and essentially related to God: and that is the difference that makes all the difference. Paul and the other writers of the New Testament never adduce the bare historical testimony to the resurrection as, on its own, decisive for belief in its reality. Always there is added the creative reality of an indirect spiritual evidence. We can therefore say emphatically with James Denney that

> The resurrection is not attested in the Gospels by outside witnesses who had inquired into it as the Psychical Research Society inquires into ghost stories; it is attested – in the only way it can be attested – by people who are within the circle of realities to which it belongs.[15]

Standing within these realities, in the light of the empty tomb in the garden beyond the cross, we cannot but enter a blank contradiction to the assertion of Goethe that 'our view into the beyond is blocked up'. The faith and experience of the Christian gospel answer, 'it is not so'. In this regard Thielicke is right to insist, 'The resurrection is certain only to those who are resolved to live with Him [with Christ], who are won by His words and His whole person, who give themselves unconditionally to Him.'[16] For them there will be 'the second Easter of His coming. This will be the moment when faith will see what it has believed and unbelief will have to see what it has not.'[17]

In a letter written by John Newton in the year 1761 to a certain Mr A.-B., the converted slave-trafficker tells of his own sureness of immortal life because of his experience of living in the possession of it; of living, that is to say, quoting his own words,

> 'in a comfortable assurance of the pardon of my sins, and habitual communion with God who made heaven and earth, a calm reliance on the Divine Providence, and

cheering prospects of a better life in the better world, with the pleasing foretaste of heaven in my soul'.

Who can doubt heaven who knows that he now possesses it? No one can be uncertain of immortal life who has faith's conviction that his life is hid with Christ in God.

Notes

1 *Christianity in European History*, 52, 53.
2 *This Life and the Next*, 8.
3 *Eternal Hope*, 97.
4 *Assurance of Immortality*, 33.
5 *The Phenomenon of Man*, 244.
6 Forsyth, *This Life and the Next*, 21.
7 Ibid.
8 *Pensées*, §221.
9 *New Essays in Philosophical Theology*, eds. A. Flew and A. MacIntyre, 269.
10 Thielicke, *A Thielicke Trilogy*, 224.
11 Ibid.
12 Forsyth, *This Life and the Next*, 20, 21.
13 Brunner, *Eternal Hope*, 94, 95.
14 *Resurrection in the New Testament*, 1.
15 *Jesus and the Gospels*, 157.
16 Thielicke, *A Thielicke Trilogy*, 191.
17 Ibid.

12

Of Present Grace and Joys Above

Brian Haymes

My purpose in this lecture is to begin to explore, tentatively, the relationship between the present calling to Christian discipleship and the Christian hope of the life of the world to come. In what way, if any, does the living of the Christian life in this world relate to the world to come? This is a particular form of the general question of the relationship of faith and ethics, of Christian believing and Christian works. What ethical implication is there in the assertion 'I believe in the life of the world to come'? What kind of difference might such a belief make to the practice of Christian living? If, under examination, it does not make any difference, can it be said to be a religious belief at all?

It will be an assumption of my argument that all theological statements are, as a matter of logic, practical or at least heavy with practical implications. Let me invoke one who has been called the first philosopher of the age, to help affirm my case.[1]

Ludwig Wittgenstein was concerned as much as anyone in the last century with the meaning of language. He came to recognise that we do many things with words, for example, we use words to refer to objects. But to insist, for example, that the literal referential meaning of a word is its one and only meaning is to end with all kinds of nonsense. Wittgenstein urged us to look and see how a word is being used because, as he argued, the meaning of a word is its use in language. When I tell you, 'My love is like a red, red rose,' I do not expect you to spray my wife with greenfly repellant. Such crude literalism would be more than a little embarrassing! To assume such a limited use and meaning of language is simply a failure in intelligence. It amounts to ignorance of how to speak the English language. So what are we doing when we say, 'I believe in the life of the world to come'?

In fact, at one point in his work Wittgenstein used the concept of belief in a Last Judgment to explore the nature and meaning of religious statements. He drew a contrast between someone who claimed that there would be a Last Judgment and someone who did not believe this would happen. What is the difference between them? You could say it was simply factual, of the same kind of disagreement between two football supporters, one of whom says that United will win the League this year and the other denying it. Time will provide the answer. So it might be affirmed about the Last Judgment. Believing, on this account, is simply taken to be a matter of asserting facts or proposing a hypothesis. But let us suppose that someone says that they believe in a Last Judgment but that the belief patently makes not the slightest difference to the way they live their life. Would we then say that this was a *religious* belief? To quote Wittgenstein:

> Suppose someone made this guidance for this life: believing in the Last Judgement. Whenever he does anything, this is before his mind. In a way, how are we to know whether to say he believes this will happen or not?
> Asking him is not enough. He will probably say he has proof. But he has what you might call an unshakeable belief. It will show, not by reasoning or by appeal to ordinary grounds for belief, but rather by regulating for all in his life.[2]

The 'meaning' of the belief, in part, and logically an essential part, will show itself in the action of the believer. Even if the belief relates to a putative future event, it will show itself as a *religious* belief by 'regulating for all in his life'. Anyone who really believes in the Last Judgment will act in certain ways. It would be misleading to assume that what this means is that they know something and therefore act on what they know. Rather, to know that there is a Last Judgment *is* to act in a certain way because the belief is held before one's mind and regulates for all one's life. However 'futuristic' the content of the belief might be it shows itself in the present or it is not properly a religious belief at all. I hold then that all religious statements are practical as a matter of logic.

There is a further fundamental assumption that I am going to make and for which I shall not argue overmuch. It is that life after death is a meaningful and proper religious belief. There have always been philosophers and theologians who have argued that we can dispense with these affirmations in the creeds, largely because little sense can be made of them. Two arguments in particular have been advanced. The first might be called the 'naturalist' position which asserts that all mental life is dependent upon the central cerebral system so that brain death, physical death, is the end of us. From dust we came and to dust we shall return – period! That is our destiny as mortal human beings. Therefore, so the argument goes, because we are psychosomatic beings the end of our *soma* is the end of our *psychē*. You cannot have one without the other. Against this position may be advanced the argument that our identity, our personhood, our 'soul', if you will allow the word, is not to be identified with our body. There is a logical distinction to be drawn between our bodies and ourselves. It makes sense, for example, to talk about standing back from ourselves in order to consider our position. This distinction creates logical space for talk about ourselves apart from our physical bodies to make sense. This logical gap means that language about our continued existence beyond our physical demise and the end of all our earthly life is not necessarily nonsense. I shall assume that such talk of life after death is not totally incoherent. Of course, this logical point is far from giving a reason as to why anyone should believe in life after death, let alone that such belief is true.

The second argument that seeks to reject all talk of life after death suggests that such beliefs are nothing more than a desire for personal survival. They arise from and express some psychological need. Now, I will agree that some kinds of Christian believing can be highly individualistic and selfish. Believing in this form becomes a kind of insurance policy, a blessed insurance perhaps, a subtle kind of seeking to save one's own life. So people believe solely in order to go to heaven, the very opposite of St. Francis Xavier's affirmation

> My God, I love Thee, not because
> I hope for heaven thereby;
> Nor because they who love Thee not
> Are lost eternally.

However, Christian believing, while I doubt it will ever escape a certain degree of selfishness, being the sinners we are, need not be so reduced. There are surely those who come near to loving God for God's own sake and glory:

> Not with the hope of gaining aught,
> Nor seeking a reward;
> But as Thyself hast loved me,
> O ever-loving Lord.
>
> E'en so I love Thee, and will love,
> And in Thy praise will sing,
> Because Thou art my loving God,
> And my redeeming King.[3]

There may be a great temptation to reduce faith to the self-centred longing for personal survival, but living Christian faith recognises that as a temptation. To believe and even long for the life eternal may have a different source than our personal desires. It may be properly religious when directed towards God. And again, even if the belief in life after death were shown to have a psychological grounding that, in itself, would tell us nothing about the truth of the affirmation.

The number of contemporary theologians who find belief in life after death untenable is not inconsiderable.[4] I note the challenge they present and the moral and intellectual weight of their arguments. But I remain a believer in the life of the world to come, life beyond our physical death. I shall assume this position without arguing further for it except to try to give some grounding to this belief as I reflect on its moral consequences.

It is often asserted that the Old Testament has no clear sense of life after death. At best, there is a developing theology of the relationship God has with his people, not simply as a people together but as individuals. The more there grew an increasing sense of relationship with God in Israel, so death was perceived as a challenge to that relationship. Psalms 16, 49 and 73 suggest this developing awareness. They contrast the life of the ungodly and proud with those who put their trust in God:

> When my soul was embittered,
> When I was pricked in heart,
> I was stupid and ignorant,
> I was like a beast toward thee.
> Nevertheless I am continually with thee;
> Thou dost hold my right hand.
> Thou dost guide me with thy counsel,
> And afterward thou wilt receive me to glory.
> Whom have I in heaven but thee?
> And there is nothing upon earth that
> I desire besides thee.
> My flesh and my heart may fail,
> But God is the strength of my heart
> And my portion for ever.
> (Ps. 73:21–26)

The point here to which I want to draw attention is that belief in life after death arises for theological reasons. It is what is believed about God that gives rise to what Israelites came to believe about themselves before God in life and death.

There is evidence within the New Testament of a debate in Judaism about life after death. The Sadducees, retaining a loyalty to the text and only the text of the Pentateuch, denied the resurrection of the dead. They taught that death was personal extinction. The Pharisees believed in a literal resurrection of the body at the Last Day. This is the faith that Martha confesses (Jn. 11:24). In contrast to these two groups, the Covenanters of Qumran believed in the resurrection life, in which they would be as 'the angels in heaven'. The Essenes seem to have taught the doctrine of the immortality of the soul.[5] What comes bursting into this first-century world is God's raising of Jesus from the dead. Whatever had been believed about life and death had to be reconsidered in resurrection light. What the first Christians proclaimed was not resurrection as a general concept but rather the particular raising up of this man. The last enemy had been met and had not utterly triumphed over him in the purposes of God. So, sin and death are not the end and this conviction rings through the New Testament. It is expressed in the great affirmation of Paul that 'neither death, nor life, nor angels, nor principalities, nor things present, nor things to come, nor powers, nor height, nor depth, nor anything else in all creation, will be able to separate us from the love of God in Christ Jesus our Lord' (Rom. 8:38–9). The relationship model, tentatively expressed in the Old Testament, now predominates. Everything must be looked at again in the light of the resurrection of Jesus. There are certainly implications here for the way that Christians will henceforth live and die.

What I wish to underline from both Testaments is the conviction that, if there is life after death, then it is so because of the nature, purpose and power of God. The natural thing for the humankind we know is for it to go down to the grave as the end. The Bible is quite clear about our mortality. But now, especially in the light of the raising up of Jesus, the 'end' of humanity is seen as being within a wider purpose of God whose hold upon his people remains faithful and sure in life and in death. The salvation that has come upon the world in Jesus Christ includes the overcoming of that which would rob us of God's own gift of life. The resurrection of Jesus proclaims, among other things, that he who had the first word and called everything into being has the last and final word and that too is a word of life. Resurrection, salvation, like creation, is a work of grace, consistent with the nature of God known in Jesus. Life after death, as life before death, is a gift of God. We may mar, scar and distort the gift, but nothing can take away the fundamental grace in creation and salvation, in this world and the world to come. Nothing, not even death, can stop God being what he is. In Christ he has affirmed that he is for us, though the cost of that divine affirmation is ever beyond human calculation or imagination.

All this amounts to a theological affirmation of some consequences. It immediately challenges any anthropology which describes humanity exclusively within its own terms. No 'natural' account will suffice. Humanity, in life, death and beyond death is always humanity before God. That we live at all is because of the divine nature. Thus there is no such animal as the Godless human. There are people who disobey and disbelieve in God. That is undoubtedly true. But simply by being human we are fundamentally, ontologically, related to God. True humanity, Christians believe, is revealed in Christ and in him humanity is inseparably related to God. To argue for the immortality of the soul as being natural to us, without reference to God, is to adopt a position that is not Christian belief. We were made by God for fellowship with God. That which is glimpsed in the Old Testament is proclaimed gloriously in the New. We are only truly ourselves in Christ. What appears to be natural to us is not to seek and do the holy will of our Father, to resist or ignore that fundamental relationship, let alone be grateful for it. The humanity we know and share lives in many ways over against God. As such it may have wistful thoughts but has no 'natural' hope of anything beyond the grave. But then, the Christian hope does not rest on the belief that life beyond death is natural to us. If life is to be ours then it comes as a gift. Our hope lies not in human nature but in the gracious God.

My argument is that the relationship between life in this world and life in the world to come is grounded in the nature of God. This, therefore, has present as well as future implications for the life of discipleship. What is yet to be received from God is already expressed in present grace.

For example, in the Fourth Gospel, a major theme of eternal life is explored. It is clear that this has both a present and a future reference. There is an element of looking forward to a salvation yet to be fulfilled. 'In my Father's house are many rooms; if it were not so would I have told you that I go to prepare a place for you?' (Jn. 14:2). Jesus speaks about raising up at the last day (Jn. 6:40). But there is also the strong contemporary emphasis, the fact of the life eternal now. 'Truly, truly, I say to you, he who hears my word and believes him who sent me, has eternal life' (Jn. 5:24). Resurrection, eternal life, judgment, all these eschatological themes have a strong present sense in John's Gospel. To live in God's salvation is not for the future alone but is a present gift and calling.

A duality of a slightly different kind can be found in Paul. Scholars working on Pauline ethics often draw attention to the fact that sometimes, for example, in the discussion on marriage in 1 Corinthians 7, the impending sense of the return of Christ influences Christian behaviour. So Paul seems to argue against Christians getting married, but the context is very particular. However, there are other occasions when it is not so much the *parousia* that shapes his moral teaching as his grateful awareness of the present life in Christ, *parousia* as presence. So vices are forbidden on the grounds of their incompatibility with the believer's present relationship with Christ. 'You are not your own; you were bought with a price. So glorify God in your body' (1 Cor. 6:19–20). For Paul, when anyone is in Christ there is a new creation (2 Cor. 5:17). This is the paradox of grace, for 'I have been crucified with Christ; it is no longer I who live, but Christ who lives in me' (Gal. 2:20). In Pauline ethics, sometimes the eschatological dimension predominates, at other times it is the present life in Christ. Either way, life depends upon the grace of God in Christ. The unity of Christian existence is in God's goodness revealed in Christ.

The gospel of the gracious God can, of course, be misrepresented in what Bonhoeffer called the offering of 'cheap grace'.[6] If Paul was hard on those who sought their salvation by way of personal works he could be equally as hard on those who, boasting in their new Christian liberty, presumed upon the grace of God. The antinomian interpretation of his gospel, wherein some could continue in sin that grace may the more abound, is a horrific thought for the apostle (Rom. 6:1). Anyone who could be so cavalier about Christian living has not appreciated either the sinfulness of sin or the costliness of grace. We cannot imagine what it must be for God to bear with the kind of world we have made and the sort of people we are, although the cross gives the all-important glimpse into what it costs God to be gracious. To see that and take it for granted, to presume upon the divine mercy, is to be on the way to spiritual death. So, although 'by grace you have been saved through faith; and this not your own doing, it is the gift of God – not because of works, lest anyone should boast', this carries the implication that 'we are his workmanship, created in Christ Jesus for good works' (Eph. 2:8–10). We are saved by grace and not by works, but we are not saved without works. To know eternal life is to do the will of God. To be in Christ is to live the life in Christ. Both present and future existence is, for the Christian, in Christ. It is possible by the saving, sanctifying work of the gracious Christ-like God.

So I would try to understand the relationship between ethics and belief. Both are grounded theologically in the grace of God. It is for this life as well as the future that Christ is our hope. Grace is sufficient for our need, in life and in death.

There are, therefore, both logical and theological reasons for arguing for a relationship between faith and ethics, between such an 'other-worldly' belief in 'the life of the world to come' and the present calling to Christian discipleship. The relationship is two-way, doctrine influencing ethics, ethics influencing what is taken to be doctrine. Both our present life, and the life of the world to come, are inseparably related in the grace of our Lord Jesus Christ. What difference, then, does it make to life now to believe in the life of the world to come as the work of grace? I shall conclude with these observations about our calling in Christ.

It seems to me that the authentic note of Christian existence, if I am right about my earlier arguments, is one of gratitude and offering. 'Freely you have received, freely give' (Mt. 10:8) sets the tone of Christian life even as it is at the heart of Christian belief. Spontaneity, generosity, sacrifice are characteristics of one who lives in Christian freedom. Here there is none of the thrust, grab and arrogance that, God forgive us, can be marks of our present personal and corporate Christian living. If we ground our ethics in obedience to law without grace, then the result inevitably is self-righteous spiritual pride or hopeless failure and dismay. Either way our existence is graceless in manifestation. If we ground our ethics in an easy liberal presumption on the goodness of God and human progress, then the same applies. Our hope of heaven is not best proclaimed by some arrogant claim to the certain knowledge by which we contemplate our personal salvation and the destruction of others. It rests on our hope of grace, of God being gracious. Gratitude, quiet trust and courage mark the life in Christ, as the offering of grateful praise is the song of heaven:

> Hallelujah!
> For the Lord our God the Almighty reigns.
> Let us rejoice and exult and give him the glory.
> (Rev. 19:6–7)

What I have been arguing for has implications for social ethics. The doctrine of grace, of life in Christ here and to eternity, implies an important relationship between earth and heaven. Indeed, the doctrine of the Incarnation requires it to be so. Christian living that is utterly earthbound, or only heavenly, is attempting to put asunder that which in God is joined together. It seems to me that there remains great value in the model for Christian existence of that of the pilgrim. It may be true that we have here no abiding city but we do have cities in which we experience the gracious call of God. Augustine's perceptive challenge to seek the shalom of the earthly city while journeying on is a true insight into Christian discipleship, and, as such, is of abiding value.[7]

In the chapel at the Northern Baptist College we have a tapestry mural. It is of the city of Manchester. You can make out the City Hall, the business centre, hospitals, library, university, council flats and even Luther King House. The artist has shot the work through with silver and gold thread so that when the light shines upon it the whole is transfigured. The piece is strongly evocative. It abides in the place of worship as a constant challenge to worshippers so to live and work in the mission of the gracious God that even Manchester be transformed more after what we imagine the kingdom of God to be. We shall be foolish, of course, if we identify our social and political programmes with the kingdom, yet the gracious calling to care for this city remains. If grace and salvation belonged only to the future it would have no present implication. But that is not the case.

To live and work in a large city can be both an experience of vitality and despair. The 'highs' and 'lows' of human existence are regularly a part of life. Despair can easily threaten to overwhelm. Yet a belief in life after death, understood as being grounded in the grace of God, means that hope is ever renewed. This is not some easy optimism. It is the faith that no situation is beyond the gracious God and his power to restore and redeem. This gives rise to that positive persistence that marks those who live and work in the inner city and other costly contexts. Worship, that celebration of the faith, is manna in the wilderness as heads are again lifted and the setting of the city and all its life is affirmed in the purposes of God. That is the work of grace, in old Manchester as sure as it is in the New Jerusalem. The eucharistic meal, that foretaste of the heavenly banquet, is the occasion when in and with Christ the things of earth are offered, only to be received again in grace.

This also sets in a particular context our talk about cheap and costly grace. The grace of our Lord Jesus Christ is revealed in the cross, that total outpouring of love in forgiveness, that birthpang in the labour that brings forth the new creation. Creation, new creation, theologically never happens in the city or anywhere else without costly suffering and pain-bearing love. God known in Jesus is gracious in this way. There are implications here for those who would be his people. Paul longed, '. . . that I might know Christ and the power of his resurrection, and may share his sufferings, becoming like him in his death, that if possible I might attain the resurrection from the dead' (Phil. 3:10–11).

Life in the city, or anywhere on earth for that matter, is ethically demanding. Some of the most important choices we have pressed upon us are far from clear of resolution. In such dilemmas there is a double temptation. One is to moral dogmatism, declaring what is right or wrong as if there were no real question at all. The other is to submit to indecision because of lack of certainty, so that nothing is done. Behind both of these responses is the fear of being wrong. But what if (1) the reality is that all our moral decisions have a quality of ambiguity about them and (2) more importantly, our life in Christ does not actually depend upon our always being right? Then we might be liberated from any belief that we are justified by correctness, orthodoxy or soundness. We might be free to take risks and live with uncertainty and integrity, trusting in our being saved not by our being right but by grace.

I cannot help but recall Dietrich Bonhoeffer again at this point. His anguish over the plot against Hitler is well known but he took the decision to play the double-life and ended in prison. From his cell came some of the most searching and inspiring theological writings of this century. He wrote about freedom and grace and death. Eventually, trusting in Christ, he was brought to the gallows. His last message to Bishop Bell was 'tell him that this is the end, for me the beginning of life'. His was a life of risk and faith.

He did not seek the martyr's death as the quick path to glory. That selfishness would have made impossible any standing with God in his suffering. Bonhoeffer was brought to death and, I believe, kept through death by grace. The road to freedom was marked by discipline, action, suffering and then,

> come now, thou greatest of feasts on the journey to freedom eternal; death, cast aside all the burdensome chains, and demolish the walls of our temporal body, the walls of our souls that are blinded, so that at last we may see that which here remains hidden. Freedom, how long we have sought thee in discipline, action and suffering; Dying, we now may behold thee revealed in the Lord.[8]

What is it that enables a young man to live, to die, like that except the reality of Christ? Here was a life, all of a piece. God is not introduced at the end to make it all come right and prove the oppressors were wrong all along. Here is life and death in trust of God.

There is no easy way we can think of death. It is designated by Paul as the last enemy (1 Cor. 15:26). For all the modern ways of trying to avoid its reality we know that death is an end of us. If there is to be a future, then it must come as gift. We are thrown back by death upon the utter mercy of God. Is it possible that we are not alone in the valley of the shadow? The gospel speaks of the good news of God who, in his Son, goes into the valley and himself suffers dying and death. Now our language is stretched to the limit. God knows in his Son god-forsakenness, dying and death. Yet God is not dead.[9] This is the proclamation of resurrection. It is the good news of God who raised Jesus from the dead. This is no doctrine of the immortality of the soul. It is the proclamation of the miracle of grace. It is supernatural not in being contra-natural, but by being that on which all creation, all nature, all life depends. Resurrection comes not as the joker in the pack but as the active, living word of the gracious God who in every place, and at every time, is working to raise up what is fallen. It is all grace upon grace even in the face of death.

What does it mean practically to believe in the life of the world to come? It means that gratitude and sacrifice mark the believer's life. It means throwing in our lot with God's present and costly struggle with the injustice and suffering of the world whenever it appears. It means having the courage to take difficult and risky decisions when they have to be made. It means, too, having hope whatever happens and even facing death in quiet trust. To be ungrateful and ungracious, to stand aside from the mission of God, to refuse the fearful responsibility of making choices, and to be anxious about our personal existence would suggest that the faith of the Christian church is either not being understood or not believed.

To believe as a Christian is to have faith and trust in the Christ-like God. This is the one who raised up Jesus Christ from the dead. This is the one who spoke the first word and whose final word will resound through creation. It is the word of life and grace and truth. Death is not the end for those in Christ for, by grace, we who are buried with him are also made alive in him and called to walk in newness of life (Rom. 6:3–4). It is grace that sought and found us, guides and keeps us, restores and enables us, and grace will lead us home.

Christ is our corner-stone,
On Him alone we build;
With His true saints alone
The courts of heaven are filled;

On His great love
Our hopes we place
Of present grace
And joys above.[10]

Notes

1. P. F. Strawson, 'A Review of Philosophical Investigations', *Mind* (1954).
2. C. Barrett (ed.), *Lectures and Conversations on Aesthetics, Psychology and Religious Belief* (Blackwell, 1970), 53–54.
3. The three verses quoted come from a hymn attributed to Francis Xavier, trans. Edward Caswell, *Baptist Hymn Book* (London: Psalms and Hymns Trust, 1962), 211.
4. See, for example, the discussion in P. and L. Badham, *Immortality or Extinction?* (SPCK, 1984), ch. 2.
5. See the useful essay by P. Badham, 'Death', in *A New Dictionary of Christian Theology*, ed. A. Richardson and J. Bowden (SCM Press, 1983).
6. D. Bonhoeffer, *The Cost of Discipleship* (SCM Press, 1976), 35–47.
7. *The City of God*, Book 19, ch. 17.
8. *The Letters and Papers from Prison* (SCM Press, 1973), 370–71.
9. For an important discussion of these themes see P. S. Fiddes, *The Creative Suffering of God* (Oxford University Press, 1988), 193–206.
10. From a sixth- or seventh-century hymn, trans. John Chandler, *Baptist Hymn Book* (London: Psalms and Hymns Trust, 1962), 267.

13

Facing the End

The apocalyptic experience in some modern novels

Paul S. Fiddes

In the last two decades there has been a spate of novels about the end of the world and the 'Last Things' that lead up to it. Using a suitably apocalyptic term, we might even speak of a great flood of apocalyptic novels, and the reason is surely not far to seek. It is not just that we have reached the year 2000, which sparks off millenarian images of crisis and cataclysm. We live at a time when the end of the world is now clearly conceivable, possible, and even – it sometimes seems – probable, for we live in the shadow of nuclear catastrophe.

The first novel I want to consider makes this point forcibly. In *Clowns of God* by Morris West, a pope is compelled to abdicate by the Roman Catholic hierarchy because he believes he has had a vision of the end of the world and the second coming, and has been called by Christ to proclaim that it will shortly happen. At first his close friend, a famous German liberal theologian Mendelius (based loosely it seems on the theologian Hans Küng) thinks he has succumbed to fanaticism; but Mendelius soon perceives that the vision is at least reasonable, in the light of the nuclear threat. As he puts it, 'the scenario of catastrophe is already a matter of informed speculation by . . . the military strategists'.[1] The inter-ballistic missiles are already targeted on the burial place of Peter the Fisherman.[2]

Two of the three novels I want to consider depict the End as a nuclear holocaust. The third, entitled *The End of the World News* by Anthony Burgess, portrays the End as caused by the collision of a rogue asteroid (code-named 'Lynx') with the earth. This reflects another scenario for apocalypse that occupies both the scientific and popular mind today, but the shadow of the bomb is also present in the novel; the president of the United States of America, just before the big bang, reflects that 'the world was already ending, though we tried to delude ourselves that this was not so . . . a war was coming . . .'[3] Lynx is, in a way, a cipher for the nuclear explosion itself. It is true that recently, following the writing of these novels, the overthrow of communism as a ruling political system in the Soviet Union and Eastern Europe in general has lifted some of the threat of nuclear war, but I venture to suggest that the dark shadow still remains. The question is still open as to whose hands will seize the nuclear command bunkers in the shattered empire of Moscow, and new nuclear powers have emerged: Israel, India and perhaps Iraq.[4]

We live then in an era when for the first time in history the end of the world is conceivable to all, whether they are religious or not. The apocalyptic novel takes a small step beyond the possibility with which we live, and portrays someone as announcing that the End is actually inevitable and near. While it also generally describes the End itself (though West's novel does not), the real interest of the plot is in the Last Things, that is the events leading up to the predicted end. The novel attempts to answer the question '*what does it feel like* when someone announces the imminent End, and we believe that he or she is right?' – that is, when we believe that person is correct within the world of the novel, which calls for a suspension of disbelief. This is why I have called my lecture 'the apocalyptic *experience*', rather than, say, 'the apocalyptic concept'.

A central figure in Burgess' novel is Dr Valentine Brodie, a writer of science fiction and a lecturer in English literature, who ends up being the leader of a spaceship which escapes the destruction of earth. Near the beginning he defines science fiction as being all about 'the ways in which ordinary human beings respond to exceptional circumstances imposed unexpectedly upon them . . . [such as] the end of the world'. One of his own stories is about a neurosis induced by a headache pill, which made people believe the end of the world was about to come; they had just been cured of this neurosis when 'the end of the world came in a form that nobody had expected'.[5] The apocalyptic novel is about response to the imminent end, before it happens; it is the experience of the Last Things that we are invited to enter. In West's novel the end is predicted by a pope; in Burgess' novel it is forecast by scientists; in a novel by Doris Lessing, *Shikasta*, it is predicted by extraterrestrial intelligences, envoys from an advanced spiritual civilisation called Canopus. For the reader, of course, it is the novel itself which is announcing the end, and it is we who are reacting to that announcement, whatever the mass of the public does in the plot. These three novels are in very different genres. West's book is in the style of an international thriller, Burgess' is a black comedy with a touch of fantasy, and Lessing's is in the style of science fiction. But all of them put the reader, imaginatively, into the position of believing that the End is about to come; we share the privileged knowledge of those few characters who know it is imminent (in the world of the story), and we live through the experience of 'before the End'. That is what I am calling 'the apocalyptic experience'; what does it feel like to live in the days just before the End?

Within that experience, three basic questions arise, which are raised in all the novels, though most articulately by the theologian Mendelius in *Clowns of God*. This novel, incidentally, is the most popular of the novels I have selected, the least literary in style and yet the most theologically acute. But in all the novels, I suggest that the way that these questions arise help us towards theological insights, not only about the End, but about living in the middle of history.

If the End is Inevitable, How Can we Prepare for it?

The first question that arises when we are plunged into the experience of the Last Things is how we are to behave in the face of an End that cannot be prevented, and an immediate problem that arises is simply how the End is to be announced. As Mendelius perceives in West's novel, to proclaim the End as imminent will cause panic and chaos; it will shut off the hope that seems to be necessary for life, and will promote the unhealthy growth of groups claiming to be the elect remnant.[6]

All the novels do in fact present a true elect, but the danger is of fanatical, exclusivist groups arising. It is a basic theme of all apocalyptic literature that there is a group of the chosen ones, the children of light, who will endure through the terrors of the last time and be granted salvation in some form. The danger is that such groups, believing themselves to be the chosen ones, will employ violence to survive: 'It was a nightmare possibility [thinks Mendelius] that the *Parousia* might be preceded by a vast and bloody crusade of the insiders against the outlanders.'[7] The pope, Jean-Marie (formerly Gregory XVII), wants at first to publish his encyclical announcing the imminent *parousia* of Christ, but Mendelius agonises over the destructive results this might have upon order and hope.

The answer to which the secular governments come in Burgess' and Morris' novels is to say nothing. Though experts know the end is imminent, the knowledge is to be suppressed and the people pacified by a mixture of lies, pleasures and repressive force. If the end is going to come anyway, why announce it at all? A sinister group of churchmen in *The Clowns of God* cooperate with the CIA (whose agent in this mission is dubbed 'the noon-day devil') in suppressing the truth of the crisis situation; they are appropriately called The Friends of Silence. By contrast, the answer formulated by the former pope and now freelance prophet, Jean-Marie, requires a religious perspective upon the End. He writes a series of letters to God, entitled 'Last Letters from a Small Planet', and presents their author as being 'Johnny the Clown', discussing the 'shutting down of the show' with the circus owner. These are given all the modern media hype and succeed in discussing the terror to come in a way that creates neither panic nor doctrinaire reactions. This indirect *form* of announcement – conversations with God – is, we notice, a form of story: like the novel itself it is at one remove from our lives, and yet gives us a way of experiencing them. The technique of proclamation by an apparently foolish story also points us to something about the *content* of the End, to which we shall need to return; as 'Johnny' (Jean-Marie) puts it in the fourth letter:

> When a man becomes a clown he makes a free gift of himself to his audience. To endow them with the saving grace of laughter, he submits to be mocked, drenched, clouted, crossed in love. Your Son made the same submission when He was crowned as a mock King, and the troops spat wine and water in his face . . . My hope is that when He comes again, He will still be human enough to shed a clown's gentle tears over the broken toys – that were once women and children.[8]

Jean-Marie here suggests that if the way to communicate the news of the End is the way of weakness, not the way of power, then this surely points to something about the nature of the last judgment itself.

While the question about how to announce the end is a particular concern of *The Clowns of God*, all three novels explore the more general question about what to do practically in the face of the coming catastrophe. The three stories come to the same conclusion: small communities must be gathered together, who may hope to survive the end in some way, and who will preserve the true values of humankind. While still pope, Jean-Marie envisages in his encyclical what the scenario for the aftermath of Armageddon should be: 'In the days of universal calamity the traditional structures of society will not survive . . . How then must Christians comport themselves in these days of trial and terror? . . . they must divide themselves into small communities, each capable of sustaining itself by the exercise of a common faith and charity.'[9] This is the 'Noah's ark' syndrome of all apocalyptic; there is a remnant, an elect but not an élite who pass through the flood of great waters. In West's novel we see a typical community being gathered in a remote Alpine valley, with the former pope as their resident priest. In Burgess' novel the ark is a spaceship that blasts off from earth just before the impact of the asteroid. Lessing's novel ends with a typical community building a new city high up in the Andes. We notice immediately that these authors do not have a total cosmic End in mind: there are survivors of the End, even if the time of survival may be short. Jean-Marie in his encyclical speaks of these communities sustaining their faith and continuing to give witness 'As they must do, even to the end.' How long that period will be to the absolute End remains open, and becomes more open as the novel proceeds; this points us to something open-ended about eschatology which is, as we shall see, by no means strange to biblical accounts of 'the End'.

But how then are these communities, these saving remnants, to be gathered? Again all these novels devote themselves to this question. *The End of the World News* makes the negative point that if the ark is to be a true one then it cannot be made by the exercise of human power. The story is an exposition of *how not* to build an ark. The man chosen to lead the project, Bartlett, is a person who is power-hungry, and whose motive is not the saving of human civilisation at all but the preserving of his own authority (he has a whole set of military uniforms he likes to wear). He drives the selected crew in a dictatorial way to prepare the ship, controlling them by the gun and by drugs when they step out of line. His power only begins to be broken when, on the eve of blast-off, he reads out a list he has prepared of the sexual couplings he proposes for the crew; the gale of laughter, in which even his accomplices join, breaks the influence of the drugs and enables a rebellion. The new leader is to be Valentine Brodie, writer of science fiction, the nearest thing they have to an artist, and previously rejected as a useless luxury on board the craft. Like the story of Johnny the Clown, weakness is stronger than human power.

The book makes this point in its very structure, which is an intertwining of three different stories. The account of the crushing of earth by Lynx is merged with an account of the life of Sigmund Freud (in the form of a television script) and an account of the visit of Leon Trotsky to New York in 1917 (in the form of the libretto for a Broadway musical). Again we notice the device of stories within a story which alerts us to the way we ourselves are in search of a story in our lives – particularly a meaningful ending. We discover later that the story of the asteroid is also a story within a story – being told to a classroom of children in the spaceship long afterwards. Now, these three stories are all about the end of history as humankind has known it; the impact of an asteroid is compared with the impact of Marx and Trotsky's doctrine of revolutionary history, and Freud's discovery of the role of the unconscious mind. All three cataclysmic events put an end to the world as it had been: the asteroid making a literal end, Marx and Trotsky putting an end to the old order of social hierarchy, and Freud putting an end to the era of 'childhood innocence'. Now, the point that Burgess makes is that each 'end' is made more chaotic by a power struggle. The emergence of a new civilisation is hindered by the struggle for control of the new situation by various groups and individuals. Freud's discoveries become confused by the struggle between the Jewish practitioners of Vienna and the clinical Protestants of Zürich (led by Carl Jung). Trotsky's socialist doctrine becomes entangled in the power games of the American workers (more concerned for patriotism and materialism than world socialism), and in the power struggle in his own Russian group. These events are parallelled by the struggle for power over the command of the spaceship, with the brilliant scientist who originated the project (Frame) betrayed as Freud and Trotsky are betrayed. The threefold fantastic structure of the book underlines that the elect who survive the end of the old era cannot be gathered by human concerns with power. A continual refrain in the musical about Trotsky's visit to New York is:

> All through history
> Mind limps after reality.
> And what is reality?

In this musical account of his life, Trotsky begins by thinking reality is dialectical materialism. He comes to see, however, that it is love – for Comrade Olga, and for his son. Positively, then, the elect are to be assembled by the weakness of love, by such gifts of love as are made by Johnny the Clown. In *The Clowns of God* the communities begin to gather spontaneously, as individuals share their love with each other, in what Jean-Marie calls 'common faith and mutual charity'. An early example of the remnant is a group of disabled and battered women who gather into a family in the Paris slums, read the Bible and pray together. One of them, a hunchbacked glass engraver, expresses their vision in the 'cosmos cup', a goblet portraying the sea in its lower part, the land in the upper. When asked by Jean-Marie where the humans are in the cosmos, she replies, 'They drink from the cup.'

In Lessing's novel, the communities are made up of those who are acutely aware of being involved in the lives of others, members one of another, incarnate in each other's consciousness; the term given to this is the 'substance of we-feeling' – SOWF for short. Many of the community members are gathered from mental hospitals where they have been banished as freaks. The report being made on the situation by the higher spiritual beings, the envoys of Canopus, stresses that when persons were 'directed to certain places temporarily or comparatively "safe", this was not necessarily with the idea of their personal survival. Certain types of Shikastan were able to respond very well: in fact their capacity to respond made them eligible.'[10]

The novel *Shikasta* is in fact the retelling of the history of the world in terms of the loss and regaining of the 'substance of we-feeling'. In her myth, Lessing portrays the earth, then called 'Rohanda' (the fruitful one), as being at first colonised by superior beings from another cosmic civilisation. These – called the Giants – built cities in geometrical patterns aligned to receive energy from Canopus, in a bond or 'lock' that is a fellowship of mind and spirit between the inhabitants of the mother planet and the colony; their whole architecture, that is, was designed to foster community. The Giants worked with the native population, to bring them into one harmony of life with them. But, through an accidental cosmic disorder, Rohanda has fallen out of the lock and become 'Shikasta', or the 'Wounded One'. The disaster could have been eased if the inhabitants had followed the way of 'Necessity', the laws laid down by Canopus for the period before the lock could be re-established; Lessing here, it seems, retells the Old Testament story of the giving of the law by Moses. Also, there was always some of the immanent influence of Canopus there, in the 'SOWF'. But the Shikastans have succumbed to a 'degenerative disease', under the influence of the evil planet of 'Shammat'; the marks of this disease are an excessive cultivation of the self as an individual, cutting a person off from a corporate life. This disease is finally to erupt in the nuclear catastrophe, and the elect communities are to rebuild the geometrical cities, preserving and fostering the vital 'substance of we-feeling'. In the last words of the novel, a young survivor is amazed at the way they had been living before the catastrophe, 'stumbling about in a thick dark, a thick ugly hot darkness, full of enemies . . .'; but now '. . . this will go on for us, as if we were being slowly lifted and filled and washed by a soft singing wind that clears our sad muddled minds and holds us safe and heals us and feeds us with lessons we never imagined. And here we all are together, here we are . . .'

So the elect communities, the Noah's arks, are to be built by the influence of love and mutuality, not by a power struggle. Lessing's novel also adds the point that if these communities are to be truly harmonious and mutual, there must be a proper racial and cultural mix within them. This is a continual concern of Lessing, a writer born in southern Africa, whose early novels were an attack upon apartheid. One of the problems of the last days is the way that the previously dominant white races have become demoralised in face of their ruin of the world through technology and their subjugation of the races of the south. This emotional reaction of guilt, 'seeing themselves entirely as villains, despoilers of the globe was', records the Canopean report on the century, 'as narrow and self-centred as their previous view when they saw themselves as God-given benefactors of the rest of Shikasta'. Both viewpoints were a failure to 'see things in interaction, a meshing of events, a reciprocation of needs, abilities, capacities'.[11] To prepare for the future, after the catastrophe, there has to be a restoration of balance, a healing of 'these woeful effects of imaginative understanding'.

A good deal of the novel relates the strategy Canopus employs for restoring a sense of 'the whole', opposing the 'Shikastan compartmentalism of mind'. A high-grade envoy of Canopus, Johor, becomes incarnate as a Shikastan (George Sherban) in the last days. His task, in preparation for the End, is to promote an international event organised by the youth armies of the world, a 'trial' of the old white races by the newly dominant black and yellow races – Africa, India, China. George Sherban (Johor) is the prosecutor, and the defendant – representing the white nations – is a man of the old British Labour left, John Brent-Oxford. He is actually another emissary of Canopus (Taufiq). The trial is so arranged that while the white nations are clearly indicted and condemned, the result is a defusing of hatred, an interchange of sympathy between accused and accusers, and some self-criticism by the prosecution. This so-called 'trial' which is tolerated in amused contempt by the authorities of the world turns out to have a power beyond any propaganda, creating the sympathy between races that was previously missing. Once again a spiritual foolishness is stronger than secular might, and it is significant that we do not realise until after the trial what its true purpose has been. It is also important that the greatest accusation against the white races is not just that they have been arrogant and contemptuous of others (though they have); it is that they just did not *notice* what they were doing – they overlooked and neglected those for whom they had responsibility. They lacked that 'substance of we-feeling'[12] which gifts us with the ability another novelist, Iris Murdoch, continually emphasises – the ability to notice others as they really are.

So these three novels, imagining a situation in which the End is imminent, make very similar proposals about how to prepare for it, about how to build the ark of salvation. But this very answer leads us on to a second major question that arises as we, as readers, share this situation.

What Sort of End is this Inevitable Event?

From the way the novels depict preparation for the event, it is clear that they do not think of the End as absolute (though West's novel is least definite about this). It is not the end of the whole cosmos, but a 'turn of an epoch'. The novels by Burgess and Lessing make this clear in their technique of flashback, with the End described from the further side, by a classroom lesson on the spaceship or by a report on the twentieth century in the Canopean archives.

We should be aware at this point of three traditional forms of eschatology that have been presented in Jewish-Christian prophetic and apocalyptic literature. Firstly, the End may be described as the literal end of this present cosmos, and its replacement by a totally different reality. Earth is envisaged as being so corrupt that it must be replaced by heaven. This is 'apocalyptic eschatology' proper, and may be called a view of 'consummation'. We find it in Jewish writings such as the book of Daniel, the Ethiopian books of *Enoch*, and some of the writings of the Dead Sea community. This kind of cosmic end is often schematised as the Two Ages, of present and future, and in Christian thought it is associated with the *parousia*, or final appearing of Christ in glory, associated with judgment and the resurrection of the dead. Christian interpreters of biblical texts (and particularly the book of Revelation) have further involved themselves in the complications of debating whether the final judgment will be preceded by a 'millennium' or thousand-year visible rule of God on earth, and if so whether the *parousia* precedes or follows this period of peace and justice. It is this cluster of images that I suspect the Drew Lecture on Immortality is usually concerned with, and I also suppose that most of its modern lecturers will interpret the term 'immortality' in the more Jewish-Christian mode of 'resurrection of the body' (i.e. the raising to new life of the whole person). Such an understanding certainly fits with the Jewish-Christian stress on eternity as a consummation of time and history, as opposed to the Platonic concept of an eternal soul.

Secondly, however, there is the kind of End that is a continuous, repeatable ending. Here 'end' is symbolic for the divine challenge that constantly comes to us, a breaking in of the eternal moment in the midst of time in a crisis that overturns all human preoccupations with the priorities of God's kingdom. This is often called 'realised eschatology', and it might be dubbed 'renewal' rather than 'consummation'. There is a good deal of this kind of eschatology in the New Testament. For example, while a large part of the book of Revelation contains a form of 'apocalyptic eschatology', its opening chapters present a different type of coming of Christ. He warns that he is about to come in judgment to the Seven Churches of Asia, and makes a promise of his coming to renewed table-fellowship with the faithful and true: 'Look, I stand at the door and knock' (Rev. 3:21). This seems to echo a very early Syriac tradition in the Eucharist, in which the cry 'Maran Atha' – 'O Lord, Come!' – certainly had a future reference, but also seems to have been an appeal to the risen Christ to come to his community here and now in the breaking of bread.[13] Such a breaking of God's 'eternal now' into the present moment was strongly articulated by the 'Dialectical Theologians' of the early part of the twentieth century, who affirmed the radical 'otherness' of God's Word and its power to strike into our existence 'from above', against theologians of the nineteenth century who had assimilated the kingdom of God to the progress of human history.[14]

Morris West's fictional theologian Mendelius presents these two types of eschatology to an audience of Protestant pastors in Rome, and they are divided about which they subscribe to. No one actually protests that these are not the only two alternatives, though West himself seems to point to another possibility in the very shape of the novel, a third kind of eschatology that also has an ancient lineage. There is what biblical scholars usually call 'prophetic eschatology' as distinct from 'apocalyptic eschatology'.[15] The idea of the 'Day of the Lord' in the Old Testament prophets is not the end of the world and history, but the day on which the Lord God will act decisively in judgment on his people and the nations, after which nothing will ever be the same again. It is a crucial turn in events; while it is not 'the' End of all things, it is not just one of a series of ends. The event about to happen is so decisive, so much a turn in human history, that it can only be described in language that seems to refer to the end of the world. Jeremiah, for instance, describes the 'Day of the Lord' as the sky rolling up like a scroll and the stars falling, but we realise as we read on that this picture of cosmic collapse is metaphor for a foreign army coming over the hill and razing Jerusalem to the ground (Jer. 4:23–6; cf. 1:14–15; 10:22).

Some New Testament scholars, and notably G. B. Caird, have similarly maintained that when Jesus spoke to his disciples about the imminent 'End' he has this kind of final event in mind – not the literal end of the world but a Day on which God will act in judgment and deliverance and after which nothing will ever be the same for his people.[16]

These three novels present that third kind of end, a decisive turn of the epoch in human history. Though there is terrible devastation, out of the ashes can come something new. This is the form of apocalypse we also find in William Blake, W. B. Yeats and even D. H. Lawrence.[17] While Blake saw the signs of the times in the French and American Revolutions, and hoped for a new coming of the spirit of the imagination embodied in Jesus, Lawrence's apocalypse is a more secular one; he believed that out of the breakdown in society caused by mindless industrialisation and the First World War could come a new era of human relationships. Lawrence was fascinated by the book of Revelation, or rather by the original myth he thought underlay it. The Christian adaptation of the myth had, in Lawrence's view, unfortunately removed the sexual element from the 'Woman clothed with the sun' and dismissed it into the form of the Scarlet Woman. The original story, he believed, told of a descent into hell followed by rebirth through sexual love, and in his own time he believed that the world was undergoing such a similar drastic catastrophe and renewal.[18] A rather different and surprising witness appears in Burgess' novel, in the figure of the popular evangelist Calvin Gropius: although depicted as a fundamentalist, he defines the second coming of Christ as 'a' final end, but not the absolute end: 'then there'll come the final conflict and the end of man as history has known him. Man will have to start again, as after the Flood.'[19]

The open nature of the apocalypse is brought out most clearly by Burgess in his threefold entertainment of Freud, Trotsky and Lynx. On the one hand, since the kind of 'ends' produced by the work of Freud and Trotsky are placed parallel with the 'end' caused by the asteroid, we are encouraged to think even of the destruction of earth as a new phase in human life. By an improbable chain of events, the only pieces of past human culture to leave earth on the spaceship are videotapes of the television play about Freud and the Trotsky musical, and the children of future ages find these works (though highly censored) to be more meaningful than the story of Lynx and their own origin, which they dismiss as a myth:

> Why aren't we told about the other myth? The myth that makes more sense than the one you've been telling us? . . . The one about the bad man called Fred Fraud who kept people strapped to a couch and the good one called Trot Sky who wanted people to do what he did and run through space . . .'[20]

On the other hand, the juxtaposition of Freud, Trotsky and the asteroid makes us see the ends represented by Freud and Trotsky in the light of Lynx. The children on the spacecraft cannot believe that they are actually on a journey, that the ship is designed for getting somewhere; they dismiss this as mere religious superstition: 'Your generation talks about a journey. Our generation knows we're just here. We've always been here . . .' We know they are wrong, and so we are the more ready to believe that we in our world are on a journey, that the ends produced by Trotsky and Freud are not final versions, an end to all movement and development. The end is a new beginning.

All three novels present the new born out of destruction. In the spaceship of *The End of the World News*, a really new culture has to be created. The removal of all music, art and literature from the survival capsule by the dictatorial Bartlett is seen as a blessing in disguise. It gives opportunity for the growth of new elements of the spirit. 'Where man is there has to be beauty, there have to be dreams,' says Val Brodie, but new dreams can emanate from human beings who are 'warm, wayward, imperfect, adaptable'.[21] Something new is needed; music created by 'the gross accidents of bowed catgut and blown reeds' has no place in a new world. There is, however, a continuity between the art of the past and the new art of the future, the patterns and accidents of chance based on the abstraction of numbers. So the unrespectable son of the evangelist Calvin Gropius who used to run a casino, Dashiell Gropius, is said to be the most important man on the ship; in his hands will be the organisation of games of skill or chance.

In *Shikasta* there is a similar birth of the new out of disaster. The catastrophe is the self-defeat of the evil Empire of Shammat. It had been parasitic upon the influence (the SOWF) that came from Canopus to Shikasta, drawing it off for its own ends; but in the last days, as a result of Shammat's own actions, 'the emanations from Shikasta herself were poisonous',[22] weakening Shammat's own life and causing divisions and wars within herself. So Shammat defeats Shammat, preparing for the new lock and new social relationship ('we-feeling') of Shikasta with Canopus. In West's novel there is a renewal of the sense of community and family in the face of disaster. Christ appears at the end, in the person of Mr Atha the speech therapist, whose full name is revealed to be 'Maran Atha', making the early Christian phrase which can either be translated 'O Lord come!', or 'The Lord comes'. Faced with Atha's claim to be the promised one, Jean-Marie makes the important point that the mere existence of a community gathered around Atha does not validate his identity; like other sects claiming to be the elect it could turn out to 'exploit people and turn them into hate'. When he challenges Atha to prove his messiahship with a sign, Atha sets a mentally handicapped child in the midst of the community; these children have already been given the affectionate title 'Clowns of God' by the founder of the institution in Paris in which they formerly lived, linking them with the motif of

'Johnny the Clown'. Christ/Atha refuses to give a sign by healing the child, since he says, 'I am not a conjuror'; instead he gives them the child as she is for a sign, for

> She will never pervert or destroy the work of my Father's hands. She is necessary to you. She will evoke the kindness that will keep you human . . . More! She will remind you every day that I am who I am, that my ways are not yours, and that the smallest dust mote whirled in darkest space does not fall out of my hand.[23]

This child is a sign of a new way of life that is possible, even in the wake of apocalypse.

Now, the way that these three novelists (one at least Christian) present the End, and set us imaginatively in the Last Days, has something to say to Christian thinking about apocalyptic. It offers the possibility of the third kind of eschatology, a decisive turn of events creating something new, even in the face of nuclear catastrophe. It warns us against a simple equation of any human act, however cataclysmic, with the divine act of the final coming of God to God's world. It urges us to consider the possibility that even nuclear warfare, reduction of the human race to a mere remnant and genetic mutation can still be a beginning and not a total end. It urges us to reflect upon a God who can do something new in the face of the worst human failing. Though none of these authors seems to have heard of the scenario of 'nuclear winter', the extension of the catastrophe into a continuing environment hostile to human life, their perception remains. The creative artist obviously finds it hard to conceive of, and depict, a total end – and this may well be a clue to the nature of God's own creativity.

Living in the imaginative world of these three novels will not lead the theologian to discount the first two meanings of the 'End', that is either a future new creation of the cosmos or the continuous challenge of our temporal existence by God's eternity. But it should prompt Christian theology to take all three meanings seriously, and to consider that they may in fact throw light on each other. Even apocalyptic eschatology in the sense of resurrection and transformation of the cosmos need not be considered simply as closure, the shutting down of creativity and the entrance into eternity as a static state. The other meanings of the 'End' invite us to envisage a future beyond a literal end of the present universe, in which God still goes on doing new things. Even if there were a total cosmic collapse, this could still be a beginning, a 'continuing consummation'[24] of growth and development of persons in new ways that we cannot imagine, but summed up in the symbol of the new creation.

Conversely, there are dangers in concentrating on the third kind of 'end', a decisive turn of an epoch in history, without the horizon of a future apocalypse. Prophetic eschatology, which is meant to place human achievement and organisation under the judgment of 'the Day of Lord' may be reduced and distorted into a validation of the present age. A particular political or ecclesiastical system may be legitimated by claiming that it represents here and now the visible rule of God on earth, that the 'turn of the age' has happened to bring it into being. Such millenarian claims have variously been made for the institution of the Christian church, dating from the ascension of Christ (so Augustine), for the Christian Empire of Constantine (so Eusebius), and for the period ushered in by the Enlightenment in Western Europe (so Gotthold Lessing). An apocalyptic hope for the final transformation of all creation keeps alive the hope of justice for the oppressed, and resistance to any system that claims absolute allegiance and submission.[25] Perhaps despite its intention, at least one of our three novels puts up a warning sign against loss of future hope. As we have already seen, the children in the schoolroom of the spacecraft, many centuries after the catastrophe of Lynx, refuse to believe that they are on a journey with a destination; they give worth only to the epoch to which this climactic turn of events has given birth, insisting that 'we've always been here, we always will . . . that's what matters'. It seems clear that a heavy price has been paid for the removal of the literature and music of the past from the survival capsule, which would have given witness to human hopes and desires.

These theological considerations about the nature of the end lead to a final question which, theologically, strikes to the heart of the matter.

Where is God in this End?

In a way that we do not expect from novelists, the theologian will ask about the relation of God to the End. In the first place, we are bound to enquire from a theological perspective whether the end has been *determined* by God. In what sense do we think that this End, which we are experiencing imaginatively, is inevitable? Is it determined in a practical sense, in that human beings are inclined to bring this kind of thing upon themselves, or in an absolute sense of a plot of the Holy Spirit in history? These questions raise the theological issue of 'types' and 'antitypes'. Catastrophic conflicts and the collapse of political and cultural systems in past ages might be said to be a type of the End. Similarly, the survival of a small group of religiously faithful people in the time when the books of Daniel or Revelation were written might be identified as a type of the 'elect' of the last times. But this typology can be understood in two ways: it could be thought to be (1) characteristic patterns of human experience that tend to emerge in similar ways from age to age, and will in the end emerge in an ultimate form; or it could be envisaged as (2) a predetermined pattern, a design of the Holy Spirit in history that brings past predictions to a necessary fulfilment.

The literary critic Frank Kermode makes the interesting point that while theologians have moved away from the latter, more archaic kind of typology, secular novelists have moved towards a secular version of it.[26] This is certainly true of D. H. Lawrence, who believed the breakdown of the old era and the emergence of the new was a predetermined pattern of history. In his own version of the three ages of history defined by Joachim of Fiore (of the Father, Son and Spirit), he proposed an age of the law (feminine) followed by the age of love (masculine), which was now about to be consummated in the age of the Spirit where law and love, masculine and feminine aspects, would be integrated. This kind of inevitable pattern of decline and rebirth, with its associated terrors and horrors, comes out clearly in Lessing's story, which is perhaps the least religious of the three we are examining. Lessing is writing a mythology, a piece of science fiction. She does not really believe that the earth has been colonised by extraterrestrials; this is a framework for talking about human loss and regain of the 'substance of we-feeling'. But when we remove the framework of external visitors, we are left with a view of human nature in which the final catastrophe is predetermined. In the myth, the lock with Canopus is lost by a predetermined movement of the planets, and it is bound to be re-established by a subsequent cosmic movement: 'Shikasta would again lock into place in the great plan that kept Canopus and her planets and colonies in an always harmoniously interacting whole.'[27] The enhancement of fellowship between the survivors after the catastrophe is again described in rather deterministic terms; now that the population of billions has been reduced to one per cent of the previous number, 'the substance-of-we-feeling, previously shared among these multitudes, was now enough to sustain, and keep them all sweet, and whole, and healthy'.[28] We may feel some sympathy with a critic of Lessing's novels, Carey Caplan, who charges Lessing with having given up hope in human development, and having become resigned to the long-term necessity of cosmic rhythms. This is a capitulation to a kind of cosmic imperialism, ironically not unlike the imperialism with which Lessing's native Zimbabwe was saddled in its colonial past as Rhodesia and against which she herself struggled.[29]

Curiously, then, the loss of a religious perspective seems to make the apocalypse more determined, not less. In fact, in the more religious approach of Morris West (and indeed, for all his jolly fantasy, in Burgess) there are protests against the idea of a 'divine assassin'. Mendelius finds the nuclear catastrophe itself to be less of a final horror than the vision of a God who 'can slam the lid on his own toy-box and toss it into the fire. That's why I can't preach your millennial catastrophe, Jean . . . not if it is inevitable, a horror decreed from eternity.'[30] In his own more gentle questioning of God in his letters of Johnny the Clown, Jean finds it hard to distinguish between a circus owner who simply knows from the beginning of the performance that his performers will murder each other and still lets it go on, and one who cuts the ropes of the big top himself. It still amounts to 'shutting down the show'.[31] Morris West is not a theologian, and never really resolves this question; he simply asserts that it is man, not God who presses the red button.[32] The theological issue is of course that of the foresight of God; exact knowledge of the future amounts, in the view of many modern philosophers of religion, to a predestined end.[33] Why announce the end at all, if nothing can be changed? asks Mendelius early on.[34] More rumbustiously, Valentine Brodie in Burgess' *End of the World News* protests that

> What I don't want to think about is some kind of predestined pattern, with God knowing all about it, creating man, knowing before he created him that he was going to be a wicked bastard, and so setting up this nice little cataclysm to get rid of him.[35]

West provides just a hint of a solution on the penultimate page of his novel, when Jean-Marie asks Atha/Christ, 'Tell me, can you really change your mind?' Like Abraham pleading for the people of Sodom and Gomorrah he wants to bargain with God, and he asks for more time before the End – 'enough to hope, work, pray, reason a little longer together'.[36] Atha does grant time, 'Not too much – but enough!', and the book ends with a postponement of the planned nuclear strikes. Yet in classical theological thought, a God who knows the future infallibly and has commissioned his servants to proclaim it, cannot change his mind. The Old Testament image of God's 'repenting' of what he had intended to do (e.g. Gen. 6:6, Jer. 18:8) cannot, Calvin tells us, be taken literally; it is simply an accommodation to our limited understanding.[37]

But such biblical expressions point us towards another picture of God and the fulfilment of God's purposes at 'the End' of human history. They invite us to consider a God who is omniscient in the sense of *knowing everything there is to know*. That is, God will not lack in knowledge if he knows perfectly all the things that are *actual* in the world of nature and history, and if he knows perfectly all the *potentialities* there are for the world. There is no need, with Aquinas, to insist that God knows all potential things *as already* actualities.[38] If God, by his own sovereign choice, has freely limited himself to knowing the future only in its potential, then there is plenty of room for the Creator to shape that potential in response to the acts and decisions of created beings. Indeed, there is room for God to invite human persons into a real partnership in making the future, to allow them to contribute to the divine creative project. This is why the note of biblical prophecy is not *prediction* and fulfilment, but *promise* and fulfilment; God is free to do new things in fulfilling his promises in quite unexpected ways. This kind of perception supports the first approach to typology in history that I mention above. As I have written more fully elsewhere,[39] this would also mean that while God knows the 'End' of all things as a certain event, the *content* of that event is open to be filled with the results of the partnership between Creator and creation. God knows that he will fulfil his purposes in bringing an end to evil and reconciling all things to himself, but the detail of what this will mean is quite open-ended. There is, then, room even for chance within the boundary markers of God's purposes for the universe. Thus far at least Dashiell Gropius in Burgess' novel is right to insist that his profession of gambler embodies a truth, that 'God's creation is all number and chance and play. Chance exists, though chance isn't really free will.'[40]

Apocalyptic novels, even if they do not explicitly ask what God is doing in the apocalypse (as do those by West and Burgess) are bound to raise profound theological questions. As we place such novels in dialogue with Christian eschatology, we must not expect them simply to verify certain theological answers; that would be to manipulate creative literature, pressing it into the service of the theologian. But the novels do allow us imaginatively to feel how various answers would strike us if we were in the times before the End. They do not prove that one model of divine action in the world is better than another, but they allow us to feel imaginatively how well each model fits and supports the reality of protest against an 'assassin God'. And we cannot help noticing that in Burgess' story at least, it seems more satisfying for Dashiell Gropius the expert in games of chance to be on board the spaceship, rather than his father whose name expresses his theology – *Calvin* Gropius.

There is also a second aspect to this question about what God is doing in the apocalypse. The theologian asks, what form will the *parousia* of Christ take? How will the one who has been appointed Judge of all appear? How will the Christ come? West's character Mendelius asks himself this constantly: 'What are we going to see? What will distinguish the Christ from the AntiChrist?' The three novels suggest an answer in the form of their plot; it is that Messiah comes quietly, hidden as a man among men, since it is in this kind of coming that he can foster the development of the small communities that are the proper response to catastrophe. In West's book, Christ comes as an insignificant speech therapist, Mr Atha, nursing Jean-Marie back to the use of words after a stroke. In Lessing the emissary Johor is born as a man, George Sherban, just as previous emissaries from Canopus had come as the great religious leaders of the past (including Jesus of Nazareth). Both Atha and Sherban travel widely and incognito throughout the world, fostering in an unspectacular way the growth of the communities. In Burgess' novel the case is not so clear, but the birth of a child, Joshua, does indirectly create the true community of the remnant; it is because the pregnant mother is determined to get on board the spacecraft that she causes the overthrow of the tyrant Bartlett, the entrance of the proper leader Val Brodie, and the inclusion of the gambler Dashiell. The child had been conceived in the first place from the aphrodisiac effect of Calvin Gropius' preaching, and so it is appropriate that the mother marries his son, Dashiell. We hear right at the end that this child Joshua 'believed he was the Son of God. He gave us our first space religion' – and a precocious pupil in the space classroom underlines the vulnerability of this gift by adding immediately, 'Which nobody believes in any more.'[41]

The theologian notices that these various presentations of a 'second coming' of a Messiah, Christian and non-Christian, tend to be modelled on the original coming of the Christ in the Christian story. They underplay the newness and the unexpected nature of the *parousia* in the New Testament, which leads to the command to 'be on the watch'; because the unveiling before the whole cosmos of the lordship of Christ, which is at present hidden, belongs to the new creation and not to the old in which we still live, it can only be described in images that keep open what cannot be wholly anticipated. But these novelistic accounts do underline the elements of humility and self-giving that were characteristic of the incarnation of the eternal Word of God as Jesus of Nazareth, and are no less needed in the face of final catastrophe. The imminence of the End calls for nothing less than the self-effacement of the Clown. It is after writing the letters to God that Jean-Marie comes to believe that the image of sovereignty which belongs to the *parousia* has to be rethought. His letters are all about childlike love, and so Jean concludes that 'the final Coming and the final Judgement itself must be acts of love. If they are not, then we inhabit a chaos created by a mad spirit, and the sooner we are released from it into nothingness the better.'[42] His practical question about how to proclaim the end has led him to a vision of its content.

Novels of the End offer the Christian reader the opportunity to see a similar vision. By living imaginatively in the days before the End, we are forced to ask questions about the nature of the End, to test and refine our beliefs in the final fire.

Notes

This present article is a slightly revised version of the Drew Lecture delivered at Spurgeon's College in 1991. Some parts of it have been drawn upon in chapter 8 of my book, *The Promised End. Eschatology in Literature and Christian Doctrine* (1999).

1 Morris West, *The Clowns of God* (London: Hodder & Stoughton, 1981), 44; cf. 25, 61, 129.
2 Ibid., 67.
3 Anthony Burgess, *The End of the World News: An Entertainment* (London: Hutchinson, 1982), 376.
4 Since the original delivery of this lecture, Pakistan must be added to this list, and Iraq's capability in weapons of mass destruction remains unknown.

[5] Burgess, *End of the World News*, 29.
[6] West, *Clowns of God*, respectively 105, 116, 96, 316.
[7] Ibid., 96.
[8] Ibid., 316.
[9] Ibid., 41.
[10] Doris Lessing, *Canopus in Argos: Archives. Re: Colonized Planet 5. Shikasta. Personal, Psychological, Historical Documents Relating to Visit by Johor (George Sherban), Emissary (Grade 9), 87th of the Period of the Last Days* (London: Jonathan Cape, 1979; repr. London: Panther Books, 1981), 426.
[11] Ibid., 428–9.
[12] Ibid., 394, 406.
[13] This view is, for example, taken by Austin Farrer, *The Revelation of St. John the Divine* (Oxford: Clarendon Press, 1964), 83. It is opposed, after a useful and careful discussion, by Richard Bauckham, *The Climax of Prophecy: Studies on the Book of Revelation* (Edinburgh: T. & T. Clark, 1993), 104–9.
[14] See e.g. Karl Barth, *The Epistle to the Romans*, trans. from the Sixth Edition by E. C. Hoskyns (Oxford: Oxford University Press, 1933), 497.
[15] This distinction was first clearly made by Stanley Frost, *Old Testament Apocalyptic* (London: Epworth Press, 1952).
[16] G. B. Caird, *The Language and Imagery of the Bible* (London: Duckworth, 1980), 265–71.
[17] See Frank Kermode, 'Lawrence and the Apocalyptic Types', in C. B. Cox and A. E. Dyson (eds.), *Word in the Desert* (London/New York: Oxford University Press, 1968), 14–38. Also now Kermode, 'Waiting for the End', in Malcolm Bull (ed.), *Apocalypse Theory and the Ends of the World* (Oxford: Blackwell, 1995), 250–63.
[18] D. H. Lawrence, *Apocalypse*, with an introduction by Richard Aldington (Hamburg: Albatross Press, 1932), chs. XV, XXIII.
[19] Burgess, *End of the World News*, 66.
[20] Ibid., 388.
[21] Ibid., 370.
[22] Lessing, *Shikasta*, 423.
[23] West, *Clowns of God*, 397. Cf. Jean-Marie's dream of the child in the cave, 307.
[24] This phrase is from John Macquarrie, *Principles of Christian Theology* (London: SCM Press, rev. edn., 1977), 209ff.
[25] On 'ecclesiastical and political millenarianism', see Jürgen Moltmann, *The Trinity and the Kingdom of God*, trans. Margaret Kohl (London: SCM Press, 1981), 191–201. Now also see, for greater detail, Moltmann, *The Coming of God*, trans. Margaret Kohl (London: SCM Press, 1996), 146–201.
[26] Kermode, 'Lawrence's Apocalyptic Types', 14–15.
[27] Lessing, *Shikasta*, 421.
[28] Ibid., 122.
[29] Carey Caplan, 'Britain's Imperialist Past in Doris Lessing's Futurist Fiction',

in Carey Caplan and Elen C. Rose (eds.), *Doris Lessing, The Alchemy of Survival* (Ohio: Ohio University Press, 1988), 149–58.

30 Morris, *Clowns of God*, 123.

31 Ibid., 295–6, 306.

32 Ibid., 123.

33 E.g. Richard Swinburne, *The Coherence of Theism* (Oxford: Clarendon Press, 1977), 167–172.

34 West, *Clowns of God*, 37–8.

35 Burgess, *End of the World News*, 252.

36 West, *Clowns of God*, 398.

37 Calvin, *Commentary on Genesis 6.6*.

38 For this approach to divine omniscience, see Richard Swinburne, *The Christian God* (Oxford: Clarendon Press, 1979), 130–34; Charles Hartshorne, *A Natural Theology for our Time* (La Salle: Open Court, 1962), 19–20, 79–82.

39 Paul S. Fiddes, *The Creative Suffering of God* (Oxford: Clarendon Press, 1988), 102–6.

40 Burgess, *End of the World News*, 369.

41 Ibid., 388.

42 West, *Clowns of God*, 319, 322.

14

Religious and Near-Death Experience in Relation to Belief in a Future Life

Paul B. L. Badham

The Primacy of Experience in Religious Believing

Claims to personal experience seem to be at the heart of religion. For although some come to belief by inheritance, some by acceptance of a revelation-tradition and some by rational argument, the belief remains at 'second-hand' until it has been appropriated through some kind of personal awareness. Only when faith is thought to have a real basis in the experience of the individual can it be said to be existentially real to the believer. In contemporary philosophy of religion, such experience is given a key role, in that in a religiously ambiguous world which can be interpreted theistically or atheistically, it is the additional evidence of personal religious experience which for the believer tips the balance in favour of theism (Hick, 1989; Mitchell, 1973; Swinburne, 1979).

In this context beliefs about a future life might seem to be an exception, for apart from Christian claims concerning Jesus Christ, no one who has died has returned to give assurance of a future hope, and it might seem therefore that of necessity this must be one belief that is forever without an experiential foundation. The purpose of this paper is to argue that this is not the case. Though there is no direct evidence of a future life there are features both in religious experience, and increasingly today in near-death experience, which do provide an experiential foundation for a future hope.

Experience and the Finality of Death

Normal everyday human experience has always pointed to the view that death is the end of any meaningful personal existence. This is very forcefully expressed in the Old Testament: 'We must all die. We are like water spilt on the ground which cannot be gathered again'; 'Human beings perish for ever like their own dung.' They are 'of dust and will return to dust'. In the grave they will rot away 'with maggots beneath and worms on top'; 'In that same hour all thinking ends' (2 Sam. 14:14; Job 20:7; Gen. 2:7; Is. 14:11; Ps. 146:4). It is true, of course, that for a generation or two the dead will live on in some kind of shadowy half-life in the memories of those who knew them. John Bowker argues that such memory traces explain why so many ancient cultures had a notion of the dead having some kind of thin, insubstantial, shadowy existence underground (the Hebrew *Sheol* or Greek *Hades*). But in neither ancient Greece, Mesopotamia, India, China nor Israel was there any notion that life in this 'underworld' had any real significance or substance. There was 'nothing after death to which one could look forward . . . For our ancestors, there was definitely no future in dying' (Bowker, 1991: 30). In the face of this universal human experience of death as the ending of personal life how is it that notions of a 'real' life after death ever got off the ground at all? To answer this question I think we need to look at those features of human experience which, as a matter of historical fact, did lead to the emergence of such beliefs.

The Experiential Basis for Belief in a Future Life in the Judaeo-Christian Tradition

Ancient Israel is a dramatic example of how beliefs can change in the light of new experiences. As we have already seen, the classic position in ancient Israel was that death must mean extinction because human beings are irreducibly physical entities who are totally at one with nature. They 'have no advantage over the beasts' and are 'like the grass that withers and the flowers that fade' (Ecc. 3:19; Ps. 90:5). However, in spite of this, a firm belief in a future life gradually evolved as religious experience came to be understood in personal terms. What appears to have happened is that conviction of a future hope grew out of the experience of individuals who came to believe that they were experiencing a personal relationship with God. This was not the original form of early Judaism, which at first thought only of a relationship between God and the whole nation of Israel. But from the time of the exile in Babylon onwards (from 597 BC) the idea of a covenant between God and humanity was increasingly seen in individualistic terms. As that conviction developed so the thought of Israel moved along a path which led to the flowering of the future hope in the intertestamental period. As Wheeler Robinson puts it, 'The faith of the Old Testament logically points towards a life beyond death, because it is so sure of an inviolable fellowship with God' (Robinson, 1962: 103). The foundation for the faith ultimately arrived at was the conviction that if human persons can really enjoy a personal relationship with God which God values, and if the believer really matters as a unique individual to the all-powerful and all-loving God then God will not allow that individual and that relationship to be destroyed by death. Throughout the subsequent history of monotheism this conviction has remained dominant. As Edward Schillebeeckx argued:

> The breeding ground of belief in life after death . . . was always seen in a communion of life between God and man . . . Living communion with God, attested as the meaning, the foundation, and the inspiring content of human existence, is the only climate in which the believer's trust in life after death comes, and evidently can come to historical fruition
> (Schillebeeckx, 1980: 797).

We shall see later that this is not wholly correct in that belief in a future destiny has also come into being in some Buddhist cultures. But within the Jewish, Christian and Islamic cultures Schillebeeckx is undoubtedly right that the experience of a direct encounter between God and the individual soul has been the prime foundation for assurance that death can never triumph over that divine love.

The Claim to Have Experience of 'the Risen Christ'

Within the Christian tradition the belief, held in common with Judaism and Islam, of knowing God has been supplemented by a conviction that the death and resurrection of Jesus provide further ground for confidence in a future hope. For many Christians faith in the resurrection of Jesus is a faith based on historical considerations, namely that the disciples' experience of seeing the risen Christ was the fount and origin of Christianity. But from the time of St Athanasius onwards other Christians have asserted a more direct experiential base (Athanasius, 1963: 60–61). They believe that Jesus rose from the dead because they claim to have come to know him directly as their personal saviour. For such Christians the primary experiential knowledge of the defeat of death is derived from this evangelical claim to know the risen Christ in their own lives.

Religious Experience Today

However, there is a problem for Christianity in contemporary Europe in that religious experiencing in its classic form does not appear to be anything like as prevalent as it once was. Many students of Religious Studies find difficulty with Otto's classic book *The Idea of the Holy* (Otto, 1923) because the sense of the numinous which Otto argued is the basis of religion seems to be something of which some have little experience. Otto assumed that a profound sense of awe and wonder at a fascinating and tremendous mystery identified as the presence of the divine was normative within Christian worship. But it does not appear any longer to be characteristic of contemporary church life in modern Europe. Similarly, the classic hymns of personal devotion display an intensity of religious feeling which goes beyond the more communal and social emphasis of much modern hymnody. And there is no longer the same expectation as there was in the past that ordinands would necessarily have felt a direct 'call' in the way church tradition presupposes. This may be illustrated by the fact that in current controversies over the ordination of women to the Christian priesthood the argument from women's sense of being called by God to this ministry has not been given much weight.

It is of course true that a succession of empirical studies has shown that religious experience of a kind is far more widespread than often supposed. For example, in David Hay's *Religious Experience Today* it is claimed that as many as 65% of postgraduate students of education in England had a religious experience which mattered to them (Hay, 1990: 59). But in most of these cases the experience seemed very diffuse and hard to clarify. The main impression left from studying them is how non-specific and vague they really were, and how different from the intense life-transforming experiences characteristic of classic conversion experience. Very few modern accounts describe the kind of personal relationship with God which historically formed a foundation for belief in a communion of love which not even death could end.

Near-Death Experiences

In this context the recent upsurge in reports of near-death experience seems particularly important. This is often a profound and life-changing experience which people never forget. It shares many of the characteristics of the deepest religious experiences known to humanity, and yet through the spread of modern resuscitation techniques it has become available to hundreds of thousands of ordinary people. Twenty-five thousand such cases have now been collected from all over the world (Kübler-Ross, 1991: 47; Becker, 1993: 77) and, as medical technology advances, so every year does the number of people who have been resuscitated from apparent death, and of these a significant proportion (somewhere between 10 and 35%) have a series of vivid experiences. The experiences include reports of 'leaving the body'; 'looking down on the resuscitation attempts'; 'feeling a sense of life-review'; 'meeting deceased relatives and friends' and enjoying a series of religious experiences of a mystical type including 'encounters' with a bright light sometimes perceived in personal terms and identified with a figure from the percipients' own religious traditions. The pattern of experiencing appears to be common across religious traditions, cultures and worldviews, though naturally the terminology used in the religious descriptions is culture-specific.

Earlier Accounts of Similar Experiences

These experiences are not new. They go back to the dawn of human history and it seems likely that in many cultures they gave rise to a belief in the possibility of a future life. Mircea Eliade suggests that some ideas about life after death may have originated in Shamanistic trances which characteristically include a notion of the Shaman leaving his body (Eliade, 1977: 17). Daniel van Egmond argues that

> it is highly probable that some types of [religious] experience suggested to man that he is able to exist independently of his physical body. For instance, the so-called near-death experiences, out-of-the-body experiences and shamanistic trances are easily interpreted this way. Indeed, the occurrence of altered states of consciousness is such a common feature in most cultures that it is very probable that such experiences were interpreted as perceptions of so-called 'higher worlds' (Van Egmond, 1993: 15).

Dean Shiels' research into out-of-the body experiences in primitive cultures showed that 64 of the 67 cultures investigated believe in the reality of such states. He tested the conventional explanations given for such phenomena by western scholars and found that they did not apply in these cultures. His conclusion was that 'When different cultures at different times and in different places arrive at the same or a very similar out-of-the-body-belief we begin to wonder if this results from a common experience of this happening' (Shiels, 1978).

Most claims to out-of-the-body experience occur near the point of death. It seems likely, therefore, that it is the fact of such reported experiences which has given rise to the traditional description of death as 'the moment when the soul leaves the body'. The experience of simply watching a person die leads to a much simpler picture of death as 'the moment when the person breathed-out (expired) for the last time'. The fact that this description has been felt to need supplementation suggests that other facts of human experiencing have been given weight as well as what is most immediately apparent.

However, in the past the distinctive near-death experience happened only to a tiny handful of people who had spontaneously recovered from apparent death or who had, after much prayer, meditation, fast and vigil, seen comparable otherworldly visions. When such an unusual experience happened to someone it was deemed to give that person very special authority on religious matters.

St Paul's 'Out of the Body' Experience and Heavenly Visions

Consider, for example, the situation of St Paul. On what did his faith in the end ultimately depend? One's immediate response might be to cite 1 Corinthians 15 and his rehearsal there of the faith handed on to him. Yet it is intriguing that when the Corinthians challenged St Paul's authority and asked him on what authority he spoke and acted, he did not appeal to the tradition he had received from others but instead felt impelled to describe his own foundational experience:

> It may do no good but I must go on with my boasting; I come now to visions and revelations granted by the Lord. I know a Christian man who fourteen years ago (whether in the body or out of the body I don't know – God knows) was caught up as far as the third heaven. And I know that this same man, (whether in the body or apart from the body I don't know – God knows) was caught up into paradise, and heard words so secret that human lips may not repeat them. About such a man I am ready to boast.
> (2 Cor. 12:1–5)

Few commentators doubt that St Paul was speaking autobiographically here, especially as a few verses later he laments that 'to keep me from being unduly elated by the magnificence of such revelations I was given a thorn in the flesh ... to keep me from being too elated' (2 Cor. 12:7). What is intriguing for our present purpose is that St Paul's experience included out-of-the-body experiences and visions of paradise, both of which are key features of the near-death experience.

Commenting on these verses in 2 Corinthians 12, St John of the Cross, the great sixteenth-century mystic, remarked that such experiences normally only occur when the soul 'goes forth from the flesh and departs this mortal life'. But in St Paul's case he was allowed these visions by special grace. Such visions, however, occur 'very rarely and to very few for God works such things only in those who are very strong in the spirit and in the law of God' (John of the Cross, 1957: 84). St John of the Cross almost certainly had a comparable experience himself, as evidenced by his poems where he speaks of 'living without inhabiting himself', 'dying yet I do not die' and as 'soaring to the heavens' (John of the Cross, 1960: 51; see also 47–57). (That secular love poems of that time use the phrase 'dying that I do not die' as a sexual metaphor does not prevent us from supposing that St John was using the expression in its primary sense.)

What is intriguing is that St Paul regarded his experience as giving him unique insight and authority, and St John of the Cross speaks of the experience as coming very rarely and to very few. What I suggest is that modern medical technology has, as it were, 'democratised' and made available to thousands an experience which has from the beginning lain at the heart of much of the world's religious perceiving and formed an important experiential basis for the future hope.

Near-Death Experience and the *Tibetan Book of the Dead*

One of the most striking features of near-death experiences is that they are not confined to theistic traditions but appear to be common across all human cultures. In particular they appear to have played a key role in both Tibetan and Japanese forms of Buddhism. In both these Mahayana traditions we can see very close parallels between contemporary near-death experience and that which seems to be reflected in their foundational scriptures. This has been widely noted in connection with the *Bardo Thodol* (the *Tibetan Book of the Dead*). The descriptions of what happens after death in this work correspond very closely to what contemporary near-death experiencers report (Evans-Wentz, 1957: 98, 101). Consider, for example, how contemporary near-death experiencers report looking down on their bodies, observing the distress of their relatives, and the activities of the medical staff. So too in the *Tibetan Book of the Dead* we read that when the person's 'consciousness-principle gets outside its body' he sees his relatives and friends gathered round weeping and watches as they remove the clothes from the body or take away the bed.

Of contemporary near-death experiencers 72% report seeing a radiant light which they often describe as a loving presence and sometimes name in accordance with a religious figure from their own traditions. A few experience a review of their past life and many experience a range of mental images which have led many commentators to suggest that the next stage of existence could be a mind-dependent world. Once again this is precisely what the *Tibetan Book* says, for it speaks of the dying person seeing the radiant, pure and immutable light of Amida Buddha before passing into what is explicitly described as a world of mental-images, in which whatever is desired is fulfilled, and in which everything that is seen is in form an hallucination reflecting the karma of the percipient.

Concerning the Being of Light which contemporary experiencers see and name in accordance with their own tradition, this also is in accord with the *Tibetan Book of the Dead* where we read, 'The Dharmakaya [The Divine Being] of clear light will appear in what ever shape will benefit all beings.' Commenting on this verse for his English translation, Lama Kazi Dawa-Samdup says, 'To appeal to a Shaivite devotee, the form of Shiva is assumed; to a Buddhist the form of the Buddha Shakya Muni; to a Christian, the form of Jesus; to a Muslim the form of the Prophet; and so for other religious devotees; and for all manner and conditions of mankind a form appropriate to the occasion' (Evans-Wentz, 1957: 94). A similar consideration applies when thinking of the vivid imagery which abounds in the *Tibetan Book*. These mental images are not thought of as universalisable. Rather, as Lama Anagarika Govinda points out in his introduction, 'The illusory Bardo visions vary, in keeping with the religious or cultural tradition in which the percipient has grown up' (Evans-Wentz, 1957: xii).

When we examine contemporary near-death accounts this is precisely what we find. What is seen appears to be cross-cultural, but how it is named depends on the religious or non-religious background of the believer. Thus it is only to be expected that a Christian evangelist in the Anglican 'Church Army' would say that he had seen Jesus (BBC, 1982), whereas the notable atheist philosopher A. J. Ayer would say, 'I was aware that this light was responsible for the government of the Universe' (Ayer, 1992). What matters is that both contemporary observers seem to have had an experience which had much in common.

Near-Death Experiences in Pure-Land Buddhism

The place where contemporary experience and foundational religious beliefs come closest together is in the Scriptures, and even the contemporary architecture of Pure-Land Buddhism, particularly in that of the True Pure-Land Sect (Jodo Shinshu Buddhism). Looking first at the Scriptures three features spring to mind. The first is that the Buddha's Pure Land seems to have many features in common with the idea of a mind-dependent world, reflecting the karma of the individual. 'All the wishes those beings may think of, they will be fulfilled, as long as they are rightful' (Conze, 1959: 233). This idea spelt out with many examples in the *Sukhavativyuha-sutra* (The Pure-Land Sutra) corresponds exactly with some contemporary descriptions by resuscitated people.

The second striking feature is the experience of so many resuscitated people of seeing and being welcomed into the world beyond by a wonderful and gracious 'Being of light'. They sense that this Being knows them completely and has limitless compassion to them in welcoming them into the life beyond. We have already noted the tendency of those who see this vision to identify this Being with a religious figure from their own tradition such as Jesus or Rama. But it is interesting that the descriptions given of the role of this being do not accord with traditional expectations in the Christian or Hindu traditions but do accord with the Pure-Land vision of Amida Buddha as 'The Buddha of Infinite Light and Boundless Life' who has vowed to appear at the moment of death. 'When they come to the end of life they will be met by Amida Buddha and the Bodhisatvas of Compassion and Wisdom and will be led by them into Buddha's Land' (Bukyo Dendo Kyokai, 1980: 218). This combination of radiant light, wisdom and compassion corresponds precisely to the descriptions given by the resuscitated of their experience of this encounter.

A third common feature is that the imagery in which the Pure Land is described is remarkably similar to the descriptions of the land beyond given by the resuscitated. I am thinking here of the imagery in the *Smaller Sukhavativyuha-sutra* (The Smaller Pure-Land Sutra) of a wonderful garden with flowers of intense vividness of colour, of bright jewels and of 'the air vibrant with celestial harmonies' (Bukyo Dendo Kyokai, 1980: 220). This corresponds almost verbatim to a description given on BBC television by a young resuscitated child concerning what she saw, and I was particularly struck by the way she too stressed the intensity of the colouring of the various flowers and jewels (BBC, 1982). Yet the rest of the description is also very interesting, for the imagery of a beautiful garden to describe heaven is common to all religious traditions, as is the notion of celestial music, and indeed the word 'paradise' was originally the word used for a Royal garden or park on earth.

The link between contemporary near-death experience and the Pure-Land religious tradition seems exemplified in the recent building of a Great Buddha Statue by the Tokyo Honganji. The statue itself was completed in 1991 and the Tokyo Honganji claim it to be the largest statue in the world. It is situated in the heart of the traditional burial grounds of the Pure-Land Sect. These burial grounds are being surrounded by beautiful gardens. One is permitted to enter the Buddha statue and ascend to eye level. As one enters the lift the lights go out and one experiences the sensation of rising rapidly upwards through a tunnel of darkness till one reaches the top. Then as one leaves the lift one sees a pillar of radiant white light reaching upwards and one looks out at the world through the eyes of Buddha and what one sees is designed to evoke images of Buddha's Pure Land, and the paradise described by past and present near-death experiencers.

What Contemporary Experiencers Report

So far I have discussed the NDE (near-death experience) in general terms and suggested that knowledge of contemporary experiences throws considerable light on key experiences of St Paul and of St John of the Cross in the Christian tradition, and on what appears in foundational Tibetan and Japanese texts in the Buddhist tradition. I propose now to look in more detail at the largest and most detailed survey of contemporary experiences to see what these tend to have in common and what the impact on the experiencer usually is.

Since the pioneering works of Raymond Moody and J. C. Hampe published independently of each other in the USA and Germany in the early 1970s (Hampe, 1979; Moody, 1973) there has been a flood of individual accounts, scientific surveys and television documentaries (Ring, 1980; Becker, 1993; Blackmore, 1993; Fenwick and Fenwick, 1995). Most of these are based on relatively small samples of between 50 and 100 cases, but recently Peter and Elizabeth Fenwick have published a comprehensive survey based on 344 British experiencers, all of whom filled in a detailed questionnaire as well as writing a long personal account (Fenwick and Fenwick, 1995 [summarised in Badham and Ballard, 1996, from which the following details derive]). This survey probably gives us the fullest account available yet of what are the characteristic features of a near-death experience.

According to the Fenwicks' report 72% of near-death experiencers speak of seeing the light. Asked to clarify the colour, 56% described it as brilliant white, 21% as golden, 6% as yellow, 3% as orange, 2% red and 7% said it had no colour. Only 5% thought of it at the cold end of the spectrum, as green (2%) or blue (3%). Seventy-six per cent talked of seeing a landscape which was invariably described in terms of a beautiful garden or an idyllic pastoral scene. Nineteen per cent heard wonderful music.

The near-death experience carries with it very strong positive emotions. Of those who underwent it, 82% felt calmness and peace, 40% felt joy and 38% felt love. Individuals write in glowing terms of their feelings, some speaking of utter peace and complete happiness: 'no person could experience such joy'; 'I was filled with elation'. Many felt that they were at peace because they understood everything: 'I was peaceful, utterly content, I knew the light held all the answers.'

For many people the experience of the transforming light was the most profound emotional experience they have ever had. Their feeling was of being overwhelmed with universal love, of being accepted by some loving being. This led a high proportion of the percipients (72%) to feel that they had been changed by the experience: 42% felt that they had become more spiritual as a result, 22% talked of becoming 'better persons' and 40% described themselves as more socially conscious.

The most common change was that 82% said they now had less fear of death. This does not necessarily mean that these all came to a firm belief in a life after death, for 48% said that they did not believe in personal survival. However, it is unclear how we should interpret this, given that some who said this also thought that some important part of them, their consciousness or soul, might yet continue. What this lack of clarity suggests to me is that an NDE can very strongly encourage belief in a future life but cannot override strongly held philosophical beliefs about what it means to be a person. We shall see a further illustration of this below when we examine the complexity of A. J. Ayer's response. On the other hand, the finding that 82% had less fear of death remains significant, as does the fact that for at least some the experience was interpreted as guaranteeing a future hope.

The near-death experience does not, however, simply change people's attitude to death, but also gives them a much more affirmative attitude to this life. Many speak of every day as a new gift, and feel that they should live life more fully and purposefully. One intriguing fact is that 47% of those who had near-death experiences felt themselves to be more psychically sensitive. By this is meant feelings of being able to predict the future, or to possess powers of healing the sick. Clearly it would be useful to check such claims to see if there is any empirical evidence to support them. But it is at least worth noting that such beliefs often follow other deeply felt religious experiences which suggests that, for many, the NDE falls into this kind of category.

Another feature which NDEs have in common with other kinds of religious experience is that they are not always positive experiences. Almost 1% talked of a hellish experience, 15% felt a sense of fear, and 9% a sense of loss. These figures are in line with other contemporary surveys, but out of line with reports from earlier cultures where hellish experiences were much more commonly reported (Bede, 1962; Zaleski, 1987). Once again this is a feature which NDEs share with contemporary religious experience which tends to focus on a sense of the love of God while earlier generations talked of a sense of 'fear'. In both cases, however, there has always been a spectrum of positive and negative experiences which might justify the speculation that beliefs about both heaven and hell may have a basis in such experiences.

On matters of religious belief most of the Fenwicks' respondents felt that their religious outlook had been broadened rather than simply confirmed. In the responses they received there was a tendency to speak of feeling in the presence of a higher Being, rather than talking of God, and in this British sample Jesus or Mary were only rarely named. The dominant characteristic was a sense of spiritual awakening which sometimes feels uneasy at any continuing acceptance of narrow doctrinal system. There was a sense that the Reality glimpsed was of more universal significance than simply to one's inherited tradition. Again this is a characteristic of experientially based beliefs in that mystics of all traditions tend to feel closer to one another than do those who base their belief-system more strongly on an inherited tradition.

Near-Death Experiences, Heaven and Hell

These findings of Peter and Elizabeth Fenwick are very much in line with the findings of other researchers in other countries. Carl Becker, Professor of Comparative Thought at Kyoto University, remarks how reminiscent modern NDEs are to accounts in Chinese and Japanese literature concerning 'those who have been to heaven and back' (Becker, 1993: 90–91), and he notes also that surveys in India and America among Christians, Jews and Hindus all present closely similar reports. J. C. Hampe in Germany comes to the same conclusion (Hampe, 1979). The experience seems to cut across all cultural and religious boundaries and yet to present the archetypal imagery of a paradisal heaven of flowery gardens, suffused in warm light and radiant with peace and joy and in the loving presence of a Being of light, of love and of compassion. However, the few negative experiences also echo archetypal imageries of hell. It seems overwhelmingly likely that reports from past near-death experiences are what have shaped our traditions and provided the content of our religious imagery concerning the future life.

These considerations are why I suggest that the experiential foundation for belief in a future life derives both from religious experience of a relationship with God, and from the reports of people who near the frontier of death believe they have caught a glimpse of a life beyond.

The Problem of Analysing Near-Death and Religious Experiences

If one tries to see any pattern in this data it does seem that to classify NDEs under the heading 'contemporary religious experience' makes good sense. It shares the ambiguity of all religious experience in that the boundaries are fuzzy and what is true of the majority of cases is not true of all. Like all religious experiences, what convinces the percipient does not necessarily influence the thinking of one who is merely told of another's experience. And while the Fenwicks' survey throws useful light on the subjective feelings of people who have NDEs, this does not solve the question of what, if any, may be the explanation we give to such phenomena.

For me one of the most impressive features of the NDE is the profound effect it has on the majority of those who experience it. Long ago William James argued that religious experiences are real because they have real effects.

In the case of the NDE this is particularly noticeable. As we saw in the survey quoted above, 72% felt their lives transformed. Comparable findings have been confirmed by others. Bruce Greyson, Editor of the *Journal of Near-Death Studies* and a Professor of Psychiatry, sums up the data thus: 'It is the most profound experience I know of . . . nothing affects people as strongly as this' (Brown, 1993). This is further endorsed by Professor Kenneth Ring in his book *Life at Death* which shows that the most impressive feature of the near-death experience is the impact it has on the beliefs and attitudes of those who have it (Ring, 1980: 81, 169, 240). Of course, as with all such experiences, the impact is not epistemically coercive, so that it remains possible for a person to be unpersuaded by it. This is both illustrated and illuminated by the impact his NDE experience had on A. J. Ayer. His first response was to think that 'on the face of it, these experiences are rather strong evidence that death does not put an end to consciousness'. However, after rehearsing some of the philosophical problems associated with life after death his conclusion was more modest, namely that 'my recent experiences have slightly weakened my conviction that my genuine death, which is due fairly soon, will be the end of me, though I continue to hope it will'. Later he retracted even this, but from a person with his long and carefully thought-out position his testimony to the power of the initial experience remains striking (Ayer, 1992).

An Important Research Project

From a scientific perspective one feature which is a permanent difficulty in the way of investigating topics like religious or near-death experiences is that the most one can normally do is to collect and analyse subjective reports. But at least we can now do this on a massive scale. Carl Becker has pointed out that the availability of modern computerised storage and comparison enables thousands of such cases to be collected from all over the world and analysed together. There is certainly value in such a project, for if it can be totally established that tens of thousands of people from totally disparate cultures, worldviews and backgrounds have all reported a common set of experiences near the point of death this does at least provide some grounds for supposing that this might actually be what happens at that point. As Richard Swinburne suggests, 'in the absence of special considerations, how things seem to be is good grounds for a belief about how things are' (Swinburne, 1979: 254).

But there is a problem in applying this to the claim that near-death experiences show that at death the soul goes out of the body and moves on to a new mode of existence, as so many NDE experiencers believe. The problem is precisely the existence of such 'special considerations', namely the mass of evidence that human consciousness cannot possibly subsist except within a functioning physical brain. But if it could ever be established that this 'limiting principle' did not apply then this barrier against taking NDEs as evidential of survival would not apply.

One intriguing fact about the NDE is that many who report 'going out of the body' at the time of apparent death not only enjoy mystical experiences such as we have already described but also claim to 'look down from above' on the resuscitation attempts, and are incredibly accurate in the observations they subsequently report which turn out to be correct in terms of what a person would have seen if he or she really had been viewing from the ceiling. These facts are accepted even by that most resolutely sceptical of the NDE inquirers, Susan Blackmore. She accepts that 'there is no doubt that people describe reasonably accurately events that have occurred around them during their NDE'. However, she suggests that a combination of 'prior knowledge, fantasy, and lucky guesses and the remaining operating senses of hearing and touch' may provide the information for the images seen which are viewed autoscopically from above because that is the perspective from which we see ourselves in memory (Blackmore, 1993: 114–15). People who actually have the experience always see such explanations as alien 'hetero-interpretations' which fail to account for the way it actually seems to them. And the very large number of correct observations which do not fit into any of Blackmore's explanatory categories (other than the catch-all category of 'lucky guesses'), suggest that the data cannot easily be accommodated in so narrow a Procrustean bed.

However, this issue could actually be resolved if a large enough prospective survey could be done in hospital contexts where it could be established on a non-anecdotal basis whether or not correct observation actually took place of a kind that could not be accounted for by any 'natural' means. For this to happen requires the collaboration of medical staff and hospital administrators in the placing of objects in cardiac wards and casualty units which could only be seen and described by an agent actually looking down from the ceiling. Such a project would be fully scientific in that it offers a proposal that is in Popperian terms unfalsifiable. On average 10% of people admitted to a cardiac ward can be expected to have a near-death experience and well over half of these will report an autoscopic experience. If out of a hundred such patients none mention seeing the objects one could safely conclude that 'seeing' from out-of-the-body does not occur and that NDEs are only subjectively real in this regard. But if a single case of correct 'seeing' could be proven beyond dispute the principle that consciousness can exist outside the body will have been established and one roadblock across the path of belief in immortality will have been removed.

Such a project is not impossible to establish since Peter Fenwick and I did successfully negotiate a pilot study in two hospitals during a two-year period. However, the handful of cases that occurred in this time did nothing but confirm the sad fact that most people resuscitated from a close encounter with death actually die without ever regaining sufficient strength to be interviewed about what, if anything, they experienced. However, if such a prospective study could be undertaken over a large enough number of hospitals for a sufficiently long time to build up a worthwhile database, the truth or falsity of the claim that near-death experiences provide evidence that consciousness can exist apart from the body could be established. Whatever the result of the experiment, it would be good to know the answer!

Conclusion

The question of whether or not there is a life after death is potentially the most important issue that could be raised. What I have sought to show in this paper is that, like most of the things we believe about the nature of reality, our answers to this question depend in part on our experiencing. A person who believes that they have truly encountered a personal and loving God, perhaps identified as the Risen Christ, is likely to believe that they have an eternal destiny. Likewise a person who has had a profound near-death experience may also come to such a belief. In neither case is the experience epistemically coercive and many will conclude that, like so much else about our world, the data are ambiguous and capable of a range of alternative explanations. However, in the case of the near-death experience there is the tantalising prospect that future research could tip the balance of probability one way or the other. Let us hope that this challenge will be taken up so that we may know whether mortality or immortality is to be our ultimate end!

References

Athanasius (1963). *On the Incarnation*. London: Mowbray. (First published AD 318.)

Ayer, A. J. (1992). 'What I Saw when I Was Dead', in P. Edwards, *Immortality*. New York: Macmillan.

Badham, P. and Ballard, P. (1996). *Facing Death*. Cardiff: University of Wales Press.

BBC (1982, March). *At the Hour of Death* [Television programme]. London: BBC.

Becker, C. (1993). *Paranormal Experience and Survival of Death*. New York: SUNY.

Bede (1962). *A History of the English Church and People* (Book 5, 284–9). Harmondsworth: Penguin. (Originally published in AD 731.)

Blackmore, S. (1993). *Dying to Live*. London: Grafton.

Bowker, J. (1991). *The Meaning of Death*. Cambridge: CUP.
Brown, M. (1993). 'Life after Death', *Daily Telegraph*, 27 March, Magazine section, 21.
Bukyo Dendo Kyokai (1980). *The Teaching of Buddha*. Tokyo: Buddhist Promoting Foundation. (Quoting from *Amitayurdhyana-sutra*.)
Conze, E. (1959). *Buddhist Scriptures*. Harmondsworth: Penguin. (Part of a series of extracts from the *Sukhavativyuha*, 15–19, 21–2, 24, 26–7.)
Eliade, M. (1977). 'Mythologies of Death', in F. E. Reynolds and E. H. Waugh (eds.), *Religious Encounters with Death*. Pennsylvania: Pennsylvania University Press.
Evans-Wentz, W. Y. (1957). *The Tibetan Book of the Dead or the After-Death Experiences on the Bardo Plane, According to Lama Kazi Dawa-Sumdup's English Rendering* (3rd edn.). Oxford: OUP. (Originally published 1927.)
Fenwick, P. & Fenwick, E. (1995). *The Truth in the Light*. London: Headline.
Hampe, J. C. (1979). *To Die is Gain*. London: Darton, Longman & Todd. (Original [German] work published 1975.)
Hay, D. (1990). *Religious Experience Today*. London: Mowbrays.
Hick, J. (1989). *An Interpretation of Religion*. Oxford: OUP.
John of the Cross (1957). *The Dark Night of the Soul* (Book 2, ch. 24). (K. Reinhardt, trans.) London: Constable. (First written AD 1579.)
John of the Cross (1960). *Poems* (R. Campbell, trans.). Harmondsworth: Penguin.
Kübler-Ross, E. (1991). *On Life After Death*. Berkeley: Celestial.
Mitchell, B. (1973). *The Justification of Religious Belief*. London: Macmillan.
Moody, R. A. (1973). *Life After Life*. Atlanta: Mockingbird.
Otto, R. (1923). *The Idea of the Holy*. Oxford: OUP.
Ring, K. (1980). *Life at Death: A Scientific Account of the Near-Death Experience*. New York: Coward, McCann & Geohagen.
Robinson, W. (1962). *Inspiration and Revelation in the Old Testament*. Oxford: OUP.
Schillebeeckx, E. (1980). *Christ, the Christian Experience in the Modern World*. London: SCM.
Shiels, D. (1978). 'A Cross-cultural Study of Beliefs in Out-of-the-Body Experiences', *Journal of the Society for Psychical Research*, 49 (775), 699.
Smith, T. (1980). 'Called Back from the Dead'. *Pulse*, 19 July.
Swinburne, R. (1979). *The Existence of God*. Oxford: OUP.
Van Egmond, D. (1993). *Body, Subject and Self: The Possibilities of Survival after Death*. Utrecht: Utrecht University Press.
Zaleski, C. (1987). *Otherworldly Journeys*. Oxford: OUP.

15

The Glory of Imagination and the Imagination of Glory

Trevor A. Hart

Let me begin by asking a question. Try to imagine, if you would, what life would be like if as human beings we lacked the capacity for imagination. How would the shape and the quality of our existence be affected were God suddenly one day to decide to delete the relevant bits of mental software which enable us to imagine, to be imaginative? What would disappear? How much would remain? Would anything survive the purging process at all? If so, would it be worth having?

It is about imagination that I want to talk in this lecture. And, as the structure of my title suggests, there are two main tasks I have set myself to achieve. I want first to consider in very broad terms the contributions imagination makes in some key areas of our common human life and experience. And then, second, I want to home in on one very specific area, that of hope. Here I shall draw upon insights offered by Ernst Bloch and George Steiner, before turning lastly to a brief consideration of the implications and applications for the explicitly eschatological elements of Christian faith and theology.

Before I embark on this possibly overambitious way of filling 45 minutes you might reasonably be expecting me already at this early stage to offer some carefully honed definition of the word 'imagination'. If I refuse to furnish one (and I do!) it is precisely because I believe the reality or realities referred to in terms of the language of imagination to be complex and highly variegated; and I would much prefer to proceed by considering what sorts of things 'imagination' does than by adopting a neat definition that rules half of them out in advance. Let's allow the reality, as we perceive it, to shape our definition for us.

Imagination – the Glorious Skeleton in Everyone's Cupboard

Ever since Plato relegated *eikasia* to the lowest rung on his ladder of human ways of knowing, and banished the artists from his ideal city-state, imagination has received a pretty bad press in the western intellectual tradition. In summary, it has regularly been disentangled and isolated from, and then rigorously subordinated to, the allegedly superior activities of reason or intellect, and conscience or will. In recent centuries this dualistic account has been both reinforced and developed by an emergent positivism that exalts some models of knowing (let's use shorthand and call them 'scientific', 'logical' and 'factual') over others. The result is a popular perception, which persists even in our postmodern culture, that some disciplines, their approaches to the world and ways of speaking of it, may be trusted as precise and reliable guides to reality (truth bearing), while others (although for the sake of appearances and tolerance a positive spin may be put upon what they do by labelling them 'creative' or 'imaginative') are inherently prone to imprecision, deception, and the positing of falsehoods, and ought therefore to be treated with suspicion. So, pulling all this together into a crude but nonetheless justifiable overstatement, the scientist (and those whose practices aspire to scientific methods) can be trusted as a worthy reporter of truth, while the novelist, poet or artist has little *intention* of reporting truth (he or she invents things and weaves fictions) and shouldn't be mistaken as doing so. Facts, truths of reason and morality are reliable and useful; imaginative, creative, 'fictive' expression is enriching and a nice escape from reality when you have the time, but in terms of *truth* it's a curate's egg, and any really useful elements in it can readily be distilled off or rendered down into facts, and truths of reason and morality. Again, if I am drawing the lines here with too thick a pencil, then it is for the purposes of clarity and in order to avoid wasting too much time in qualification *ad infinitum*; but in any case I don't think the pencil is *much* thicker than it deserves to be!

This relative suspicion of the fruits of imagination within our culture is reflected clearly in the western Christian (and especially the Protestant) tradition which has tended to be overly rationalistic and empiricist in both its theology and its piety. One clear example in which the two areas come together is its attitude towards the Bible. Whether it is the conservative evangelical's concern for a certain sort of infallibility to be ascribed to the texts, or the liberal's passion to identify and pare away the trimmings of myth and theological elaboration, very often the same basic set of assumptions is operative; namely, that what is of permanent value for faith must be reducible in the final analysis either to fact (history), or to eternal truths which can be shown to be rationally and morally satisfying. Both conservative apologetics and liberal attempts to reconstruct the tradition, that is to say, buy uncritically into the dualism I have been describing.

Very often neither group seems to be able or willing to recognise any positive contribution or role for imagination and its various products *per se* within the mainstream of Christian faith and theology. If we allow dramatic sketches in our services, we nonetheless want the point they are making to be explained later in a sermon of a mostly conceptual nature.

Garrett Green, in *Imagining God*,[1] directs us helpfully to one vital aspect of the context for this contemporary Christian suspicion of imagination; namely, the direct linkage between religion and imagination that arose during the nineteenth century and that, in terms of the prevalent dualistic scheme of things, effectively relegated religious and theological discourse without further discussion to a fictive and non-truth-bearing status. By far the most influential factor in this development was Hegel's analysis of religion and religious language as a poetic handmaid to philosophy. The positive forms of religion were a clothing of the truths of reason with imaginative garb (*Vorstellungen* – 'representations') that would enable those incapable of dealing directly with conceptual truth itself (*Begriffe*) to obtain some purchase at least upon it. Thus theological statements should not be treated as conceptual truth claims, but as an illustrative and imaginative mediation between reason and sense, dressing rational truths up in sensory form, using picture language in an imaginative but ultimately fictive manner, incarnating concepts in an impure mixture from which truth itself must finally be distilled and purified. The Logos must become incarnate in order for us to grasp it; we shall not find truth, however, in its incarnate, but only its discarnate and pure form. Religion, in other words, is one big dramatic sketch, and we need philosophy to enter into the pulpit and to explain it to us by translating its meaning into pure conceptual terms.

Hegel's analysis (intended positively, to rehabilitate religion in a sceptical age) was subsequently taken up and used in various ways. We can but mention in passing the hugely influential developments of it by Hegelians such as Strauss, the significance of whose introduction of the category of 'myth' into theology can hardly be overestimated, and Feuerbach whose book *The Essence of Christianity* insisted that religion is not so much an imaginative laying hold of eternal truths about God, but rather an imaginative *projection* of truths about humankind, which we then worship under the illusion that they are God. Karl Marx's evaluation of religion as the 'opiate of the people' belongs in the same line of development, but pursued now in a political direction. The substance of religious belief is not merely an illusory product of the corporate imagination; it is in fact a deliberately engineered illusion designed to generate and sustain fantasies and dreams that will divert the attention of the oppressed masses from the actual awfulness of their situation long enough for their labour to be thoroughly exploited. What is required, on Marx's diagnosis, is a regime of cold turkey sufficient to permit reality to break through the illusion, and to provoke in due course a thoroughly justifiable reaction against the pushers.

This linkage between religion and imagination was not, then, quite the advantage to faith that some of those who first pursued it supposed it might be. At its best it secured a place for religious forms of life and discourse at the price of their effective removal from the sphere of serious intellectual engagement with reality. At its worst it led to their construal as illusory and even damaging untruths, which should either be outgrown or even purged. One response to this, I have suggested, is that which seeks to show the intellectual and historical soundness of the faith, and ignores, plays down or pares away its imaginative component. An alternative response seeks instead to rehabilitate imagination as an alternative but complementary route to knowledge of reality of certain sorts. Thus, for example, Brian Horne in his recent work *Imagining Evil*[2] does a fine job of showing how imagination functions to uncover depths of truth and meaning that elude the merely empirical or rational approach to things. 'The baroque paintings and sculpture of sixteenth century Italy', he writes, 'will convey truths to the viewer that all the readings of the proceedings of the Council of Trent will never convey; T. S. Eliot's Four Quartets will awaken in the reader an awareness of the nature of religious experience that no textbook on the psychology of religion could ever provide.'[3] Religious truth, in other words, is of such a sort as to need to be embodied or incarnated in forms fashioned by the imagination before it can be laid hold of and rendered fully meaningful to human beings. Here, unlike Hegel, *imagination alone* is held to be capable of reaching the parts other ways of knowing cannot reach, and is hence elevated from its subordinate or penultimate status to an equal standing alongside the intellect.

But this, it seems to me, does not go anywhere near far enough, for it allows the basic construal of imagination as a faculty or activity essentially separable from that of intellect to stand unchallenged. And it seems to me that it must not be allowed to stand any longer, for if anything deserves the tag of dangerous illusion then it is this very perception itself. The alternative claim I want to present for your consideration (and which I shall only be able in the time available to go so far towards demonstrating) is the strong one that *it is virtually impossible to identify any human activity or capacity from which imagination is entirely absent, or in which it does not play some basic role, either directly or indirectly*. Let me now try to suggest how this is the case by referring briefly to some key areas in our experience.

First, we may consider what is arguably our most basic level of engagement with the world; namely, the perception of objects, that on which scientific and factual knowledge, we might note, is securely founded. What is interesting, but often overlooked, is that David Hume and Immanuel Kant, both of whose names lend themselves to an association with attempts to delimit genuine knowledge to the spheres of reason and experience, both willingly admit that imagination plays a vital role in the acquisition of knowledge in these very spheres. Hume's *Treatise of Human Nature* identifies several key functions of imagination in this context, among which we may list just three. First, imagination fills in the gaps between discrete but essentially similar perceptions, and thereby posits the existence of distinct and continuous objects in the world. Second, and in similar vein, imagination enables the inductive construction of abstract ideas. When, in other words, we have had a number of similar but distinguishable perceptions, we apply a common noun to the objects discerned, and when we subsequently hear this word used imagination is stimulated to image the idea attaching to the word, and so enables us to identify the relevant object as a dog, a tree, an exam paper, or whatever it might be. Third, for Hume it is the imagination that makes those links between one perception and another that we refer to as causal relations, relations with which natural science, we may suppose, has a considerable amount to do. Turning to Kant, we may observe two basic functions he ascribes to *Einbildungskraft* or imagination in the *Critique of Pure Reason*: first, the construction of the objects we experience (the fashioning of composite wholes out of a manifold of distinct bits of raw sensory data), and second, the application to these percepts of the a priori concepts with which the mind makes sense of experience. If, in other words, concepts without percepts are empty, and percepts without concepts are blind, then it is the imagination that we have to thank for bringing the two together and facilitating the resultant understanding. Without its prior activity, there could be no knowledge of anything.

Both Hume and Kant also note the role of imagination in rendering knowledge of the past, calling to mind experiences, objects and events which it stores away in the somewhat complicated and elusive banks of what we call memory. This central imaginative function is taken up and pursued at length by R. G. Collingwood in his classic study *The Idea of History*.[4] Not only is imagination responsible for recalling events we ourselves have experienced or witnessed; it is a vital component in all those acts of sympathetic self-projection or translation in which we seek to put ourself in someone else's shoes so far as it is possible to do so, and thereby better to understand their thoughts, their experiences and their actions. Such a hermeneutic feat, Collingwood reminds us, is involved in every attempt to reconstruct the past. Again, to a considerable extent, it is a matter of filling in the gaps left in our data, and constructing a coherent and meaningful picture of things. The same is true, therefore, not just in history, but in any and every attempt to interpret, to translate, to make sense of things, whether events, texts, other persons or whatever. We leap over the boundaries of our own particularity and seek to enter into another perspective. So imagination is central to ethics, for example, where we are constantly involved in attempts to understand the motivations of others, or to see how general principles might be applied in different contexts, or even to picture what the future consequences of different possible courses of action in the present might be. None of these things would be possible without extensive exercise of and fundamental input from imagination.

There are so many things that could be mentioned, but we must rest content with just one more example; namely, the role of imagination in the theoretical side of science. What is a hypothesis if it is not an imaginative construct to be tried and tested by empirical means? What is a model, but an imaginative attempt to envisage one less well known and understood thing in terms of another much better known and understood thing? Even in that allegedly most pure of the sciences, mathematics, the activity of imagination is clearly discernible. No form of logical problem-solving could even be attempted without the capacity to envisage and pursue different possible solutions (i.e. to picture possibilities other than and lying beyond the actual or given) and this is a function of the imagination.

We need, and may, labour the point no further. The attempt to disentangle imagination from these various aspects of human intellectual endeavour, and subsequently to treat both its activities and its fruits with relative suspicion will not bear careful scrutiny and must be abandoned for good. If theology owes a considerable debt to imaginative activity and strategies, then so too, it must be admitted, do all these other disciplines and features of human life, given that the ways in which imagination functions in each may differ quite widely. The simple point to be established here is that its presence cannot any longer be held to call some project or activity automatically into suspicion or to devalue its outcomes, and that its complete absence is not even imaginable, let alone desirable.

Imagination and the Grammar of Hope

I want to turn now to one particular sphere in which imagination functions; namely, our capacity as historically located beings to venture in thought beyond the boundaries of the present moment into the future. And what I am interested in specifically is the way in which certain aspects of that capacity exercise a necessary and transformative reflexive impact upon our ways of being in the present. I want, in other words, to think about imagination and eschatological hope, and the ways in which that hope shapes who we are and what we do today.

Let me clarify at once and make it plain that I am not thinking of the sort of crude appeal to self-interest which has too often been deployed in energising 'repentance' and 'obedience' in evangelistic strategies: the threat of eternal perdition and the promise of paradise, each colourfully imagined and illuminated in Dantesque style so as to scare the hell out of people. As William Temple observed in his Drew Lecture for 1931, whatever the logical status of the language of heaven and hell may be supposed to be, its graphic elaboration for this purpose appeals to all the wrong motives in us, and generates a response less than truly moral.[5] The transformative function of hope is, I want to suggest, quite other than this.

George Steiner in his classic work on the nature of language and translation, *After Babel*[6], notes that our ability as human beings to think about (we might reasonably substitute the word 'imagine') temporality, to construe past and future as distinct from the present, is in large measure bound up with our use of language. Our possession of a grammar complete with tenses is what makes such imaginative projection possible. 'Language', Steiner writes, 'happens in time but also, very largely, creates the time in which it happens.'[7] Language, that is to say, shapes our perception of the moment of speech or thought as present, and of other times as either past or future. Especially in the case of the future this capacity to transcend the present, to speak of or imagine a state of affairs other than the present, is vital to the direction of our ways of being in the world. 'The status of the future of the verb', he observes, 'is at the core of existence. It shapes the image we carry of the meaning of life, and of our personal place in that meaning.'[8]

As we have already noted, the potential shaping impact of such linguistic or imaginative projection was clearly grasped by Karl Marx who, in reference to what he deemed illusory hopes of a religious nature, construed that impact in negative terms, as debilitating the urge for political reform in the real world. But Steiner turns this around, and reminds us of the deliberate suppression in former communist regimes not this time of hope, but of memory. The outlawing of the past, the careful editing of national memory was designed precisely to mould and shape present consciousness, and thereby to control it and direct it in particular ways. 'One can imagine a comparable prohibition of the future' he ruminates. 'What would existence be like in a total (totalitarian) present, in an idiom which limited projective utterances to the horizon of Monday next?'[9]

His point is clear. The suppression of imaginative projection into the future, the enforced removal of the future tense from the language, would just as surely be debilitating with respect to present activism and energy, because future tenses necessarily entail the possibility of change of one sort or another. Without them, hope for a better future is simply not possible.

Steiner proceeds to suggest that human life as such is characterised (and distinguished from other forms of life) by its essential directedness towards the future, and its fundamental capacity for hope. And the capacity to imagine and to speak of what lies beyond the given here and now is vital to this direction. 'We move forward', he writes in characteristically graphic vein, 'in the slipstream of the statements we make about tomorrow morning, about the millenium.'[10] Through imaginative construction we posit what he calls, paradoxically, 'axiomatic fictions' which, as it were, drag us forward in their wake and energise our living towards tomorrow rather than merely in today. We live in hope. Apart from it we are inert and, like sharks in water, would quickly drown in our own despair, trapped in an eternal and 'total' present. Change, progress, intention, excitement, anticipation, all the things that enable us to cope with and overcome the undoubted pains and trials and disasters we experience, these are bound up with our movement towards the future. 'The conventions of forwardness so deeply entrenched in our syntax make for a constant, sometimes involuntary, resilience. Drown as we may, the idiom of hope, so immediate to the mind, thrusts us to the surface.'[11] This ability to imagine ahead, to see beyond the given to a better and brighter future, Steiner avers, furnishes distinct advantages in the evolutionary process, and has doubtless contributed to the survival and superiority of humankind. 'Natural selection', he suggests, 'has favoured the subjunctive.'[12]

We may, I suppose, prefer a more specifically theological construal of that claim, but its essential point is well made. The capacity to construct futurity, we may rather say, which is a central function of the imagination, is essential to our humanity and to its movement forward in the creative purposes of God.

Steiner identifies another closely related imaginative function as equally important in this regard which I must mention briefly; namely, our capacity for counter-factuality, for the deliberate construction of falsehoods or alternatives. The generation of 'counter-worlds' is, of course, the source of fantasy, illusion and lies. But it is also the source of our ability to see how things might be different, to refuse to accept the world as it is. Indeed, insofar as the language we habitually use to describe the world, the ways in which we image and construe it are a vital component in the shaping of our experience of it – to the extent, that is to say, that reality is a social and linguistic construct (and there is no need to capitulate altogether to radical accounts of this in order to recognise some truth in the claim), the capacity to picture and to speak of the world otherwise than in accordance with the currently favoured social construct is itself a capacity to change reality, to deconstruct and then reconstruct it for ourselves. As Christians, for example, we shall probably want to construe the world in which we live as one in which Christ is Lord, rather than as a meaningless and random series of subatomic fluctuations; and this insistence on describing the world differently will generate quite distinct ways of being in the world.

Turning now from Steiner to Ernst Bloch, we find a strikingly similar recognition of the essential directedness of human life towards the future, and of the vital contribution of imaginative hope in the realisation of this futured existence. In his massive *magnum opus*, *The Principle of Hope*[13] Bloch, an atheist, a Marxist and a Jew, traces the patterns and manifestations of this constant 'venturing beyond', as he calls it, in the forms of human life.

Human existence, Bloch observes, is driven by cravings, urgings, desires and strivings, all of which are forms of discontent with the way things are.

Some of our cravings are duly clothed by imagination with particular form, and transformed into wishes. But the nature of wishes is to be somewhat detached from moral commitment. We may entertain two or more mutually exclusive wishes at once. Only when we choose between them and begin to invest them with moral intent, acting towards their eventual fulfilment, do they become wants. The central category with which Bloch deals in expounding all this is that of dreams, and especially daydreams. In daydreams, he notes, we are more in conscious control of our imaginings than in dreams, and we bring our wishes and wants to fictitious fulfilment. All freedom movements, he notes, are guided by such utopian aspirations, and revolutionary interests are kindled by the ability to posit a disjunction between knowledge of how bad the world is, and 'recognition of how good it could be if it were otherwise'.[14] Daydreams are not, therefore, merely contemplative (the stuff of nostalgic armchair aspiration), or analgesic, but invigorating and empowering. 'The pull towards what is lacking never ends . . . . The lack of what we dream about hurts not less, but more. It thus prevents us from getting used to deprivation.'[15]

Bloch insists, however, on drawing a distinction between imagination's construction of daydreams on the one hand and what he calls 'mere fantasizing' on the other. Genuine hope is possessed of both subjective and objective aspects. As a component of human consciousness it is, nevertheless, soundly rooted in real ontological possibilities. Hope, that is to say, as manifest in daydreams, intuits what Bloch calls 'a Not-Yet-Being of an expectable kind'. It 'does not play around and get lost in an Empty-Possible, but psychologically anticipates a Real-Possible'.[16]

Here we need to identify Bloch's framework as a metaphysic of the world, and history as an incomplete process that moves forward, above all, through the capacity of hope to lay hold of the 'Not-Yet-Existent' and the 'Not-Yet-Conscious' and, precisely in anticipating them, to transform the present, energising us in the here and now to transcend the here and now with its apparent limitations and actual deprivations. Hope empowers our striving towards its realisation. But it must be genuine hope, and not mere fantasy. Only a Real-Possible has the resources to draw us into the future in this way. The *Novum* (genuinely new thing) which hope attaches itself and looks forward to is, paradoxically, in one sense not new at all. It is wholly new in as much as it has never previously existed, and in as much as the conditions for the possibility of its existence may not yet even exist. But it is, nonetheless (and in retrospect will be able to be seen to have been) a real possibility, because the conditions for its possibility are already latent within the conditions and possibilities of the present.

What the imagination does in hope, its 'utopian function' as Bloch calls it, is thus twofold. First, it leaps over the limits and perceived discontinuities that lie between present reality and the utopian future; even though it cannot yet see clearly the route from here to there – it intuits it as a real-possible. Second, through setting this vision before us and enabling us to 'look forward' to it, hope drives us forward, empowering and guiding ways of being in the world in the present, which themselves serve to create the conditions in which the object of hope becomes possible. There is no hint of a rationalistic prediction or plotting of the future here, therefore. We cannot, for Bloch, *know* the future, or precisely how it will arise. (In passing it is perhaps worth asking whether, if we could, there would always be aspects of what lies in front of us that would so cripple us with fear as to render us incapable of action?) Hope, as Bloch sees it, is that activity of the imagination that lays hold intuitively of something that may or may not actually come to pass, but the potential for which lies genuinely within the latent capacities of the system or process of human history. 'The historical content of hope', he writes, 'is human culture referred to its concrete-utopian horizon.'[17]

One final observation must suffice to bring my account of Bloch to a conclusion. He sees death understood as personal extinction as an insurmountable obstacle to hope, refusing to endorse attempts to be stoical in the face of it, or to transfer hope from the shoulders of the individual to the tribe or race. There is something insatiable, he indicates, about the human desire for and drive towards 'life in all its fulness'. Even those of us who live good and satisfying lives, seeing out our threescore years and ten, when we contemplate the enormities of what life has to offer can only feel regret and frustration at what we have missed, and how our opportunities have been cut short too early. Bloch sums up the sentiment in these wistful words: 'Been in Egypt and never saw the pyramids.'[18] What, then, of those whose lives were cut shorter even than our own, or whose existence was blighted by tragedy or evil never to be set to rights if death has the final word on their personal lot? 'The world is full of slaughtered goodness and of criminals enjoying a long and peaceful old age; martyrs do not experience their resurrection, the criminals of white terror are seldom brought to judgment, in both cases death makes everything irreparable.'[19] Hope, therefore, Bloch concludes, if it is to perform the utopian function, must not only be intuition of a Real-Possible, but must be personal, and must therefore entail the indestructibility of the person, and the assured presence of all persons at the end, a view that led him towards a fascination with the Christian category of resurrection, but ultimately to embrace the doctrine of *metempsychosis*, or the transmigration and reincarnation of souls.

The Imagination of Glory

There is not time left in this lecture (indeed there would hardly be time in a whole series) to trace the implications for a Christian eschatology of all that could be gleaned from Steiner's and Bloch's analyses of the utopian function of imagination. All I can do is to raise some questions that may direct us to some points of divergence and possible convergence.

I begin by noting that one major Christian theologian at least has already begun the task of engaging with this agenda, although surprisingly not in terms that lay bare the vital function of imagination in hope and its transformation of the present. I refer, of course, to Jürgen Moltmann whose creative interaction with Bloch's thought in particular is evident throughout his corpus, but especially in the early *Theology of Hope*[20] and the very recent *The Coming of God*.[21]

Moltmann's borrowing of some of Bloch's central categories shows how, if they are to be taken up into a Christian eschatology, they must nonetheless be carefully modified. The most notable instance of this, perhaps, is Moltmann's refusal to embrace the key theme of hope as that which intuits a 'Real-Possible' the conditions for which lie latent within the process or scheme of history. Moltmann is not a process theologian, and he sees that Christian hope rests not on the latent capacities or potentialities of nature (however new and unexpected these may seem to be from the perspective of the present), but rather in the capacity of the God of the gospel to summon forth life out of death, to create *ex nihilo* the possibilities of a new life, a new creation, where none presently exist. This is a theme that recurs time and time again throughout Scripture, from creation itself, the calling of Israel out of slavery in Egypt, the virgin conception of Christ in the womb of a virgin, and (centrally and supremely of course) the resurrection of the crucified Jesus from death. It is a pattern that recurs in the life of the church, in the granting of faith and new life by the Spirit where the potential for it is wholly lacking. And it is the paradigm for Christian hope, the creation of a new heaven and new earth which is (like the risen Christ in his relation to the crucified Jesus) continuous with the old, but utterly transcends the potentialities latent within it, and relies wholly on the faithfulness and promise of God.

Here we touch upon the key category for Moltmann's own theology of hope. It is rooted not in an imagined or daydreamed possible future, but in the certain future of God's *promise*. Perhaps this accounts for his notable avoidance of the category of imagination, a word, as we have noted, linked readily with the uncertain, the imprecise, even the patently false. But there is no need to avoid this category. Indeed, a promise, just as much as a daydream, is a construction of imagination both on the part of the one who makes it and those who receive and trust it. What this forces us to reckon with in passing is yet another key function of imagination in Christian theology; namely, its role as the vehicle or locus of God's self-revealing activity. John Baillie in his book *Our Knowledge of God* hints at this important connection:

> The new convert may long have known and believed all that the Church teaches about God and Christ, but somehow only now has the meaning of it all 'come

> home' to him. He has never, we say, 'taken it home to himself' before. What is this 'coming home,' this 'taking to oneself,' which alone gives to faith a salvific power? It is, of course, something that God brings to pass in the soul; but perhaps it is more in the realm of the imagination that He brings it to pass than in the realm of the intellect.[22]

This theme of revelation and saving faith as being bound up with God's capacity to seize not primarily our mind or our will, but first and foremost our imagination, is one well worthy of exploration in itself. The promise of God, of a new creation in Christ, must be imagined before it can be believed and trusted, and before we can live in the light of it.

For Christians, then, the hope of which we speak is a matter of trusting in a God-given promise about a future glory we can imagine and speak about if not fully, then at least sufficiently to transform our ways of being in the present. Hence it is a certain hope, and not, as in Bloch's analysis, merely a matter of a future that may come to pass, but equally may not. But does this built-in certainty not seem likely to reduce (if not remove altogether) the motive force of such hope? One might suppose so perhaps. After all, if the eventual outcome is secure regardless of our striving or lack of it towards the goal of our hope; if redemption does not rest on our strivings and works towards the realisation of the kingdom, then surely the more economic (and certainly the more comfortable) option is to sit back and wait for it all to happen? Is Bloch's model, with its inbuilt risk factor, not more likely to generate the sort of enthusiasm and effort necessary to see the kingdom at least approximated to in this world?

It should not be surprising that such a question is raised. But it seems to me that the answer to it must be an emphatic negative. To begin with, we may observe that if this were so, then it would not truly be the principle of *hope* about which Bloch is writing at such length, but rather a principle of *fear* or *anxiety* (generated by risk) that drives humans forward in an energetic bid to work out their own salvation for fear of the consequences of inaction. To suppose this would in fact be to have missed the entire point of Bloch's case: *hope* energises and transforms human action in the present. But it does perhaps raise a reasonable counter-question; namely, whether, without the introduction of some transcendent guarantor of the outcomes of hope, without the receipt of a divine promise such as that to which Christians lay claim, hope can really be the *genuine* source of a transformed present at all. Within the Christian gospel of grace, with its rejection of every attempt at self-redemption and self-justification, the priority of indicatives over imperatives is everywhere apparent. The fact that redemption comes to us as a free gift, created *ex nihilo* rather than seeking some potential or partial contribution from our side, far from creating a context for antinomian lethargy actually liberates us from the culture of fear and anxiety, and thereby sets us free to act with confidence, secure in the knowledge that failure is itself forgivable and redeemable. But act we do and must, not in order to secure or bring about the kingdom, but precisely because such action is in itself a blessing, a good thing worth doing and sharing with others. And we are sustained and encouraged in this action by the certainty of the final endorsement of what we seek to anticipate here in God's wholly new future.

We are called and enabled, through the activity of the Holy Spirit in the church, to become what we already are in Jesus Christ, and what we will finally be and be seen to be in the new creation of which his resurrection is the decisive anticipation in history. Here, it seems to me, the structure of Bloch's analysis, and the insights offered by Steiner into the vital transformative impact of our capacity to imagine and speak of the future, or to offer an alternative construction of the world and our place within it to that presented by our culture at large, is enormously helpful. We are, as I have put the matter elsewhere, committed as Christians to 'the story which the Christian community tells about the way things are in God's world. The Christian is one who believes this story, who integrates it into his world view, and thereby deploys it as a basis for living in the world.'[23] 'Always be prepared', writes the apostle Peter, 'to respond to anyone who asks you to give the reason for the hope that is in you' (1 Pet. 3:15). That reason is, of course, the promise of God made in Jesus Christ and communicated to us by the Holy Spirit. That this promise can seize us, that we are able to picture this hope to ourselves and to one another, that it can thereby become the motive force for that radically changed way of being in the world, repentance and discipleship – that we can, in short, indulge in the imagination of glory, is part and parcel of the glory of imagination.

Notes

1 New York, 1989. See especially ch. 1.
2 London, 1996.
3 Ibid., xiii.
4 Oxford, 1946. See 231ff.
5 See 'The Idea of Immortality in Relation to Religion and Ethics', in Charles Duthie (ed.), *Resurrection and Immortality* (London, 1979), 7.
6 Oxford, 1992[2]. See especially ch. 3, 'Word Against Object'.
7 Ibid., 144.
8 Ibid., 145.
9 Ibid., 146.
10 Ibid., 168.
11 Ibid., 167.
12 Ibid., 228.
13 3 vols., ET Oxford, 1986.

[14] Ibid., 95.
[15] Ibid., 451.
[16] Ibid., 144.
[17] Ibid., 146.
[18] Ibid., 1105.
[19] Ibid., 1106.
[20] London, 1967.
[21] London, 1996.
[22] *Our Knowledge of God* (Oxford, 1939), 77.
[23] See Trevor A. Hart, *Faith Thinking* (London, 1995), 145.

16

The Year 2000 and the End of Secular Eschatology

Richard J. Bauckham

I

The year 2000 – or, as popular parlance has rather oddly come to call it, the millennium – is a secular event, not a Christian one. I am not just referring to the relative lack of Christian significance given to the event in the Millennium Dome. I do not mean simply that the two-thousandth anniversary of the birth of Jesus has certainly already passed, because in the fifth century Dionysius Exiguus miscalculated the date and Anno Domini years have been wrongly numbered ever since. These are relatively trivial points. The issue to which I wish to draw attention is the metanarrative within which the date 2000 can be treated as of some kind of epochal significance. By the word 'metanarrative' I mean a grand story about the character and meaning of the world, the kind of story by which human societies live. The biblical Christian story, which offers a kind of narrative sketch of the meaning of history, from creation to the end of history, is a metanarrative. It shares with other modern metanarratives a form of eschatology, that is, an expectation that the story will come to a meaningful end, in the Christian case that God will bring the story to an end. There are, of course, some Christians for whom the year 2000 has a special significance within their version of the Christian metanarrative. But they are insignificant. If the year 2000 has any substantial significance for western people in general, this is due not to the Christian metanarrative, but to the modern metanarrative that dates from the eighteenth century, the myth of historical progress. That human history moves forward along an upward sloping path, which either continues indefinitely into an ever improving future or else reaches its zenith in an ultimate utopia – that has been the myth by which the modern age has lived, the grand story that has functioned to give meaning to historical experience in the modern period. What I have called in the title of my lecture 'secular eschatology' is the expectations of the future integral to this metanarrative: the utopian hopes of unlimited human improvement.

This modern myth of progress had its roots in the Renaissance but especially expressed the eighteenth-century Enlightenment's vast confidence that human reason, once freed from the shackles of traditional authority and religious superstition, would take humanity into a new age of freedom and prosperity. Much of the success of the idea of progress in the nineteenth century was connected with science and technology. Human advancement was sought in mastery of nature, coercing nature to serve human ends, reconstructing nature into a world more accommodating to human habitation, tapping the resources of nature for the material benefit of humans. A major factor powering this whole project of domination and advancement was economic. The relatively new idea that human wants and desires for material goods of all kinds were potentially unlimited made continuous economic growth a major imperative of western civilisation. The typically modern economic process of creating constantly expanding demands in order to meet them was underway. But progress was by no means conceived in purely material terms. Democratic freedoms and human rights evolved slowly but steadily from the principles of the Enlightenment. The confidence in reason gave education a central role in progress, and, since human nature was understood as fundamentally rational and good, the dispelling of ignorance and the triumph of reason were confidently expected to lead to the general moral betterment of the race. Progress meant the steady progress of humanity towards perfection. And, although highly Eurocentric, the myth of progress was universalistic in its goal of extending the benefits of European progress to the rest of the world. More than any other ideology, the modern myth of progress has sought meaning within history, in a teleological understanding of history's orientation towards a utopian goal.

It is this notion of history that the use of the era Anno Domini has suited so well. Although of Christian origin, thinking AD was appropriate, perhaps even necessary, to the modern myth of historical progress. In place of the reigns of kings or the passage of generations or the other ways in which people used to measure and divide historical time, the AD era allows us to think of the history of the whole world measured in regular, quantitatively equal periods: decades, centuries, even millennia. With AD dating it became possible to situate one's own time within a sequence of regular periods marking the forward march of history into an unlimited future. It is no accident, surely, that the dominance of AD dates in western consciousness of time and history occurred coincidentally not, as one might expect, with the Christianisation of western society, but rather with the beginnings of its modernisation.

The fact is that until the seventeenth century few people noticed the year-date Anno Domini. Few seventh-century people, for example, knew that they lived in the seventh century. It is true that there was, as we have often been told recently, some anxiety and excitement accompanying the end of the first millennium AD, but only because ordinary people heard of the special significance some scholars attached to this date. Even when dating by the Christian era became common in official usage, ordinary people did not think in such terms. They did not use AD dates in letters or conversation. Our sense of living in a particular period defined as the umpteenth century probably only began in the sixteenth century, while it was the growing use of calendars in the seventeenth century that spread the typically modern sense of AD time. And still only gradually did transitions from an old to a new century come to be treated as appropriate points at which to look backwards and forwards, taking stock of the point reached in humanity's temporal advance. And it was only at the end of the nineteenth century, the great century of progress, at the apogee of the modern metanarrative, that the approach of a new century provoked a nearly obsessive assessment of the progress.

All this suggests that we shall grasp the significance of the year 2000 for contemporary western society, not by comparison with the year 1000, but rather by comparison with the year 1900. In 1892 a columnist for the *Spectator* wrote this:

> The fact that we are approaching the end of another century of our era, strongly affects the popular imagination. It is supposed that, in some undefined way, we must be better or worse merely because of this chronological fact. Were it the end, not of the nineteenth [century], but of the twentieth, we should be still more excited. Even now, the idea of that Annus Mirabilis, the Year of Grace 2000, begins to affect us. We feel that if we could live to witness its advent, we should witness an immense event. We should almost expect something to happen in the Cosmos, so that we might read the great date written on the skies.[1]

The author's tone is a little ironic, but the mood he reflects is the famous *fin de siècle* mood of 1890s Europe. If *fin de siècle* – the end of the nineteenth century – created such an outpouring of angst and excitement, what, he not unreasonably wonders, would *fin de millénaire* – the approach of the second millennium – be like?

The *fin de siècle* mood of the 1890s entailed a process of reviewing the past century and looking forward – enthusiastically or fearfully – into the next. The mood was an unstable mixture of optimism and pessimism, the assessment a kind of weighing of progress and decadence in the balance. Some intellectuals harboured a feeling of imminent perdition, but more prevalent was eager anticipation of a twentieth century propelled by the accelerating momentum of the nineteenth into a qualitatively better era. Frederic Harrison put it like this: 'We *are* on the threshold of a great time, even if our time itself is not great. In science, in religion, in social organisation, we all know what things are in the air . . . It is the age of great expectation and unwearied striving after better things.[2] Enthusiasm was not uncritical: there were end-of-century failures which required to be surmounted in the better future. Alfred Russel Wallace, assessing the past century in a book called *The Wonderful Century* published in 1898 (and notice, incidentally, how unlikely it is that a book published in 1998 could describe our century in such a title) – Wallace catalogued the extraordinary technological advances of the century, but castigated his contemporaries for neglecting hypnotism and phrenology while taking up the harmful practice of vaccination. More significantly (so it seems with hindsight), he deplored the militarism which harnessed technological advance to the development of ever deadlier machines of war. But the dogmatic optimism of the century was not easily crushed. Alexander Sutherland, writing a year later under the title 'The natural decline of warfare', argued that a trajectory of progress over recent centuries pointed to the elimination of warfare in the not too distant future. At the end of the century, he pointed out, it was already the case that absolute peace reigned among civilised nations, though not yet on the borders of the civilised world.[3] This kind of thinking lay in the background to the devastating effect the First World War was to have on progressivist optimism just a few years into the new century on which so much expectation had so recently been focused. There followed what George Steiner recently judged 'the most bestial period in recorded history'.[4] He meant the twentieth century.

So, at the end of the twentieth century, are we, as the 1892 *Spectator* thought we should be, still more excited than they were? I suspect not. Certainly, to the extent that the new millennium does stir our imagination and provoke a sense of the need for stock-taking, even celebration of human achievements, it is the myth of progress that gives the year 2000 this magic. But the power of the myth of progress has long been waning. It has so dominated and permeated the culture of modernity that we cannot easily leave it behind, but it lingers in people's minds more as an unexamined assumption than as a working faith. The twentieth century has robbed it of its plausibility and its allure. I doubt if even the year 2000 can give it more than an artificial new lease of life.

The *fin de millénaire* is hardly turning out to be a *fin de siècle* to the power of ten. Books which take the turn of the millennium as a cue for a back-and-forth-looking assessment of where we are and how we should be aiming to get where we wish have been appearing, but even the optimists are highly chastened, while secular pessimism focuses not merely on decadence, as in the 1890s, but on truly apocalyptic danger. *Shall We Make the Year 2000?* (the title of a book published in 1985)[5] captures this mood. One of the most recent of these stock-taking books, called *The Age of Anxiety*, aims to encounter the 'millennial anxiety', the fear of the future which characterises British society in the

1990s. The book's authors themselves offer varying degrees, none too extreme, of optimism and pessimism. They take the anxiety seriously, and none proposes a return to the ebullient optimism of the nineteenth-century myth, on which the editors comment: 'For perfectibility read corruptibility, for belief in progress read naiveté.'[6] But it is surely no accident that the scientist among the authors retains more than his co-authors do of the nineteenth-century's faith in progress, science-based as that was to a large extent. He ends by exhorting us, 'if the going gets *really* anxious', to try to believe that science reassures.[7] But he would probably not be surprised if most of his readers failed to believe this. Increasingly, in public opinion, scientists are no longer benevolent magicians, but sorcerers' apprentices letting loose forces they cannot control and whose effects they cannot predict.

The difference from the 1890s resembles a paradigm shift. Then it was a matter of drawing up a balance sheet of successes and failures of the century: credit for building the railways, debit for stockpiling armaments, and so on. The difference now is not just that many find our balance sheet to be more or less in overall debit. Nor is it just that we disagree about the evaluation of many changes (is the decline of the traditional family progress or regress?). The most disturbing thing is that progress itself has turned threatening. Increasingly we have had to recognise that many of the most apparently benign advances of technology are having calamitous results. The exponential continuation of the line of nineteenth-century progress is putting the future of the planet itself in the balance. The dominant myth by which the whole modern age has lived – the idea of historical progress – has not only failed us but turned against us.

The more we recognise this, the more the *fin de millénaire* must seem to be a time, not just for taking stock of the past century, but for taking stock of the whole modern age. With the *fin de millénaire*, the time has come to assess not progress, but the myth of progress itself. But have we anything else with which to face the future? Perhaps, after all, we do not need to. If the year 2000 proves, as I suspect it may, banal, then perhaps it will show that contemporary society is abandoning that hopeful sense of direction to an ever new and better future which after all was not at all the way in which most societies in human history have lived. It is arguable that, whereas pre-modern (traditional) societies gave priority to the past and modern (progressive) society has given priority to the future, with the decline of the idea of progress a postmodern society is emerging in which priority is given to the present. We have cut ourselves off from the past that used to give meaning to the present; we have closed off the future that used to be the wide-open horizon of hope in the present; perhaps only the present itself is left to us and this is compressed time into which we seem increasingly driven to squeeze as much as possible. The year 2000 may prove a convenient date to mark the end of the secular eschatology of progress.

II

Before turning to the Christian metanarrative, I suggest we consider three anti-metanarratives, as I think we might call them, all three formulated in deliberate opposition to the modern myth of progress. In their different ways all three throw considerable light on the decline of the myth of progress and the condition of western society after its end. Their authors are all seminal thinkers. I take them in chronological order.

First, Friedrich Nietzsche, a postmodern thinker in the heyday of modernity, pioneer of much that we now think characteristically postmodern. Famously, Nietzsche proclaimed the death of God – the loss of credibility of the idea of God in the modern period. He proclaimed it as an event whose unprecedented significance had not yet been perceived even by the atheists of Nietzsche's time. The death of God entails the end of truth and morality as objective and universal values. For the typically modern, humanist atheism that found inherent meaning in the historical process as progress towards a goal, Nietzsche had only scorn. It was merely an atheistic continuation of Christian values. It had failed to see that the death of God entailed also the death of meaning and progress in history. Nietzsche in effect foresaw the incredulity towards all metanarratives that a century later would be said to define the postmodern. The death not only of the Christian metanarrative but also of its stepchild the modern myth of progress follow from the death of God.

In their place Nietzsche offered an anti-metanarrative: the idea of eternal recurrence. Postmodernists have in this respect not followed Nietzsche, but the idea plays an important role in his thought. We can think of it as the antithesis of any metanarrative that seeks meaning in history or in eschatology. Nietzsche presents it vividly like this:

> What, if some day or night a demon were to . . . say to you: 'This life as you now live it and have lived it, you will have to live once more and innumerable times more; and there will be nothing new in it, but every pain and every joy and every thought and sigh and everything ultimately small or great in your life will have to return to you, all the same succession and sequence . . . The eternal hourglass of existence is turned upside down again and again, and you with it, speck of dust!'
>
> Would you not throw yourself down and gnash your teeth and curse the demon who spoke thus? Or have you once experienced a tremendous moment when you would have answered him: 'You are a god and never have I heard anything more divine.' If this thought gained possession of you, it would change you as you are or perhaps crush you. The question in each and every thing, 'Do you desire this once more and innumerable times more?' would lie upon your actions as the greatest weight. Or how well disposed would you have to become to yourself and to life *to crave nothing more fervently* than this ultimate eternal confirmation and seal?[8]

The idea of eternal recurrence functions as a kind of illumination of what it would really mean to accept fully the lack of meaning and purpose in the world. To live without a metanarrative, liberated from the Christian and modern dream of a reality different from what actually is, should mean to be able instead to affirm the totality of life just as it is, to crave nothing more fervently than that one's actual life, just exactly as it has been and is, should recur infinitely. But Nietzsche himself knew that it would take the Superman to be able to do that. It must mean, for example, that survivors of Auschwitz must crave nothing more fervently than that the sufferings of Auschwitz recur, just as they did, infinitely.

Auschwitz is a good test of both metanarratives and anti-metanarratives. As representative of the evils of the twentieth century, Auschwitz negates the myth of progress. It exposes the myth's inability to deal with the horror of history. In the face of Auschwitz, no one may say that the evils of history are a price worth paying for a better future. The modern attempt to find meaning inherent in history founders on Auschwitz, but does not Nietzsche's rejection of meaning also? Who would not say that to affirm Auschwitz as part of the totality of life, to want nothing to be different, to crave its eternal recurrence, would be not super- but subhuman?

Nietzsche died, insane, long before Auschwitz. Walter Benjamin, the German Jewish philosopher, died a year before Hitler decreed the Final Solution. But Benjamin already saw the reality of his time as one of mass murder when he wrote, only months before his own death in 1940, the following meditation on a painting by Paul Klee which he owned and which had long fascinated him:

> A Klee painting named 'Angelus Novus' [the new angel] shows an angel looking as though he is about to move away from something he is fixedly contemplating. His eyes are staring, his mouth is open, his wings are spread. This is how one pictures the angel of history. His face is turned toward the past. Where we perceive a chain of events, he sees one single catastrophe which keeps piling wreckage upon wreckage and hurls it in front of his feet. The angel would like to stay, awaken the dead, and make whole what has been smashed. But a storm is blowing from Paradise; it has got caught in his wings with such violence that the angel can no longer close them. This storm irresistibly propels him into the future to which his back is turned, while the pile of debris before him grows skyward. This storm is what we call progress.[9]

The typically modern view of history as inevitable progress looks resolutely forward, but Benjamin through the staring eyes of his angel of history faces backwards, his eyes fixed on the victims and the wreckage of history that pile up before him. Progress leaves the victims behind. The future cannot repair the past. What Benjamin sees so clearly is that history cries out for redemption and progress cannot provide it. Even were the angel to be finally blown to a standstill in utopia, the debris of history would remain before his eyes. Utopia can be no compensation for those who have suffered history. It leaves the dead dead. While Benjamin here, in this bleakly back-to-front vision of progress, offers no hope for the redemption of history, he refutes any notion that the modern metanarrative can offer such hope.

The French philosopher who famously in 1979 defined the postmodern as incredulity towards metanarratives, Jean-François Lyotard, offers an anti-metanarrative of his own, which he calls a postmodern fable.[10] It is too long to read now, but it tells in purely scientific terms the story of the origin of the earth, the process of Darwinian evolution, and the story of humanity up to the time, many millions of years in the future, when the sun is about to explode and absorb the solar system into itself. Whatever it is that the human brain has then become escapes the catastrophe by leaving the planet forever before its destruction. This can be thought possible because the human species will have foreseen and prepared for the death of the solar system millions of years before it happens. Nevertheless the story has no human meaning. It is not the story of human beings, but of energy. It is the story of the conflict between the two processes that affect energy: entropy and increasing differentiation or complexification. The former leads to the death of the solar system, but the latter makes possible the escape of the highly complex form of organising energies into which the human species will have evolved by then. That will not be humanity but as different from us as the human species is from the amoeba. Humans are merely one transitory form in which energy is organised. The escape, with which the fable ends, cannot be an object of human hope as utopia has been for modern progressive humanity, for it is not humans who escape, and, in any case, the hero of the fable is not humanity or even what humanity will then have become, but energy. Humans are objects of history, not subjects, and even energy is not the subject of history, for it has no intentionality.

The fable is postmodern in that its content signifies 'the end of hopes (modernity's hell)', as Lyotard puts it, while the form is no more than a fable, self-consciously imaginary. It expresses what Lyotard calls 'the postmodern state of thought': the 'suffering for lack of finality', which eschatology, Christian and modern, used to assuage, but the postmodern fable cannot. The fable seems to me appropriate to these last years of the second millennium, when there seems considerable interest in scientific cosmology and Darwinian evolution. As substitutes for the grand narratives of religion and modernity, these scientific narratives can only be anti-metanarratives, offering explanation but not meaning.

III

How then should Christians view the end of secular eschatology, if I am right that its end is approaching? The answer is certainly not obvious, since the postmodern incredulity towards metanarratives is directed against the Christian metanarrative as well as the progressivist modern one. Nietzsche and Lyotard see the modern myth of progress as no more than a modern version of Christian eschatology. Moreover, Christian theologians in the modern period have often tried to give theological legitimation to modernity by claiming its major characteristics to be based on Christian premises. In so doing they have assimilated the Christian metanarrative to liberal progressivism, and that assimilation still lingers not only in the expected but also in quite surprising Christian places. I would not be surprised if the modern myth of progress, in liberal Christian dress, survived in some Christian circles longer than in secular ones.

It is undoubtedly the case that the modern metanarrative owes its historical origins to the Christian metanarrative that preceded it as the dominant myth of European culture. The Christian metanarrative, like the Jewish and Islamic ones, but unlike most other pre-modern worldviews, is a story whose end is still to come. Historicity and futurity are integral to it, as they are to the modern myth of progress. It is certainly very doubtful whether the modern metanarrative, with its concentration on a movement of history towards a future goal, could have come about had the Christian metanarrative not preceded it as a major influence on European culture. But the transition from the Christian to the modern metanarrative entailed two decisive novelties that radically distinguish the modern from the Christian metanarrative.

The first is the rejection of transcendence and the reduction of eschatology to the immanent goal of human history. In the Christian tradition the end of history and the new creation had not been considered the end product of the historical process, a goal history itself could achieve, but a fresh creative act of the transcendent God who would thus make of his creation what it had no immanent capacity to be. And while the Christian tradition had envisaged the activity of the Spirit of God at work in the world and already anticipating the new creation within history, this had not been seen as a cumulative process bringing the world gradually into the perfection of the kingdom of God. Moreover, the coming kingdom of God was not understood as merely the final period of history, to be reached at the end of a continuous temporal line stretching into the future. The end of history was to happen to the whole of history, entailing the resurrection and the judgment of all the dead. This is eschatological transcendence that necessarily disappeared with God when Enlightenment humanity replaced God by taking the reins of history into their own hands.

In doing so they took over far more of the Christian eschatological hope than mere history without transcendence could bear. Education and technology were now the means to the goal of history, which could only be understood as an immanent goal, the product of the historical process. By these means human beings were perfectible and the world infinitely adaptable to human needs. Education replaced grace and technology replaced creation. The whole scientific-technological project of the modern age has been a kind of new creation, a remaking of the world, as though humans had the creative power of God and the creative wisdom of God. This was promethean eschatology that crucially failed to recognise the limits of this world. In assuming limitless power over a limitless future of unlimited resources, humanity reached for the eschatological freedom of God and is now discovering the limits only as we risk catastrophe in colliding against them.

The end of secular eschatology is the end of eschatology without transcendence. Christian eschatology, by contrast, trusts the final future to God the creator and lord of all things. Therefore it can sustain hope and inspire action without needing these to be underpinned by the myth of incremental progress towards a utopian goal. Christian hope neither attempts what can only come from God nor neglects what is humanly possible. Sustained by the hope of everything from God, it attempts what is possible within the limits of each present. It does not overreach itself in striving for a post-historical goal. It does not value what can be done only as a step in a linear progress to a goal. It does what can be done for its own sake, here and now, confident that every present will find itself, redeemed and fulfilled, in God's new creation of all things.

The modern metanarrative differed from the Christian in rejecting transcendence; it also, secondly, differed in its attitude to the evils of history. The myth of progress in its heyday was a kind of immanent theodicy or justification of history. All the pains and losses were justified by the goal. They were the eggs broken to make the utopian omelette. This is the sense, as I remarked earlier, in which Auschwitz negates the myth of progress. In the face of Auschwitz, no one can say that the evils of history are a price worth paying for a better future. But if they are not, then progress can do nothing but leave them behind. Progress can only forget the victims of history. The victims of progress itself indeed *must* be forgotten if progress is not to be exposed as a sham. One has only to turn around and look back, with Benjamin's angel of history, to realise that history cries out for redemption that progress cannot provide.

Unlike the myth of progress, Christian eschatology does not privilege future history over past history. The end of history will happen to all of history. In the resurrection all the dead of all history will rise to judgment and life in the new creation. There is no danger that people in the past or the present be considered mere means to the greater good of people in the future. The countless victims of history, those whose lives were torture and those who scarcely lived at all, are not to be forgotten, but remembered in hope of the resurrection. And not only the dead, but also those of the living for whom there can be no more hope in this world, those who can neither assist nor benefit from the onward march of progress – the desperately and incurably sick, the dying, the wretched of the earth – must not be left behind, but be cherished with the special care God has for the most hopeless. The future we cannot give them is promised them by God.

The horror, the tragedy and the loss, which are as much a part of history as fulfilment and achievement, can be fully acknowledged in the Christian metanarrative, since it is a narrative of redemption. At its heart is a story for which the secular narrative of modernity has no equivalent: the story of Jesus, his cross and resurrection. The cross, where Jesus drank to the dregs the cup of God-forsaken death, is not a stage in the upward ascent of human history, but a descent to its depths in order to bring God into those depths. Since the cross cannot be edited out of the Christian metanarrative, it forbids those who tell the Christian story any whitewashing of history, any progressivist tale of success that neglects the victims. It forbids any form of hope that minimises or justifies evil. Instead it affirms the crucified God's loving solidarity with all who suffer and proffers hope for the end of history, when God will wipe away every tear from every eye and take his whole creation beyond the reach of evil.

It seems that taking transcendence seriously and taking evil seriously belong together. Immanent eschatology, in which utopia must come from the resources of history itself, cannot cope with radical evil and must almost inevitably play it down. There is, however, a kind of counter-charge, which, in conclusion I think we must consider. Many champions of the myth of progress themselves recognised the radical difference between the transcendent eschatology of the Christian tradition and the immanent eschatology of its secular stepchild. But they charged the former with other-worldliness of the pie-in-the-sky-when-you-die variety. The otherworldly hope distracted attention from efforts to improve this world. I do not think this charge was fair to most of the Christian tradition, but it does bring me, finally, to relate my lecture to the aims for which the Drew Lecture was founded. Personal immortality and the destiny of the soul were to be its concern. I have preferred to speak of the resurrection of the dead in the context of God's new creation of all things. Secular eschatology fails most obviously in offering no hope for the dead, but Christian eschatology makes the opposite mistake if it offers only immortality for souls extracted from history and the world. Christian eschatology gives hope to human persons most genuinely when it looks to God for the redemption of all history and all creation. One day the angel of history will fly back to Paradise, and as he goes he will awaken the dead and make whole all that has been smashed.[12]

Notes

1 Quoted in H. Schwartz, *Century's End: A Cultural History of the Fin de Siècle from the 990s through the 1990s* (New York: Doubleday, 1990), 275.

2 Quoted in D. Thompson, *The End of Time: Faith and Fear in the Shadow of the Millennium* (London: Random House, 1997), 119.

3 C. Townshend, 'The Fin de Siècle', in A. Dancher (ed.), *Fin de Siècle: The Meaning of the Twentieth Century* (London: Tauris, 1995), 202, 207–9.

4 G. Steiner, *Errata: An Examined Life* (London: Weidenfeld & Nicolson, 1997), 103.

5 J. G. de Beus, *Shall We Make the Year 2000?: The Decisive Challenge to Western Civilisation* (London: Sidgwick & Jackson, 1985).

6 S. Dunant and R. Porter (eds.), *The Age of Anxiety* (London: Virago, 1997[2]), xv.

7 Watts, 'Can Science Reassure?', in Dunant and Porter, *The Age of Anxiety*, 187. It is typical that his account of science makes no reference to the commercial motives that direct most scientific research.

8 F. Nietzsche, *The Gay Science*, trans. W. Kaufmann (New York: Random House, 1974), 273–4 (§341).

9 W. Benjamin, *Illuminations* (ed. H. Arendt; trans. H. Zohn; New York: Schocken, 1969), 257–8; and cf. R. Alter, *Necessary Angels: Tradition and Modernity in Kafka, Benjamin and Scholem* (Cambridge, Mass., Harvard University Press, 1991), 114–15.

10 J.-F. Lyotard, *Postmodern Fables*, trans. G. Van Den Abbeele (Minneapolis: University of Minnesota Press, 1997), ch. 6.

11 Lyotard, *Postmodern Fables*, 100.

12 For a fuller treatment of the subject of this lecture, see R. Bauckham and T. A. Hart, *Hope against Hope: Christian Eschatology in Contemporary Context* (London: Darton, Longman & Todd, 1999); US edition: *Hope against Hope: Christian Eschatology at the Turn of the Millennium* (Grand Rapids: Eerdmans, 1999).

17

'Until he Comes'

Towards an eschatology of church membership

Colin E. Gunton

Eschatology and the Church

It is often said that our era is one in which eschatology has been rediscovered, although there is neither clarity nor agreement as to how that eschatology might be understood.[1] If we merely review some of the responses to the rediscovery there will be enough evidence of the disarray. Some late nineteenth and early twentieth-century biblical scholars and church historians took the discovery of Jesus' essentially eschatological message as Christianity's death warrant. Jesus saw himself, they held, as the prophet of the end; but the end did not come, and so he was mistaken. The genius of Barth is that he took the very same discoveries to be a life warrant: 'If Christianity is not thoroughgoing eschatology, it is nothing.'[2] Yet the eschatology of the second edition of *The Epistle to the Romans*, like that of Bultmann's not finally so dissimilar proposals, owes, it is often enough claimed, more to Kantian dualism than to the peculiarly elusive biblical representations of eschatology. The later Barth replaced his early eschatology with what was effectively a realised eschatology of revelation. In Jesus Christ, who is the *eschatos*, the end has already come, because in him God's covenant purpose, to reconcile all people in him, was realised. In their response to the later Barth, however, Moltmann and Pannenberg discerned a similar flaw to that of the early work, this time in a tendency to reduce eschatology, effectively disarming it by the orientation of Barth's theology to the beginning; or at least, in the more subtle criticisms of Robert Jenson, weakening its impact.[3] But are Pannenberg and Moltmann any more successful in maintaining the right relation of beginning, middle and end, for that is surely the key to the matter? Not in every way, it must be said. Pannenberg's employment of Plotinus' concept of time in his recent work does not inspire confidence that he has solved the problem,[4] while the emanationist aspects of Moltmann's recent writing on the Spirit work against eschatology rather than for it.[5]

Here we must beware of supposing that it is primarily the calling of the theologian to solve problems. Part of the point of eschatology is that it warns us that certain central questions are not patient of solution this side of the end. We are part of a culture that seeks to bring in the kingdom, or some kind of kingdom, by human activity, and it is a recurring feature of the overrealised secular eschatology of the day that we are so prone to seek to solve that which is beyond immediate solution.

That is one clue indeed to our frantic modern restlessness and to the ineffective attempts of modern governments of all stamps to bring in the kingdom by legislation. In all life, and especially in the life of the church, eschatological reserve should be the hallmark of thought and action: a recollection of the limits of our possibilities, given at once both human finitude and the sin that continues to hold back even, sometimes especially, those who are on the way to final redemption.

In this lecture, I want to look at something of the limits we should place on what we might expect of the church. I accept that in many ways we expect too little, but it is equally the case that expecting too much often derives from an overrealised eschatology which distorts the community's life and witness. Let me instance three symptoms of an overrealised eschatology in matters ecclesial. The first is historical, and well described in Moltmann's recent study of eschatology.[6] Making excessive claims for the church's capacity to represent, even to be, the kingdom, has led to some of the political excesses which have disfigured church history, and are still a major feature of secularist attacks on Christianity. The story is too well rehearsed to require further comment. The second danger characterises the thought of that recent ethical thinking often labelled Anabaptist and represented by John Howard Yoder and Stanley Hauerwas. These are two seminal and important thinkers, and one might cautiously apply to them the much overused adjective, prophetic. Yet in their tendency to reject or minimise the importance of the doctrine of justification by grace alone they risk placing upon the faithful a burden greater than they can bear. Let me be cautious, for once. Their call to the church to be a distinctive and holy community, *for* the world by being self-consciously *other* than it, is salutary and, indeed, right – especially in view of the perceptive recent observation that the mainline denominations have generally succeeded in being of the world but not in it. And the charges against them of sectarianism are mostly merely silly. Yet the function of the law or of ethical teaching in eschatological perspective does require clearer exposition than it is sometimes given if we are not to impose ethical overload by a failure to recognise limits.

The third example comes from the other end of the ecclesial spectrum, and concerns christology, specifically the overweighting of the theology of the body of Christ. It is often enough observed that the difference between Luther and Calvin on the Lord's Supper derives from a difference in christology; indeed, at a time when the Chalcedonian Definition of the person of Christ remained for the most part unquestioned, Reformation christological dispute was centred on that topic. Luther's christology, tending as it does to the monophysite, and holding the communication of attributes – roughly, that anything you can say of divinity of Christ you must also be able to say of his humanity – led to the conclusion that because God could be everywhere, so could Christ's human body, and hence it could be present in with and under the elements of bread and wine. Calvin has often enough been accused of separating the divine and the human, though that has been shown by Bruce McCormack to be mistaken.[7] His christology was essentially Cyrillian, while his teaching of the union of the faithful with Christ also militated against a mere transcendence of the ascended saviour. Yet the ascension did imply for him that Christ's body is located at the right hand of God, and could not therefore be ubiquitous. To be bodily is to be particular and to be located in space, and this ruled out the claim that Christ's body could be everywhere at once. This gives greater space for the Spirit's distinctive work in relation to the church rather than to the bread and wine. The Spirit is primarily seen as one who lifts worshippers into the presence of God rather than achieving a transformation of the elements. But it is in conversation with a representative of the Lutheran tradition that our theme can best be developed.

In our day, with the continued fading of the Constantinian settlement, the problem of the nature of the church and of her relation to the social order in which she is set – the question of what kind of political entity the church is – is receiving renewed attention. And it is here that a recent ecclesiology is of great interest to us. Let me say briefly first what I cannot, and then what I can, take from Robert Jenson's account of the church in his recent *Systematic Theology*. Insofar as Christ is risen, he is for this writer risen into, almost as, the church:

> The church, according to Paul, is the risen body of Christ. She is this because the bread and cup in the congregation's midst is the very same body of Christ.[8]

The monophysite undertones of this are apparent in other formulations:

> For the proposition that the church is a human body of the risen Christ to be ontically and straightforwardly true, all that is required is that Jesus indeed be the

> Logos of God . . . He needs no other body to be a risen man, body and soul. There is and needs to be no other place than the church for him to be embodied, nor in that other place any other entity to be the 'real' body of Christ.[9]

The church is repeatedly described in this work as Christ's availability for the world, just as our bodies are our availability for others. 'That the church is the body of Christ . . . means that she is the object in the world as which the risen Christ is an object for the world . . .'[10] Despite a brief obeisance to transcendence – to the church as the bride, and therefore other, of Christ – it is immanence that dominates: 'that the church is ontologically the risen Christ's human body . . .'[11] Here the 'Lutheran' christology is fully at work, apparently denying that the risen and ascended Christ is 'at the right hand of the Father' in anything other than an immanent sense.[12] The church, it would seem, not just represents but actually *is* the presence on earth of the eschatological kingdom. This, for reasons that we shall come to, simply will not do.

On the other hand, there is something I would like to appropriate from Robert Jenson, and this is his teaching that the church, as church, is a socio-political reality in its own right. It has, or more accurately is, a polity, a way of being politically and socially in the world. In this respect, Jenson points out, first, 'that when the New Testament does refer to the church as God's people, this is in every case but one done at least in part to identify her with Israel'.[13] It follows that if the church is identical or continuous with Israel, then like Israel she is a polity, an organised way of being in the world. Second, the discontinuity with Israel which is also involved centres on the rite of baptism, in which one becomes, in Aquinas' words, 'a member of Christ', and receives the gifts of the Spirit which 'are all in fact "rights and privileges" of the *community* into which the rite initiates'.[14] 'A *people* united in a common *spirit*, that is, a people who have become a community, is a *polity* . . .' And the polity is for Jenson an anticipated eschatology. 'The church anticipates [the] eschatological peace [of the Kingdom] in the imperfect but real concord of her members, situated in mutual and complementary modes of leading and obeying.'[15] Third, the distinctive polity entails a distinctive ethic, which Jenson elaborates in terms of the Decalogue. With all these features I am in agreement, though not with all the details of their articulation.

Aspects of 1 Corinthians

I shall in this second section concentrate not, as might be expected in the light of the text (1 Cor. 11:26) contained in the title, on the Lord's Supper, but on the prior question of the nature of the church, and in particular on the sense in which we can say that the end is realised in her life. Is the church an eschatological reality, and in what sense? Let us, at least for the sake of discussion, begin by treating the Supper as a subspecies of the meal in general. Jenson again:

> All meals are intrinsically religious occasions, indeed sacrifices, and were so understood especially in Israel. For all life belongs intimately to God, so that the killing involved in eating – which we do not at all avoid by eating vegetables – is an intrusion into his domain . . . Sharing a meal is therefore always a communal act of worship and establishes fellowship precisely before the Lord.[16]

In this regard, the interest of the words 'until he comes' derives at least as much from the sharing of meals in general as from what we think, because of the tradition, of its specifically eucharistic significance.

Three aspects of the broader context will enable the case to be made. It is evident, first, that much of the argument of Paul's letter concerns the domain within which the members of the infant church have their being and to which they give their allegiance. Sharing meals is at the heart of it. Speaking purely theologically, so to say, to share the meals of the pagan temples is harmless, because their gods do not exist. Paul has, however, a number of reasons for discouraging his flock from so indulging. The first is moral: it is a sin against love to offend the Christian neighbour unnecessarily. But a second goes further. There are, he writes, gods many and lords many (8:5), and, even though in one sense they are non-existent, they yet exercise authority over those who enter their realm. To eat with the non-existent idols is to enter a social and political sphere in competition with that of the God of Israel. It is the same with those who have recourse to pagan law courts to settle inner-churchly disputes. In this instance the eschatological dimensions of the matter come into view. Those who are to judge angels place themselves under the authority of the demonic. The church is a social and political reality that does things differently from other institutions, because it is eschatologically different, which means that the basis of its being and authority are also radically different. Here Hauerwas and Yoder are right. It follows that in so far as all meals are of religious significance, to share table fellowship with idols is, to use the fashionable expression, to sleep with the enemy. I use that metaphor because it opens up another related aspect of the Corinthian church's situation. For Paul, transgressing sexual boundaries is another way of entering the realm of that which is demonic because it is opposed to the rule of God; that is, it is a way of entering into relations that are constitutive of our human being contrary to those of the eschatological kingdom. In all these realms of action, the Corinthians' errors are of a piece in that they place themselves outside the authority of the ascended Christ.

That takes me to the second piece of context. For Paul we are at once – and here we meet the eschatological tension that characterises the whole of this work – what we do in the body and what our bodies are eschatologically. We are what we do and yet we are what we shall be. The human body, that which is nourished by the meals of which we have spoken, is the way we are in the world, and by this is meant not the world distinct from the church but the world that is God's creation. This is especially the case in the way we are related to our fellow human beings, those made in the image of God. What we do with and in the body anticipates – or, I suppose we should say, *may* anticipate – what we shall be. Let us here simply listen to part of the outcome of Paul's discussion of sexual morality and pagan eating alongside one another:

> Food for the stomach, and the stomach for food' [presumably Paul is here quoting his opponents] – but God will destroy them both. The body is not meant for sexual immorality, but for the Lord, and the Lord for the body. By his power God raised the Lord from the dead, and he will raise us also. Do you not know that your bodies are members of Christ himself? Shall I then take the members of Christ and unite them with a prostitute? Never!
> (1 Cor. 6:13–15, NIV)

Paul then proceeds, citing Genesis, to say that sexual union is literally a form of union, which in the wrong context displaces union with Christ. Then follow some points whose trinitarian logic should be noted:

> But he who unites himself with the Lord is one with him in spirit . . . Do you not know that your body is a temple of the Holy Spirit . . . You are not your own; you were bought at a price. Therefore honour God with your body.

To be at once a member of Christ and the place of the Spirit's activity; that is the high status of the body in Paul's theology. And the reasons are twofold: atonement and eschatology. 'You were bought with a price'; 'God will raise us also.'

The third contextual consideration follows naturally from this. The verses we have just heard from chapter 6 anticipate chapter 15, that eschatological climax which, like all eschatology, throws its light back on what has gone before. That later chapter also introduces the trinitarian considerations on which depend the way in which we shall understand the relation between past reconciliation and eschatological fulfilment, and therefore life in the church. There, too, is to be found the basis for the differences between what for the sake of simplicity we can call Lutheran and Reformed christology and ecclesiology. 1 Corinthians 15 describes Jesus Christ as a particular human being rather than the apparently social or corporate person we have met in Jenson and possibly in earlier chapters. Jesus is the first and only one to have been raised, and indeed, part of the heresy Paul appears to be combating is the denial of this unique resurrection in favour of ascribing some such realised status to all the members of the church. So, he insists, there is a distinction to be made between the time of Christ's resurrection and that of ours: 'Christ, the first fruits; then, when he comes, those who belong to him' (v. 23). Here, Christ is patently distinguished from the church. He is, to use Irenaean language, one of God the Father's two hands whose *present* reign, as the risen and ascended Lord, will be completed only when every enemy – 'all dominion, authority and power' and, ultimately, death; that is to say, those 'gods many and lords many' into whose hands the erring Corinthians were placing themselves – has been defeated. Only when those bodies which are the location of human being and activity have been raised and transformed, will Christ's incarnate work be done.

Alongside, therefore, the close identification of Christ with the church which Jenson has rightly observed is the polar pull in another direction: he is one with the church only as also its transcendent Lord. Transcendence is not swallowed up in immanence, any more than death is yet finally swallowed up in victory. That is why we must attempt to hear the passage from chapter 11 with ears freed as much as possible from traditional debate about the presence of Christ in the bread and the wine. 'In memory of him . . . until he comes' presupposes, according to Richard Hays, that he is in fact absent.[17] *In that respect*, Paul is speaking of real absence, not real presence. The passage, furthermore, is devoted to the church's polity, its social and political constitution, as much as to its eucharistic worship, indeed, more than that, at least if the latter is narrowly conceived. Let us follow the logic of Paul's argument. Chapter 11 begins with the much discussed passage about the covering of women's heads, which I shall take it as concerned essentially not with who takes part in the leading of worship, but with the due and dignified order in which that takes place; that is to say, with proper ecclesial polity. There then follows a second discussion of the church's political order: of the scandal of the carrying over of worldly social divisions into the meals that they share. Only at this stage do we hear what are called the words of institution, which are a simple recollection of what Jesus once did.

After that comes Paul's lapidary comment: 'For whenever you eat this bread and drink this cup, you proclaim the Lord's death until he comes.' Notice that in parallel with the bread is not 'wine' but 'cup'. As Caird writes, 'In Paul's account, as in the others, the parallel to "bread" is not "wine" but "cup". Elsewhere in the recorded words of Jesus the cup is a symbol of his crucifixion (Mk. 10:38; 14:36).'[18] It is the narrated passion and resurrection that determine the church and its worship. Therefore I believe that the notion, much touted in ecumenical conversations, that the eucharist makes the church should be rejected. The church is the creature of the Word, as the broad context of this epistle – the main support of Jenson's sacramentology – makes absolutely clear.[19] Must we not therefore qualify the immediacy of talk of the church as

Christ's availability to the world? Is not the priority rather to be given to the word, first of Scripture and then of proclamation, to which the visible word of the Supper is appended, and on which it is dependent for both its being and its intelligibility? '[A] sacrament is never without a preceding promise but is joined to it as a sort of appendix, with the purpose of confirming and sealing the promise itself . . .'[20] Sacraments are appendixes to the Word, and that means secondary to the atoning work of Christ which is, for eschatological reasons, first a heard and proclaimed word by virtue of the fact that we are the church between that which we remember and that to which we move.

But let us continue our review of chapter 11. After the words I have discussed, Paul returns to – ethics and judgment. Talk of eating and drinking unworthily returns us to the problem of the church's polity. Here we meet what may be an insoluble problem of interpretation. The almost universal translation of verse 29, 'anyone who eats and drinks without recognising [or discerning] the body eats and drinks judgment on himself' is at best a guess. According to Caird, 'nowhere else in Greek literature does *diakrinō* mean "to recognise", and this sense hardly fits the second occurrence of the word at v. 31 ("we shall not be *judged*").'[21] Listen to the repeated allusions to judgment:

> Anyone who eats and drinks [offending in whatever way is intended] eats and drinks judgment (*krima*) on himself. That is why many of you are weak and sick, and a number of you have fallen asleep. But if we judged (*diekrinomen*) ourselves, we would not come under judgment (*ekrinometha*). When we are judged (*krinomenoi*) by the Lord, we are being disciplined (*paideuometha*), so that we will not be condemned (*katakrithōmen*) with the world (vv. 29–31).

Whatever else is the case, the one thing that 'the body' that is not discerned – or whatever – cannot refer to is the eucharistic elements. If a body is being unrecognised, that body is the community whose social structure is being torn apart by bad behaviour rather than inadequate sacramentology. It would seem that Paul is deploying a series of puns on the theme of judgment, to the effect that to share the cup is to undergo judgment (meaning godly discipline) and so avoid judgment (meaning eschatological rejection), the latter of which is the unintended outcome revealed in some of the symptoms of the church's disordered life.

It is in this light that we should refer back to the previous chapter, 1 Corinthians 10, which begins with the theme of judgment: with the death in the wilderness of thousands of Israelites. 'Therefore . . . flee from idolatry'; that is to say, flee from the worship of anything that is not God, from entering any sphere of influence than that of the God of Israel. *That is to say*: join yourselves to this community of worship and not to any other solidarity of sacrifice. If all meals are of religious significance, then it makes all the difference with whom you eat. (What does it imply that the Archbishop of Canterbury recently sat to eat with the President of China, for example?)[22] That is the religious, moral and political context of the Corinthians' meal, and that is the primary connotation of participation in the blood and body of Christ. The blood is a reference to the cross, to the atonement, which is, according to Paul, the only thing he wishes to proclaim (1 Cor. 1:18–2:5); and the body to the community that is what it is because it eats and drinks together. It is a matter of polity: 'You cannot drink the cup of the Lord and the cup of demons too . . .' (1 Cor. 10:21).

Here a question needs to be asked. Am I seeking to moralise this passage, to turn this into a matter of mere ethics? The answer is a qualified denial. It is a denial because the calling of the church is to worship God simply in and for himself before it is a call to act morally and politically. Yet that denial must be qualified because of the character of the being and action of the God who is worshipped. The triune God is one whose triune *koinōnia* has overflowed into the creation and redemption of a world he loves, and particularly of those creatures he has made in his image and remade in the image of his Son Jesus. It is for that reason – because God is himself communion – that the worship of the church cannot be disentangled from its social and political matrix and outcome. That is the message Paul and Jenson share. How are we to bring together in due relation to one another these two interrelated realms of worship and life? In two ways, it seems to me, and here I can only be exploratory.

First, much depends on the meaning of the words from moral and political philosophy that are being so freely used in this interpretation of 1 Corinthians. It can never be forgotten that this is a book whose roots are in the Old Testament rather than in Aristotle, and we employ the latter's pagan heritage at our peril. In chapter after chapter of this letter, Paul is concerned with what can only be called Torah, which means not merely law but the whole gracious divine dispensation for human living on earth and in the body. It is consistently a matter of the sphere of authority within which one places oneself: of whom or what one worships (hence the concern with the idolatry which is to be shunned) and of the source of one's authority for the shape of one's life on earth. In both realms, there is an absolute choice to be made. For members of the body of Christ to enter the sphere of pagan worship or to have recourse to pagan law courts is, as we have seen, to enter the sphere of the demonic. Rather, as chapter 6 continues, one must give one's allegiance to the Torah, and here the Decalogue is summarised and repeated as the canon by which membership of the community of salvation is measured. And the reason? The fact of that past atonement which has achieved through trinitarian agency a transfer of allegiance: 'But you were washed, you were sanctified, you were justified in the name of the Lord Jesus Christ and by the Spirit of our God' (1 Cor. 6:11).

The second way of understanding the relation of worship and polity is with the notion of sacrifice. Let us again recall Jenson's point: 'All meals are intrinsically religious occasions, indeed sacrifices . . .' We therefore need to pause to consider some of the things that sacrifice is according to the Scriptures. Here, it seems to me, there is a definite hierarchy. First, although there is no one satisfactory 'explanation' of the meaning of sacrifice, worship and thanksgiving come high up the list of meanings. For Scripture, giving thanks and praise to God is a large part of what sacrifice means. We cannot moralise this passage if it means taking it out of its prior context of worship, which is praise and thanks to God for the price Christ has paid – another sacrificial term, used, as we have seen, in this letter. And yet, second, as prophet and psalmist point out repeatedly, indeed, relentlessly, right worship is inseparable from right conduct. For both Old and New Testament, sacrifice is inseparable from obedience. If Jacob Milgrom is right, the priestly writer achieved what is in effect a moralisation of sacrifice by taking it out of paganism's merely cultic and religious realm. For Leviticus, whose influence penetrates deeply into the letter we are examining, sacrifice is largely a matter of Israel's social and political reality, in ways directly analogous to the situation of the Corinthian church. The priestly writer achieved a demythologisation of sacrifice, which was concerned not now with the exorcism of the demonic, as in the pagan peoples around, but with holiness conceived in mostly ethical terms.[23] Life or death – precisely as in 1 Corinthians – is the issue, not ritual impurity. Similarly, for Paul, if we may cross-refer to another of his letters, the primary sacrifice under the new dispensation, is that of the body: 'offer your bodies as *a* living sacrifice . . .' (Rom. 12:1–2). In that parallel passage in Romans, where too the relationship of the body and its members is at issue, we find again the socio-political concern that the diverse offerings of the distinct members of the body *together* make a single sacrifice of praise. How we are to hold the two dimensions of worship and ethics in right relation is surely in part a matter of eschatology, and to that we now turn.

Towards an Eschatology of Church Membership

'Until he comes'. Christ's rule is exercised through the church, but it is the very church whose members from time to time go to pagan temples and law courts, and generally behave in ways which would frustrate that rule. Therefore any too close identification of the church with Christ after the manner of Jenson risks two offences against eschatology. The first is the empirical self-deception or special pleading that presumes upon the judgment of God – which, after all, begins with the people of God. To suggest that the church is *literally* Christ's body raises expectations beyond that attributable, in eschatological perspective, to the body with which we are actually concerned. Second, it also claims for the church an immediacy that is simply unjustifiable because it derives from an overrealised eschatology. This serves as a recipe for the clericalism and sacerdotalism which has historically militated, and still does militate, against the participation of the whole people of God in *koinōnia* and mission. Against this, Paul's position, it seems to me, implies that while it may be necessary in particular cases to exclude from fellowship those who commit serious offences and remain unrepentant, the body of Christ remains those very people who are doing the things he deplores – so long, that is, as they submit to the godly discipline consequent upon membership of the body, accepting the need to become what they eschatologically are in promise.

The key to ecclesiology as to eschatology is pneumatology, and in this connection, that means the role of the Spirit in enabling the church to be the church at once in worship and in the obedience that is definitive of its being. If, as Calvin held, the Christian life is that which takes place between the resurrection and return of Christ, then the Father's Spirit is the one who determines the ascended Christ's relation to the world during that period. Crucial here is an important distinction: that the presence of Christ is not *as* but *through* the Spirit, who is the mediator of both Christ's presence and his (eschatological) otherness. Here we must engage with Calvin's teaching that the body of Christ is in some sense spatially 'in the heavens' with the Father. Jenson is perhaps right that this becomes impossible on a Copernican worldview, although how far we should allow our christology to be determined by a natural theology must be doubtful.[24] The weakness in Calvin, as Douglas Farrow has recently argued, is that he 'handled the dialectic of presence and absence almost exclusively in spatial terms, and to that extent in a *non*-eschatological fashion'.[25] The aspect of his christology that must not be lost, however, is his maintaining of Christ's otherness in the relation mediated by the Spirit. While being other than the church even when that is understood as his body, he is present to and in it in so far as the Spirit enables it from time to time to be that which it is elected to be.

What does this imply, first, for ethics? Let me return to the place where I began, with the recovery in the last century or so of the eschatological moment of New Testament faith. One of the most celebrated of the rediscoverers, Albert Schweitzer, spoke of the moral teaching of Jesus as an interim ethic: the unworldly behaviour recommended for those for whom the return of the Lord was an immediate expectation.[26] He thought that it was designed only for a church that expected to be around for a very short time. Here, in this letter that is among the earliest of New Testament writings, we see a rather different picture, whatever is to be made of some of the recommendations about marriage in chapter 7. Paul's ethic is highly concrete, and concerns obedience and love rather than an emergency dispensation. If we alter the eschatology, we shall be able to extend the meaning and content of this 'interim ethic'. The 'unworldly' behaviour enabled from time to time by the Spirit is the worldly obedience and love that all too rarely characterise the kingdoms of this world – including, we must confess, the realm of the church, as 1 and 2 Corinthians make all too clear. Here we must say: insofar as the church's mode of life does from time to time anticipate that of the age to come, it is enabled to do so by the Spirit who both makes present the life-giving death of Christ and will complete its eschatological perfecting on the last day. That is why worship, and especially what we call sacramental worship, cannot but be the focus of the church's life, for in both baptism – which is in part concerned with anticipation of eschatological judgment – and the Lord's Supper we are, so to speak, positioned in the realm of the eschatological kingdom while we live in created time and space.

The kingdom that Christ will hand over to the Father is his rule over the created world as that is entrusted, for the time – the interim? – of the covenants, to those made in his image. For Paul, our engagement with that world is centred on two things, what we do most intimately with our bodies in eating and drinking and in relations between man and woman. There also is to be found the heart of our social being. Our being in relation to God is inextricable from our closest relations with the world – ingesting it – and our most intimate relations with one another. It is from these that flow all those things which we have come to call justice, often in abstraction from that justice of God which justifies the godless: our economic, political, legal and other institutional forms of relation with the kingdoms of the world which are not yet the kingdoms of our God. The greatest disservice that the church can do to the world is to believe that it can concern itself with the latter in abstraction from *both* of the former. The relation between eucharist and economic justice has been much treated, and in various ways, but not, I think in the broader terms of the Torah as Paul republishes it.[27] The space which God the Father opens up by the death and resurrection of his Son is given shape by this ethic which is now ordered to him, the embodiment of God's dispensation for the world. It is the shape to be taken by the life of those who live between the atonement and the end. It is thus an eschatological 'interim' ethic.

What does this development imply, second, for sacramental worship? Much Protestant theology has been uncomfortable with the apparently 'material' implications of Patristic talk of the Lord's Supper as the medicine of immortality. But we should recall the disturbing verse we have met, so far without comment. 'That is why many of you are weak and sick, and a number of you have fallen asleep' (1 Cor. 11:30). The tenor of our argument suggests that in the things that shape our human being in the present we encounter a choice between life and death, eschatologically construed. To be related to God the Father through Christ and in the Spirit – to be in the church – is to be elect for the former, for eternal life. That is made especially the case in the gospel sacraments, those things so intimately bound up with our membership of Christ. On the one hand, water is a natural substance, that which at once maintains life, cleanses it and can destroy it by drowning, so that Jesus' baptism in the Jordan, and consequently the new life of the Christian, constitutes the end of the old world, the world in which life is swallowed up by death, by the acceptance of eschatological judgment on that world. On the other hand, in the Lord's Supper we encounter nature manufactured, substances which are at once nature and culture, the creator's gifts handled and changed – killed – by human hand. The outcome of Jesus' life, especially as that is expounded by 1 Corinthians 15, carries the promise that what human beings do with and in their world will in some way be taken up into the reign of God, so that man and nature may alike praise the one who is their maker.

'Until he comes'. As the terms of this lecture prescribe, we are primarily concerned with personal immortality, with the promised resurrection of those made in the image of God and being remade in the image of the risen Jesus. Even, especially, in an age of non-discrimination and of ecological anxiety, we must reaffirm with Isaac Watts that the saints are God's supreme delight, and so reiterate that law, even – especially – when considered in eschatological framework, is a function of gospel, and secondary to that worship through the eternal Word, incarnate, heard and seen which is the church's primary calling. It is the incarnation that provides the key. The sacrifice of praise that is the worship and ethic of the church is eschatological in that it is bracketed by two other sacrifices: the remembered one that is at once the Father's gift of his Son and the Son's gift of his life for the life of the world; and the anticipated one that is his handing over of all rule and authority to the Father. In the interim, Christ's presence in all its manifold forms is realised only through anticipation, and that means through the mediation of the eschatological Spirit, as anticipated eschatology. Our eschatological membership of the body and bride of Christ belongs in that period of fulfilment and promise, in sure hope of the resurrection of the dead.[28]

Notes

1 The Drew Lecture on Immortality, Spurgeon's College, London, 11 November 1999. It might be subtitled 'a conversation with Robert Jenson, with particular respect to the first letter to the Corinthians'.

2 Karl Barth, *Epistle to the Romans*, trans. E. C. Hoskyns (Oxford: Oxford University Press, 1933), 314.

3 Robert W. Jenson, *God After God: The God of the Past and the God of the Future, Seen in the Work of Karl Barth* (Indianapolis and New York: Bobbs Merrill, 1969).

4 Wolfhart Pannenberg, *Metaphysics and the Idea of God*, trans. Philip Clayton (Edinburgh: T. & T. Clark, 1990), 75ff.

5 Jürgen Moltmann, *The Spirit of Life*, trans. Margaret Kohl (London: SCM Press, 1992).

6 Jürgen Moltmann, *The Coming of God: Christian Eschatology*, trans. Margaret Kohl (London: SCM Press, 1996).

7 Bruce McCormack, *For Us and Our Salvation: Incarnation and Atonement in the Reformed Tradition* (Princeton: Princeton Theological Seminary, 1993), 7–8.

8 Robert W. Jenson, *Systematic Theology* vol. 1, *The Triune God*; vol. 2, *The Works of God* (New York and Oxford: Oxford University Press, 1997, 1999), vol. 1, 205. For Jenson Christ is risen 'almost' as the church, because the position is more nuanced than some of the citations I shall use suggest. In a forthcoming paper on the roots of Jenson's ecclesiology in the thought of his teacher Peter Brunner, David Yeago argues that Jenson tends to conflate two things that Brunner more carefully keeps apart. 'Brunner . . . continues to distinguish . . . *two* modes in which the risen body of the Lord exists. Jenson on the other hand regards a *distinct* mode of existence before God's throne as unnecessary, simply identifying "heaven" with the eucharistic assembly.'

9 Jenson, *Systematic Theology* 1, 206.

10 Jenson, *Systematic Theology* 2, 213.

11 Ibid. The distinction appears merely to be this, 'just in that the church gathers around objects distinct from herself, the bread and the cup, which are the availability *to her* of the same Christ'.

12 Jenson, *Systematic Theology* 1, 204: 'Although Paul clearly thinks of the Lord as in some sense visibly located in a heaven spatially related to the rest of the creation, the only body of Christ to which Paul actually refers is not an entity in this heaven but the Eucharist's loaf and cup and the church assembled around them.'

13 Jenson, *Systematic Theology* 2, 191.

14 Ibid., 196.

15 Ibid., 204. I leave on one side here, for the sake of brevity, the important additional point that polities require government, and this polity one which 'forswears all coercion', 205.

16 Ibid., 185.

17 '[T]he meal acknowledges the *absence* of the Lord and mingles memory and hope, recalling his death and awaiting his coming again' (Richard B. Hays, *First Corinthians* [Louisville: John Knox, 1997], 199).

18 G. B. Caird, *New Testament Theology*, ed. L. D. Hurst (Oxford: Clarendon Press, 1994), 229.

19 Christoph Schwöbel, 'The Creature of the Word: Recovering the Ecclesiology of the Reformers', in C. E. Gunton and D. W. Hardy (eds.), *On Being the Church: Essays on the Christian Community* (Edinburgh: T. & T. Clark, 1989), 110–155.

20 John Calvin, *Institutes of the Christian Religion*, ed. J. T. McNeill, trans. and indexed F. L. Battles, *Library of Christian Classics* vols. 20 and 21 (Philadelphia: Westminster Press, 1960), 4.14.3. Where I would differ from Calvin is

in taking exception to his view that all of this is 'for our ignorance and dullness, then for our weakness'. Does it not indicate a suspicion that the materiality of the thing is somehow secondary?

21 Caird, *New Testament Theology*, 228.

22 See a discussion of its significance by Paul Johnson, *The Spectator*, 30 October 1999.

23 'The purification offering taught the ecology of morality, that the sins of the individual adversely affect society even when committed inadvertently . . . The ethical thrust of these two expiatory sacrifices can be shown to be evident in other respects as well' (Jacob Milgrom, *Leviticus 1–16* [London: Doubleday, 1991], 51). Milgrom evinces also the book's concern for the poor, and that 'the blood prohibition is an index of P's concern for the welfare of humanity', 47.

24 Jenson, *Systematic Theology* 1, 202, 205.

25 Douglas Farrow, 'In Support of (something like) a Reformed View of Ascension and Eucharist', p. 15 of typescript.

26 'The ethics of Jesus are concerned only with the attainment of inner perfection. They renounce moral works. They have nothing to do with the achievement of anything in the world' (Albert Schweitzer, *The Kingdom of God and Primitive Christianity*, trans. L. A. Garrard [London: A. & C. Black, 1968], 98).

27 William T. Cavanaugh, *Torture and Eucharist: Theology, Politics and the Body of Christ* (Oxford: Blackwell, 1998). Robert Jenson is on surer ground in remarking on the relation between sexual disorder and criminality: 'the simultaneity of the lack of sexual regulation in young males of American cities' *Lumpenproletariat* and their criminality is regularly taken as coincidence. It is nothing of the sort; the first causes the second' (Jenson, *Systematic Theology* 2, n. 81, 91).

28 Parts of this lecture are marked by interaction with at least four of my former and present students, John Colwell, Steve Holmes, Douglas Knight and Douglas Farrow, the first two listed being members of Spurgeon's College. See Douglas Farrow, *Ascension and Ecclesia: On the Significance of the Doctrine of the Ascension for Ecclesiology and Christian Cosmology* (Edinburgh: T. & T. Clark, 1999).